SURVIVORS OF A KIND

Survivors of a Kind
Memoirs of the Western Front

Brian Bond

continuum

Continuum UK, The Tower Building, 11 York Road, London SE1 7NX
Continuum US, 80 Maiden Lane, Suite 704, New York, NY 10038

www.continuumbooks.com

First published 2008

British Library Cataloguing-in-Publication Data
A catalogue record for this book is available from the British Library.

ISBN 978 1 84725 004 9

Typeset by Pindar NZ, Auckland, New Zealand
Printed and bound by MPG Books Ltd, Cornwall, Great Britain

Contents

Illustrations   vii

Acknowledgements   xi

Introduction   xiii

1   Robert Graves and *Goodbye to All That*   1

2   Rebutting disenchantment: Charles Carrington and *A Subaltern's War*   13

3   Survivors of a kind: Guy Chapman and Edmund Blunden   27

4   Fire-eaters: Alfred Pollard, VC and John Reith   45

5   Grandeur and misery: the Guards   59

6   Voices from the ranks: Frederic Manning and Frank Richards   75

7   Protesters against the war: the contrasting cases of Siegfried Sassoon and Max Plowman   93

8   Martinet, militarist and opponent of war: the strange career of Brigadier-General F. P. Crozier   113

9   The war in the air: Cecil Lewis and Billy Bishop   131

10   Having a 'good war': Anthony Eden and Harold Macmillan   147

Afterword   163

Notes   167

Appendix: Chronology of publications   181

Select bibliography   183

Index   187

For my dear wife
Madeleine
who has typed all my books

Illustrations

Maps

1   The Somme Battlefield

2   The Ypres Salient

Plates

1   Robert Graves

2   Siegfried Sassoon

3   Frank Richards

4   Guy Chapman

5   Royal Welch Fusiliers Officers

6   Frederic Manning

7   Captain W. A. 'Billy' Bishop

8   A. O. Pollard

9   Stephen Graham

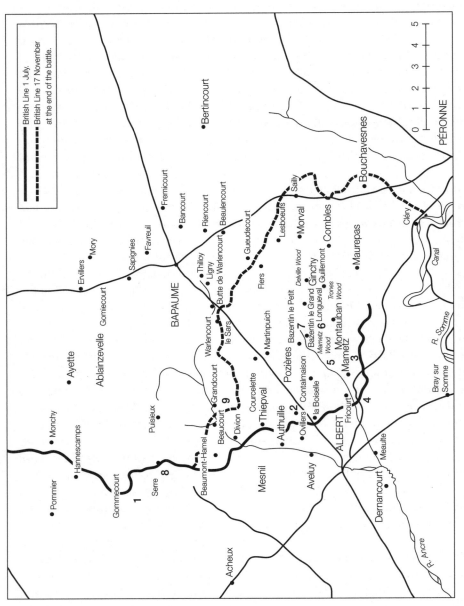

1. The Somme Battlefield 1916.

SOMME

1. Carrington observes 56th Division's failed attack on Gommecourt, 1 July 1916
2. Carrington's battalion (5th Warwicks) leads successful flank attack to capture Ovillers, 15–16 July 1916
3. David Thomas killed in a raid near Mametz on 19 March 1916
4. Bois Français. Graves and Sassoon served here early in 1916, the latter winning his MC nearby on 26 May
5. Sassoon occupies Quadrangle Trench, 4–5 July 1916
6. Seventh Battalion, King's Shropshire Light Infantry shattered in a failed attack on 14 July 1916, shortly before Manning joined it
7. Graves badly wounded on 20 July 1916. Two days later his mother was erroneously informed of his death
8. Manning's battalion takes part in 3rd Division's failed attack on Serre, 13 November 1916. His hero 'Bourne' is killed
9. Pollard wins MC in an advance towards Grandcourt, January to February 1917

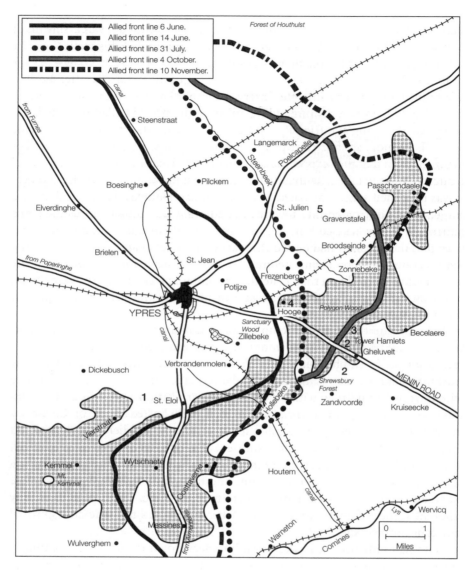

Allied front line 6 June.
Allied front line 14 June.
Allied front line 31 July.
Allied front line 4 October.
Allied front line 10 November.

2. The Ypres Salient.

YPRES

1. Eden's battalion takes part in 41st Division's successful attack on the Messines Salient, 7 June 1917
2. Chapman served here in the autumn of 1917
3. Blunden served here August–November 1917
4. Pollard served here, June–September 1915
5. Carrington's ordeal on the night of 4 October 1917

Acknowledgements

Among the numerous individuals who have helped and advised me, I should particularly like to thank Geoffrey Blades, Nigel Cave, Hugh Cecil, Sebastian Cox, Carl Bridge, Tony Hampshire, Colin Hook, Jonathan Marwil, Ian McIntyre, Brian Owen, Brian Holden Reid, Gary Sheffield and Peter Simkins. Catherine Boylan generously allowed me to make unrestricted use of her research and published article on Alfred Pollard, VC. Max Egremont kindly read my draft chapter on Siegfried Sassoon and Max Plowman. Tim Bowman not only offered critical comments on my chapter on Brigadier-General F. P. Crozier, but also, most helpfully, supplied me with his notes on Crozier's files in War Office Papers at the Public Record Office. Above all, Tom Donovan deserves special thanks for reading my whole typescript in draft, pointing out several errors, and making suggestions for changes. At the proof stage Ian Howe spotted several slips and ambiguities which I had missed. Needless to say, I am entirely responsible for the published text.

Several of the draft chapters were adapted as lectures and discussed at the following: the Military History Seminar at the Institute of Historical Research; the Senior Essay Society at Stonyhurst College; the Sherborne Historical Society; the Thames Valley Branch of the Western Front Association; and the Buckinghamshire Historical Association Branch at Aylesbury.

I am most grateful to the following museums and archives for supplying photographs with permission to publish them: the Regimental Museum of the Royal Welch Fusiliers (Robert Graves, Siegfried Sassoon, Frank Richards and the group of RWF officers); and the Honourable Artillery Company Archives (Alfred Pollard, VC). In addition, Jonathan Marwil provided me with a photograph of Frederic Manning, and Hugh Cecil provided me with photographs of Stephen Graham and Guy Chapman. I am also grateful to the Trustees of the Imperial War Museum for permission to use John Nash's painting *Over the Top* as cover picture. The maps have been adapted for this book by David Appleyard of Leeds University. I am also pleased to acknowledge the help and encouragement I have received from my editor, Ben Hayes.

Finally, my long-suffering wife, Madeleine, has again struggled to decipher my difficult longhand, besides offering acute comments on stylistic lapses. To her the book is gratefully dedicated.

Introduction

This study developed from my earlier concise survey *The Unquiet Western Front: Britain's Role in Literature and History* (2002). In an excellent pioneering work, *The Flower of Battle* (1995), Hugh Cecil showed that British fiction of the First World War was of considerable interest and value for historians, so it seemed reasonable to assume that war memoirs would be at least of equal importance as historical sources. This aspect of war literature has received little attention from scholars. The late Andrew Rutherford included an admirable chapter on the other ranks (especially Frederic Manning) in *The Literature of War* (1978); and Paul Fussell's *The Great War and Modern Memory* (1975) includes some highly perceptive sections, notably on Edmund Blunden and Siegfried Sassoon. But these, and a few other relevant publications, approached the genre essentially from the viewpoint of literary criticism rather than history.

An important personal consideration in my choice of subject was that in retirement I wanted to study books which I knew I should enjoy reading and re-reading, and with the hope of communicating some of my enthusiasm, appraisals and insights.

Where could I make a livelier start than with Robert Graves's *Goodbye to All That*; first read as an undergraduate in a new edition in 1957? Other obvious literary classics included Sassoon's *Memoirs of an Infantry Officer,* Blunden's *Undertones of War* and Manning's *Her Privates We* which I had offered for many years as a text in an MA course on 'The Face of Battle', making the case that despite its fictional dressing it could legitimately be treated as a memoir closely based on the author's military service.

Personal interests aside, I felt it was important to demonstrate the tremendous variety of war memoirs in, for example, their style of presentation and in their authors' attitudes to the war, beyond the handful of classics admitted to the literary canon. Most of the accounts selected are elegantly written and, while they contain harrowing descriptions of battlefield squalor, horrific incidents and anguish over injuries and deaths, the more positive aspects such as comradeship, pride in the regiment and enjoyments out of the line are also prominent. Indeed disenchantment and defeatism feature less strongly than might be expected if approaching the subject from some of the most publicized war poetry.

In broad terms, then, my aim has been to open up a neglected aspect of First

World War literary and historical studies by employing particular books to illustrate specific themes rather than attempt a more comprehensive coverage. I have also concentrated mainly on British (and Dominion) authors, leaving the great foreign language classics (such as the works of Barbusse, Jünger and Remarque) to a later occasion or to another hand.

The chronology of the publication of war memoirs is very interesting and is conveyed in more detail in an appendix. Although quite a few memoirs appeared during the war or soon after the Armistice, many early attempts were abandoned or consigned to the bottom drawer. Would-be authors, including Robert Graves, Edmund Blunden and Charles Carrington, found they were too war-weary, distracted by the need to earn a living, or psychologically disturbed to be able to concentrate or put their experiences into perspective. These were, after all, mostly very young men who had had a normal lifetime's excitement, danger and responsibility, packed into three or four years. They had known no other life but school, college and combat. Consequently it took about a decade before a real outpouring of 'war books' appeared in the late 1920s and early 1930s. By then the excessive hopes placed in the 'brave new world' after victory had been disappointed, and many ex-soldiers in particular felt that their sacrifices had not been recognized or rewarded. More specifically, Sassoon, Graves and other writers were angry that the public still had no real understanding of what they had been through, deluded by wartime propaganda, misleading war reporting, sentimentality and escapism. Thus several authors, such as Charles Carrington, had a strong incentive to counter a perceived public mood of 'disenchantment' with the war and to convey as graphically as they could what the war had really been like for their generation, and why they had endured to the end. We should not however discount the perennial writers' incentives of winning fame and fortune. Given the enormous commercial success of E. M. Remarque's *All Quiet on the Western Front* (published first in German and then in an English translation early in 1929), it is not surprising that Robert Graves and many other hard-up authors should now dash off their memoirs and look for a publisher. Nor were the latter indifferent to the sudden boom in war books. Peter Davies, for example, himself a veteran of the Western Front, cajoled both Frederic Manning and Cecil Lewis into writing what proved to be outstanding memoirs. The boom, however, was short-lived. Frank Crozier and Alfred Pollard nearly 'missed the boat' with books appearing in 1930 and 1932 respectively. Frank Richards and Guy Chapman were certainly latecomers in 1933, though both their books received a favourable welcome from reviewers and were eventually reprinted.

With a few exceptions, the flow of First World War memoirs dried up in the later 1930s and did not resume until the late 1950s. By then the consumers of war memoirs and biographies were becoming sated with the controversies involving Montgomery, Auchinleck, Rommel and Patton and discovered a new interest in the grimmer side of the earlier war, exemplified by Leon Wolff's *In Flanders Fields* (1958). This publishing trend was given the boost of a precise timetable with the fiftieth anniversaries occurring from 1964 onwards. Graves's, Richards' and Chapman's earlier memoirs were all republished and John Reith's *Wearing Spurs*, though written in the 1930s, made a belated appearance. Among politicians Oliver Lyttelton (Lord Chandos), Harold Macmillan and Anthony Eden all published recollections of the First World War late in their careers, revisiting 'another world' in the light of their very different experiences in the Second World War – and after.

Most of the memoirs were written by 'temporary gentlemen', young subalterns and captains who did not intend to, or were dissuaded from making careers in the post-war Army. Frank Richards represents a genuine 'old sweat' with pre-1914 regular service in the ranks, while other wartime volunteer rankers, including Manning, Stephen Graham and Norman Cliff, are also featured. Brigadier-General Frank Crozier is given prominence as an eccentric and very irregular career officer who achieved senior rank and whose three rambling autobiographical volumes deserve to be better known.

A major theme for the early memoir writers was the need to escape from the overwhelming spell exerted by their war experience; to write it out of their systems and free themselves to begin a new civilian life. Robert Graves tackled this challenge boldly in a polemical spirit and largely succeeded in saying goodbye to 'all that', embracing not only the war but his unhappy pre-war memories of public school and his chaotic domestic life after 1918. His break with the past was marked by going into voluntary exile on Majorca, and by writing poetry and prose unrelated to the First World War. Sassoon, Blunden and Guy Chapman found it much harder to escape from enthralment to lost and surviving comrades, the enveloping sense of still belonging to their battalions and, in Chapman's case, the perverse attractions of war itself.

Although Britain produced no fervent, mystic nationalist with the wide philosophical interests and literary skills of Ernst Jünger, she too had her unapologetic warriors or fire-eaters. Alfred Pollard, VC and John (later Lord) Reith in their very different ways enjoyed the war, relishing its challenges and the opportunities to win medals and glory.

For self-evident reasons of limited education, lack of leisure and ignorance about how to write and get published, only a few genuine rankers published war memoirs in the 1920s and 1930s. Frank Richards was the shining exception but it is doubtful if *Old Soldiers Never Die* would have been published but for the considerable help of his former officer Robert Graves. In complete contrast Frederic Manning was a gentleman ranker and a scholar who eventually gained a commission but wrote in the guise of a private soldier, albeit with qualities, such as a command of fluent French, which marked him out as different. Despite its fictional overlay *Her Privates We* so closely follows the chronology and experiences of Manning's brief sojourn with the 7th Battalion, King's Shropshire Light Infantry that it can be rated a war memoir.

Sassoon's work also raises questions of definition since his fictional alter ego, George Sherston, was neither a poet nor a homosexual, and reacted to critical aspects of the war in very different ways to Sassoon. However, in his diaries and in his factual retrospect *Siegfried's Journey* (1945) he provides ample evidence to differentiate his actual war experience from Sherston's. Rather than traverse again ground so fully explored by his recent biographers, I have focused on his famous public protest in 1917 against the continuation of the war, comparing this with the far less well-known, and more morally committed protest by another author and infantry subaltern, Max Plowman.

In seeking to show how elite regiments continued to aspire to standards of excellence, based on an almost Prussian approach to dress, discipline and drill, I found the perfect starting place in Lord Chandos' brilliant account of his service with the Grenadier Guards in his *Memoirs*. But the Guards' unrivalled standards of excellence on the drill square, on parade, in training and, above all, in combat were achieved and ruthlessly maintained at a high cost to the rank and file whose private misery was the reverse side of the Guards' undoubted distinction and glory. In their differing styles two educated rankers, Stephen Graham and Norman Cliff, testify to this darker side of the Guards' profile.

Without wishing to encroach on the preserves of the experts on the war in the air, it seemed essential to touch on the conflict above the trenches which inspired powerful myths of a chivalrous contest between 'knights of the air' and exerted a strong appeal to the public imagination. I chose just two authors for my case study. Cecil Lewis' *Sagittarius Rising* is one of the most attractively written, reflective and interesting of all the war memoirs, though it covers only a small part of a life so long and eventful that it invites the hackneyed phrase 'stranger than fiction'. Like several of the authors discussed, Lewis' war recollections contain fearful predictions about the horrors of the impending conflict in the 1930s, particularly as regards aerial bombing of civilian targets. By contrast, the Canadian fighter ace, Billy Bishop, published *Winged Warfare* in a gung-ho spirit in 1918 while he still had another tour of duty to perform in France as a squadron leader. In some respects a fascinating and attractive personality, Bishop was a renowned hunter of enemy aircraft whose number of 'kills' was exceeded by only three other pilots. His subsequent life as aviation pioneer, businessman and tireless worker for the Royal Canadian Air Force is full of interest, but perhaps he 'peaked' too early in life and found nothing later that matched the excitement, risk-taking and fame that he had experienced as a very young man in France.

'Having a good war' remained an almost essential qualification for ambitious Conservative male politicians until quite recently. Several, who achieved high office in politics, like Alfred Duff Cooper, had successful albeit brief military careers in the First World War and published autobiographies, but only two, Anthony Eden and Harold Macmillan, reached the 'top of the greasy pole' to become successive prime ministers. Eden had an outstanding war as an infantry officer and wrote a short but beautifully written and moving book about this long-vanished world at the very end of his life. Macmillan, a Grenadier Guardsman, also displayed conspicuous gallantry until badly wounded on the Somme in 1916. Both seemed to come to terms with their war experience quickly when embarking on their political careers, but Macmillan would suffer continuous pain from his wounds for the rest of his life.

Some readers may disagree with my choice of certain memoirs to illustrate my themes, or feel that I should have cast my net wider. But, though acutely conscious of omissions and limitations, I must reiterate in concluding that I have selected particular authors and themes because they interested me and demonstrate the variety of the literature. If I have managed to enthuse new readers with the war experiences of these men and stimulated them to explore further then I shall be content.

Robert Graves and Goodbye to All That

Robert Graves's *Goodbye to All That*, first published in November 1929, is justly regarded as one of the outstanding memoirs to be inspired by the First World War. It is irreverent towards authority, scathing in its criticism of fools and knaves and packed with anecdotes, both comic and tragic. Graves needed to write a best-seller to make money, and he succeeded: his book remains immensely readable when other more sober and accurate narratives have faded in memory. Graves wrote (or dictated) his book in a hurry and in a depressed and angry mood. He did not write as a scholar, historian or chronicler of military events so the book is seriously flawed as a factual record. Nevertheless his account of regimental soldiering is serious and convincing in essentials: it most interestingly illustrates the ambivalent views of so many young, reflective officers about the meaning of their military experience and the justness, or otherwise, of the war. In sum, Graves combined bitter denunciation of all that was squalid and inglorious in the war while showing profound admiration for the traditional military virtues: *esprit de corps*, bravery in combat and stoic endurance of discomfort and suffering.

It needs to be stressed that Graves's title accurately embodied his intention to bid farewell to 'all that' and not merely to the war years. In a classic example of the 'before-during-and-after' triptych, Graves traced his own development from childhood (he was born in 1895), through the traumatic experience of war as a young man, to his survival, gradual recovery, and emergence as an adult in the 1920s. His memoir has been termed 'a paradigm of the process of social and cultural transformation' over these three decades.[1] Graves's Edwardian family life was comfortable, bourgeois and claustrophobic. Added to the usual religious doubts, uncertainty about his future career and demoralizing anxieties about sex, Robert Graves was saddled, in a period of rapidly growing Germanophobia, with the name of his mother's distinguished German family – von Ranke. This handicap, and his early passion for poetry at Charterhouse, an anti-intellectual, games-obsessed public school, made his life a misery until he found a partial escape-route and countermeasure in boxing. It was a completely male-dominated, authoritarian world with strict hierarchies of power and a culture of homoerotic yearnings and shame which would be transposed, unchanged in essentials, to the womanless world of military ranks and regimental traditions on the Western Front. As several literary critics have noted, these ingredients account for much of the personal anguish and the themes explored by the war poets and others deeply affected by the fighting, including Siegfried Sassoon, Wilfred Owen and the playwright R. C. Sherriff.[2]

The post-war world depicted by Graves contrasted sharply with the pre-war and wartime episodes. True, the war had left him a nervous wreck; shell-shocked, fearful of rail travel or using the telephone, and subject to fits of trembling and weeping. But at least he was free to lead an irresponsible, penniless and bizarre tragi-comic bohemian life; he had made a reputation as a poet; and he was determined never again to be in a position where he had to take orders from anyone.

In the Prologue to the second, much-revised edition of his memoirs, published in 1957, Graves described the genesis of the book as follows:

> I partly wrote, partly dictated, this book twenty-eight years ago during a complicated domestic crisis, and with very little time for revision. It was my bitter leave-taking of England where I had recently broken a good many conventions; quarrelled with, or been disowned, by most of my friends; been grilled by the police on a suspicion of attempted murder; and ceased to care what anyone thought of me.[3]

Hard to credit though it may be, this detached retrospective actually understated his chaotic circumstances in 1929. He had briefly tried – and abandoned – a job of teaching English in Egypt. His attempt to run a village store near Oxford had failed miserably; his feminist wife Nancy had recently left him, after a stormy marriage, for an Irish writer, Geoffrey Phibbs, who was sending Graves threatening letters. Robert himself was having an affair with the American poet Laura Riding, an intensely possessive and egotistic virago who had badly injured herself by jumping out of a fourth-floor window in a temper. When Nancy suddenly left him on 6 May 1929 Robert was trying to look after the crippled Laura, while suffering the effects of lower-level defenestration himself;[4] in this tragi-comic incident Graves had jumped from a second-floor window! He began writing (or dictating) his autobiography on 23 May and, apart from an additional month for revision, finished the draft on 24 July – his 34th birthday. When the revision was completed, he wrote, 'I shall have parted with myself for good'.[5] He admitted there must be many slight errors but claimed, disingenuously, that 'no incidents are invented or embellished'. Among his achievements to date he had rejected formal religion, won fame as a poet and 'been killed' in the First World War. His demise had indeed been gazetted in *The Times*, thus permitting him to read with malicious delight the insincere tributes of individuals who had detested the living 'von Runicke', as he was nicknamed in the regiment.

Graves, then, wrote his autobiography in an angry, rebellious and reckless mood, determined to say 'goodbye' to all that he characterized as 'godawful' including, as well as the war, family, politics, friends, arguments, unhappiness and even literature.[6] His mordant contempt for all the conventional values of the time endowed his writing with a particular zest which other more elegant and consciously literary accounts lacked. He captured the essence of what his war had been like in a way which would appeal – and indeed still does – to a wide readership. Moreover, whether consciously or not, Graves managed to exorcise the war experience, after a decade of trauma, by transforming it into his own brilliantly colourful myth. Unlike some contemporary memoir writers, Graves really did want to draw a heavy line under his previous career so as to start a new life. This he did shortly afterwards by emigrating permanently, except for an enforced return to England in the Second World War, to Majorca. In effect 'he had written his war book so that he could stop writing about war'.[7]

In a now little-read sequel to his memoirs, *But It Still Goes On* (1930), Graves admitted that he had deliberately aimed to write a best-seller by including 'frank answers to all the inquisitive questions that people like to ask about other people's lives. And not only that, I have ... mixed in all the ingredients that I know mixed into other popular books'. Thus, for example, there has to be a ghost story and something about T. E. Lawrence, with whom Graves was well acquainted, having published *Lawrence and the Arabs* in 1927. But, in confronting his numerous critics, he asked 'what is *truthfulness* in war books', and answered that strict accuracy was only to be sought in unit and campaign histories. As regards personal memoirs, 'high explosive barrages will make a temporary liar or visionary of anyone'. He had supplied dates and place names wherever possible, but was unrepentant about the essential truth of his recollections.[8]

In order to reach these underlying truths the reader has to penetrate behind the dazzling superstructure of theatrical episodes or 'caricature scenes' rich in tall stories, satire, horrors and farce.[9]

To give a few examples: it strains credulity to believe that the first and last dead bodies Graves sees in France are British suicides. It is impossible to tap out Morse code messages to the enemy by removing bullets from a machine-gun belt. Over-heating machine guns to obtain boiling water for tea in the cooling-jacket would not produce a drinkable beverage. Of the many hilarious anecdotes reminiscent of the music halls or *Punch* this example must suffice: two men appear before the adjutant and report that they've just shot their company sergeant major:

> The Adjutant said: 'Good heavens, how did this happen?'
> 'It was an accident, Sir'.
> 'What do you mean, you damn fools? Did you mistake him for a spy?'
> 'No Sir, we mistook him for our platoon-sergeant'.[10]

The 'bloody balls up' which historians more politely refer to as the battle of Loos provides an ideal set piece for Graves's black humour. Adverse winds make the discharge of gas – comically known as 'the Accessory' – very risky, so the gas company telegraphs: 'Dead calm. Impossible to discharge accessory'; only to be ignored by the staff who order 'Accessory to be discharged at all costs'. The costs, borne by the British troops attacking, are predictably disastrous. This suicidal order to attack is attributed to 'Paul the Pimp', an inexperienced captain on the general staff alleged to wear the red tabs of his calling not only on his chest but even on his undervest.[11] Sassoon later remarked that Graves was inordinately interested in unpleasant sights and smells, and the latter certainly leaves nothing to the reader's imagination in describing horrific deaths and putrefying corpses. He records in a deadpan way the most horrific details of trench life:

> Cuinchy was one of the worst places for rats. They came up from the canal and fed on the many corpses and multiplied. When I was here with the Welsh a new officer came to the company, and, as a token of his welcome, he was given a dug-out containing a spring bed. When he turned in that night he heard a scuffling, shone his torch on the bed, and there were two rats on his blankets tussling for the possession of a severed hand. This was thought a great joke.[12]

Here and elsewhere he adopts a stance of cold and perhaps protective callousness which he may not consistently have displayed at the time. Lastly, we must mention Graves's merciless treatment of knaves and fools who, together, comprise the majority of his characters. Knavery and foolery abound at all times, but war provides the perfect theatre: it gives a platform – and authority – in Graves's opinion, to 'all the terrible people'.

It would be unrealistic to expect the persona projected by the Robert Graves of 1929 precisely to reflect his young, immature self at the beginning of the war. In 1914, when he volunteered and joined the Royal Welch Fusiliers, he had just left Charterhouse and was relieved to delay going up to Oxford. He was devoted, almost certainly chastely, to a younger boy at school, was rebellious towards authority, aspired to be a poet and was saddled with a German middle-name. His early experience as a subaltern, particularly in a conservative, tradition-conscious battalion, dominated more than most others by regular officers, was therefore likely to be difficult. Graves, however, had learnt at Charterhouse to conceal traits which might make him appear 'wet' or unmanly and to repress his feelings. He adopted a cool, nonchalant attitude mimicking that of hardened regulars, and his apparent callousness is reflected in many of the anecdotes in his memoirs.[13]

Although Graves irritated some senior officers in the battalion, who found him untidy and insufferably opinionated, he quickly showed that he possessed the one quality vital for acceptance – bravery in combat. The battalion's medical officer and later chronicler, Captain J. C. Dunn, admired the young subaltern and valued his post-war friendship despite grave reservations about his mixing of fact and fiction in his writing. One of the battalion's commanders whom Graves *did* respect, Colonel Crawshay, wrote to him after his miraculous recovery from his recorded 'death' in 1916: 'I once heard an old officer in the Royal Welch say the men would follow you to Hell; but these chaps [heroes in the struggle to capture High Wood after Graves's near-fatal wounding], would bring you back and put you in a dug-out in Heaven'.[14]

Graves had been fortuitously posted to the Second Battalion, Royal Welch Fusiliers where, despite a hostile reception and his fury at the terrible bungling at Loos, he soon developed an intense devotion to the regiment and its traditions. In December 1915, for example, he wrote to his literary patron, Edward Marsh, 'I have to live up to my part here as I have learned to worship my Regiment: in sheer self-defence I had to find something to idealize in the Service and the amazing sequence of R.W. Fus. suicides in defence of their "Never-lost-a-trench" boast is really irrestible'.[15] He even became a fervent supporter of parade-ground drill. He admired the soldiers' bravery and stoical endurance and was proud to have earned their respect as a platoon and later company commander, but he does not appear to have sentimentalized his relationship with the other ranks, partly perhaps due to his class consciousness and prudery in sexual matters, but also because he was not basically homosexual. Except in the turmoil of battle and immediately afterwards, when strict discipline was relaxed 'as though we were all drunk together', formal relations were enforced and intimate conversation between officers and other ranks was impossible.

By the time of Siegfried Sassoon's public protest against the continuation of the war in July 1917, if not before, Graves too had come to see the war as madness and had no belief in its political objectives or strategic conduct. Yet, while privately endorsing Sassoon's reasons for protesting, Graves deplored his action because he was letting down the regiment and, more generally, because the latter believed that the war must be fought to a finish. Graves's pride in being a Royal Welch Fusilier was what most sustained and motivated him. Despite the rudeness and unfairness he so bitterly chronicles, he believed in the Regiment's high soldierly standards and his loyalty to it was never disappointed.[16] The ethic behind Graves's remarkable pride in his Regiment was the heroic, warrior code which insists on courage in battle and doing one's duty regardless of the cause or the prospect of success: he does not seek self-sacrifice or personal glory but believes that orders must be carried out – though he rages at lives being thrown away in hopeless attacks. It may be suggested that, after his futile protest against the war, Sassoon also came to share Graves's stoic determination to 'stick it out' to the end, as demonstrated by his (brief) return to the Western Front in 1918.

Graves's delight in his good fortune in blindly choosing to join the Royal Welch Fusiliers runs like a scarlet thread through his memoirs. He details the battle honours won by the two battalions and believes that the inculcation of regimental history helped to sustain morale after numerous actions in which the battalions suffered very heavy losses. The Welch (more 'Brummies' than

Welshmen in Graves's time at the front) genuinely believed they were much better trench fighters than the Germans; consequently as soon as they arrived in a new sector they sought to gain fire ascendancy and to dominate no-man's-land by frequent, aggressive night patrols. These were the marks of an 'elite' regiment which was frequently thrown into fierce battles and did not accept the 'live and let live' conventions which were welcomed by less aggressive units. Both battalions boasted that they had never lost a trench; meaning that if forced out they had always recaptured it during the action. Retirement on higher orders or due to lack of reinforcements did not count. Graves was surprisingly enthusiastic about the value of arms drill as a factor in sustaining morale. In his view the best fighters were those with guts who were also good at drill: he told a group of brave but sceptical Canadians they could only afford to neglect their drill when they were better at fighting than the Guards.[17] Graves's proudest moment as an admirer of his battalion's exploits surely came on 24 July when he was near to death on the Somme:

> A brigade-major, wounded in the leg, who lay in the next bed, gave me news of the battalion. He looked at my label and said: 'I see you're in the Second Royal Welch. I watched your High Wood show through field glasses. The way your battalion shook out into artillery formation, company by company – with each section of four or five men in file at fifty yards interval and distance – going down into the hollow and up the slope through the barrage, was the most beautiful bit of parade-ground drill I've ever seen. Your company officers must have been superb.[18]

This undoubted pride in his regiment sits awkwardly with Graves's bitter remarks about his (and Sassoon's) boorish and hostile treatment by senior officers in the Second Battalion – in contrast to the First Battalion which both found more relaxed and humane. Though he had already had combat experience with another battalion and had been promoted to full lieutenant, Graves and another subaltern were received very coldly when joining the Second Battalion RWF in 1915. Another young officer told him they would be treated like dirt. 'The senior officers are beasts. If you open your mouth or make the slightest noise in the mess, they jump down your throat. Only officers of the rank of captain are allowed to drink whisky or turn on the gramophone … It's just like peacetime.' Graves protested that all this was childish: was there a war on or wasn't there? 'The Royal Welch don't recognize it socially', his friend replied, but in the trenches he would rather be with this battalion than any other. Graves admits that he secretly cursed them: 'You damned snobs! I'll survive you all. There'll come a time when there won't be one of you left in the battalion to remember this (officers') mess at Laventie.'[19] When he rejoined the battalion in July 1916 after recovering from wounds, he was delighted to find that his prophecy had come true: his enemies had all been killed or wounded. Even so he was once again coldly received due to a resentful officer spreading the rumour that he was a German spy. Sassoon complained about his unpleasant treatment in the Second Battalion as late as March 1917.[20]

Graves served briefly in the First Battalion and found it much easier to live in, though equally regimental in enforcing traditions and seniority, and even more successful in combat. The two battalions seem to have retained their contrasting characters throughout the war despite the fact that both were broken several times by heavy casualties. In his opinion the difference was that:

> in August 1914, the Second Battalion had just finished its eighteen years overseas tour, whereas the First Battalion had not left England since the South African War and was, therefore, less old-fashioned in its militarism and more humane.[21]

However, the sharp contrast in the character of the two battalions must be treated with caution since Graves and Sassoon only served for brief periods in each and, as Graves acknowledged, a change of commanding officer could make a big difference. Also, though Sassoon and Graves were friends during their active service, the former unsparingly revealed the latter's character defects as 'Cromlech' in his Sherston trilogy. According to this characterization Graves was very bad at hitting it off with (the majority of) officers who disliked cleverness. The Colonel was said to have remarked that 'young Cromlech threw his tongue a hell of a lot too much, and that it was about time he gave up reading Shakespeare and took to using soap and water'.[22]

Like so many young officers, Graves found home leave so disturbing – in the ignorance, insensitiveness and complacency of friends and family – that he was relieved to return to the 'real world' of soldiering in France. In late summer 1915, for example, he writes that 'London seemed unreality itself'. Family and friends recounted a Zeppelin raid and a bomb dropped only three streets away, to which Graves replied that a bomb had recently fallen in the house next to him, killing three soldiers, a woman and a child. When they discovered that this had happened in France 'the look of interest faded from their faces'. To the bewilderment of fellow-officers Graves spent the remainder of his leave walking alone on the Welsh hills.[23]

Recuperating from his 'death' a good year later he felt estranged from England. At home 'war madness ran wild everywhere, looking for a pseudo-military outlet'. Civilians talked a strange, newspaper language and he found conversation with his parents virtually impossible. In his memoirs Graves particularly selects for criticism the cloying publications of 'A little mother' whose patriotic letters to the press excited enormous interest. Again he sought refuge in Wales, this time accompanied by Sassoon.[24] This strong belief, on Graves's part, that the 'real world' lay in France with his battalion in the front line, contrasted with the 'unreal world' of profiteers, shirkers and vicarious warmongers at home, surely contributed to his dismay at Sassoon's public protest against the war since this seemed likely to keep him at home with the pacifists who had strongly influenced his decision.

Sassoon's defiance of the authorities in July 1917 by publishing a statement in the press calling for an immediate end to the war will be discussed in detail elsewhere so here we need only mention Graves's part in his friend's courageous but fruitless gesture. Although he entirely agreed with Sassoon about the 'political errors and insincerities', Graves believed his friend would be made a martyr as a spokesman for pacifists who did not understand or care about his mental and physical exhaustion. Sassoon would face court martial, imprisonment and disgrace, while his courageous act would be appreciated neither by the public nor the regiment. Worst of all, the gesture would be futile: the war would continue until one side or the other cracked.[25]

Robert Graves went to remarkable lengths to save his friend. He argued his way out of a military hospital at Osborne on the Isle of Wight, pulled strings to muffle the publicity given to Sassoon's protest when the matter was raised in the House of Commons, and persuaded the military authorities (and a very reluctant Sassoon) to give him a medical board. Furthermore, Graves did his best to 'fix' the board and appeared as a witness before it to give a histrionic account of Sassoon's precarious mental state. As a result Sassoon was assigned to a convalescent home for neurasthenics at Craiglockhart, near Edinburgh, where he came under the care of Professor W. H. R. Rivers. Sassoon dropped his protest against the war and eventually returned, albeit briefly, to active service. Curiously, Sassoon seems not to have appreciated Graves's tremendous efforts on his behalf because he believed the latter had lied in swearing to him (on oath) that the authorities would not risk court-martialling a war hero and would instead confine him to a padded cell. Graves later claimed he had not lied but had simply exaggerated an unofficial warning as to Sassoon's likely fate.[26] Their friendship survived this crisis but was much more severely strained when *Goodbye to All That* was published.

Graves wrote his autobiography in a tearing hurry, desperate to make money and start a new life. In these aims he succeeded magnificently. Though not such a worldwide best-seller as Remarque's *All Quiet On The Western Front* (it was less popular in America and only translated into two foreign languages), the book sold 300,000 copies in the first month, brought its author celebrity, and enabled him to begin a new life (with Laura Riding) in Majorca.

Graves, however, paid a high price for his reckless truth-telling, tactlessness and tendency to exaggerate. His family, and especially his father, were deeply offended by his revelations about his pre-war unhappiness and irritation with his parents' attitudes during the war.[27] He managed to infuriate a large number of Scots by mentioning that Scottish units had run away at Loos and High Wood, even insisting in 1930 (in *But It Still Goes On*) that his strictures were essentially correct if mistaken in a few details.

The Second Battalion's distinguished medical officer, Dr J. C. Dunn, was particularly angry at Graves's aspersions against Scottish units since he had returned to his native Glasgow and feared he would be embroiled in the resulting controversy. More generally Dunn, who had been 'got at' by Sassoon and Blunden with forewarnings about Graves's irreverent tone and numerous errors, adopted a censorious attitude to the book and refused to accept any contribution from its author to the battalion history which he was then compiling. Moreover, though himself critical of some of the battalion's senior officers and its performance in the latter phases of the war, Dunn felt that Graves had been unfair to some officers whom he admired, notably Colonel O. de L. Williams, who had been caricatured as the rude and reactionary 'Buzz Off'. Dunn also resented Graves's mentioning that he, the medical officer, had seized a machine gun and taken temporary command in a crisis on 26 September 1917, but this seems to have been true. Nevertheless Dunn's admiration for Graves remained strong and their mutual respect was evident in their regular correspondence until 1943.[28]

The person by far the most angered and pained by Graves's attacks was his old friend Sassoon, whose counter-attacks were aided and encouraged by Edmund Blunden, the latter apparently motivated by jealousy. Sassoon had good reason to be deeply upset. Graves had failed to send him an advance copy, which was both discourteous and unprofessional. Graves, for example, proposed to include an unpublished poem of Sassoon's without permission. He had also given a graphic, indeed hair-raising anecdote of Sassoon's mother's spiritualist attempts to contact her dead son in the middle of the night when Graves was a guest. Although no names were mentioned, Sassoon understandably felt that this was an abuse of his hospitality which would mortify his mother. Moreover Graves had stated that this nightmare incident had so disturbed him that he had left the next morning whereas he had in fact stayed on for several more days.[29]

Sassoon acquired a copy too late to stop publication completely, but to avert legal action the publisher (Cape) was obliged to delete the most offensive passages and issue the volume with blank spaces. It later emerged that Sassoon and Blunden had been brooding over an advance copy for three weeks and intended to do a demolition job which they hoped would prevent publication. Graves's biographer calculates that there are 5,631 words of annotation in ink on approximately half the book's 448 pages.[30] Together Sassoon and Blunden compiled a long list of factual errors, most of them trivial, and entirely ignoring the author's satirical intentions and his admission that he was not aiming at producing a factual history.

Sassoon was reluctant to quarrel with his old friend but, as his voluminous correspondence with Blunden painfully demonstrates, he worked himself into such a fury over the book that a complete reconciliation became difficult. On 12 November 1929, for example, he tells Blunden that Graves's book is 'mad-

dening': the anecdote about his mother's efforts to contact her dead son reveals
Graves's 'callous egotism'; and the author has misused Sassoon's wartime
correspondence in which he was only responding to Graves's 'own neurotic
temperament'.[31] In another letter dated 9 December 1929 Sassoon alleges that
Graves deliberately timed his nasal operation in 1916 to avoid ten weeks in the
line and that this was resented by his battalion. Furthermore, he writes, Graves
was spoken ill of in both the First and Second Battalions. In subsequent letters
Sassoon becomes almost incoherent with rage, sketching a punch-up with Graves
and showing how battered he looks afterwards, and in another sketched cartoon
referring to him as 'Von Rubberneck Sarcophagus'. Apart from these schoolboy
jokes, humour and tolerance were conspicuously lacking, and Graves did not
help by his unapologetic replies. On 28 January 1930 Sassoon writes to Blunden:
'I know I am prejudiced against R.G. but surely he *is* in a very swollen-headed
state of mind?'[32]

The quarrel over *Goodbye to All That* petered out in 1930, but Sassoon clearly
remained resentful towards his old friend and was also puzzled by his development as a poet; believing, mistakenly, that he had 'gone off the rails'. Graves took
the robust view that it was Sassoon who had picked the quarrel and who had
lost the more by it. Their reconciliation was consequently superficial, and when
Graves's biographer asked his opinion of Sassoon in 1963 he replied tersely
'Twisted from birth'.[33]

Did Robert Graves succeed in saying 'goodbye' to all that he found so repellent
in British society, the war, and his own personal circumstances? The answer seems
to be almost entirely positive. He had made enough money to settle comfortably
in Majorca. He set aside his war poetry completely, excluding it from all collected
works. In Samuel Hynes's apt words 'it was as though ... the man who wrote those
poems was the Captain Graves who had been declared dead on the Somme'.[34]
He became a world-famous author, not only as an outstanding poet, but also as
a biographer and critic. His bohemian lifestyle, unremarkable now, must have
seemed eccentric and even reprehensible to some in the 1930s, but he succeeded
in living by his pen without ever again having to obey other people's orders.
In writing so frankly about his marital and other personal problems, and in
particular the effects of 'shell-shock' which were still so troublesome for him
in the 1920s, Graves felt he had completed a rite of passage and given himself
an opportunity to start afresh.[35] His reported death in 1916 could be seen as
symbolic, marking the end of one phase of life and the start of another. In both
his life and work he was able to distance himself from his military experience
more successfully than several of his contemporaries, including Sassoon and
perhaps Blunden also.

But, as other chapters in this book will demonstrate, such a searing experience
as war on the Western Front, endured in Graves's case between the ages of 19

and 23, was certain to leave permanent scars, both psychological and physical. Graves remained proud that he had served with the Royal Welch Fusiliers, and on the outbreak of war in September 1939 at once volunteered to serve with the infantry. When offered only a sedentary appointment on account of his age he declined, and turned aside to write a biography of Sergeant Roger Lamb, who had fought with the First Battalion of the Royal Welch Fusiliers in the American War of Independence.[36]

Finally, in writing a new introduction to the paperback edition of Frank Richards' autobiography *Old Soldiers Never Die* in 1964, Graves remarked that the 'grossly mismanaged First World War ... gives us infantrymen so convenient a measuring stick for discomfort, grief, pain, fear and horror, that nothing since has greatly daunted us. But it also brought new meanings of courage, patience, loyalty and greatness of spirit; incommunicable, we found, to later times'.[37]

2

Rebutting disenchantment: Charles Carrington and A Subaltern's War

In 1929 Charles Carrington published, under the pseudonym 'Charles Edmonds', memoirs of his experiences in the First World War which had been written ten years earlier. With his former comrades in mind he sought to counter 'the uniform disillusion of most authors of war books'. Readers needed to be reminded that among the millions who had served there were other types than 'Prussian militarists' and the equally conventional 'disillusioned pessimists'. In his account there would no disenchantment: 'No corrupt sergeant majors stole my rations or accepted my bribes. No incompetent colonels failed to give me food or lodging. No casual staff officers ordered me to certain death, indifferent to my fate.'[1]

In 1965 Carrington returned to the subject in *Soldier from the Wars Returning*, surveying Britain's role in the war from a much broader perspective and providing a much fuller account of his own military career. He remained convinced that Britain's cause had been just; that there had been no alternative to sticking it out until victory was won; and that the nation had reason to be proud of the Army's achievement. These views once again put him out of step with prevailing attitudes to war (and particularly the First World War) in a decade notable for hostility to the ruling classes in general and military authority in particular. Alan Clark popularized the notion that the ordinary soldiers were heroes or 'lions' led by the 'donkeys' of the high command and their staffs. Joan Littlewood launched a savage, but entertaining, left-wing assault on the whole officer class in *Oh! What a Lovely War*, which reached huge audiences, first as a stage performance and later as an internationally popular film.[2]

Carrington himself had enjoyed an interesting and successful career and was neither disillusioned nor embittered, but when I knew him in the mid-1980s he was a lonely widower who did tend to display (perhaps reasonably) some irritation at the failure of the current generation of students to grapple imaginatively with the meaning of the First World War and especially the nature of combat in the trenches. Among contemporary military historians he felt that John Terraine was almost alone in being on the right track in defending Haig's reputation and the record of the British Army. As his obituary in the *Sunday Telegraph* remarked (on 24 June 1990) he was 'not altogether reconciled to the modern world' and died 'having survived the majority of his numerous friends'.

Charles Carrington was born at West Bromwich in 1897 but moved as a young boy to New Zealand where his father became Dean of Christchurch. His family background was cultured and upper middle class. He achieved literary distinction with his biography of *Rudyard Kipling* (1955); two of his brothers and a sister would also publish scholarly books; and his eldest brother became Archbishop of Quebec, Primate of All Canada. Charles was educated at Christ's College, Canterbury but returned to England shortly before the outbreak of the First World War to prepare for taking a scholarship examination for Oxford or Cambridge.

Although under age he at once enlisted in the ranks of a service battalion of the Royal Warwickshire Regiment but soon began to fear that the war would be over long before his unit would be ready for active service. In February 1915 an uncle pulled strings to obtain for him a commission and a transfer to the 9th (Service) Battalion York and Lancaster Regiment. There he was tremendously happy, wholly engaged with the care and training of his platoon of 40 Yorkshire miners: 'To see their healthy faces, to hear their North Country accents, to feel myself one of them ... gave me the deepest contentment I had yet known.'[3]

Consequently he was bitterly disappointed when, in August 1915, he was deemed to be too young to accompany the battalion to France. This unit suffered a tragic fate ten months later when, on 1 July 1916, it was in the leading wave against the fortified strongpoint of Ovillers and was shot to pieces on the unbroken wire. Thanks to further avuncular intervention Charles obtained a transfer from the Kitchener Army to a Territorial Battalion of his former regiment, the Royal Warwicks, and sailed to France in December 1915 with the 5th Battalion. He was still under 19 years old and, on his own admission, a somewhat romantic and innocent young man.[4]

Full of excitement and eager to experience the real war after more than a year of dreary training and disappointments in England, Carrington was fortunate to spend six months in a comparatively 'cushy' part of the line opposite the formidable fortified stronghold of Gommecourt before being plunged into the very centre of the Somme offensive in July 1916 at La Boisselle and Ovillers.

Shortly after demobilization in 1919 he wrote a concise account of his part in this battle and in that of Passchendaele in October 1917. Using war diaries and other confidential battalion papers, as well as his personal journal and letters, he strove to recapture the vivid personal experience while it was still fresh in his memory, realizing, most perceptively, that in ten years' time recollections would have faded and later considerations would inevitably creep in. He aimed to be completely honest, ridding himself alike of modesty and shame. He was too modest to hope that the two essays were publishable but changed his mind when the sudden spate of war books began to appear in the late 1920s. In order to achieve dramatic impact he omitted a considerable amount of interesting narrative about his experiences before, between and after these two notorious battles of attrition; and also decided to change all the names (including his own) and unit numbers since so many of the people discussed were still alive. These decisions were justified in so far as *A Subaltern's War* was an immediate success with reviewers and sold well, but we must be grateful for the volume *Soldier from the Wars Returning* for its fuller coverage, inclusion of real names, and more considered reflections on political and strategic issues.

In his epilogue to *A Subaltern's War* Carrington launched a bold counter-attack against what he took to be the characteristic theme of disenchantment in the current outpouring of war books. He entitled this vigorous riposte 'An Essay on Militarism', using the word not pejoratively but rather to mean the soldiers' viewpoint, their patriotic pride in the Army and its achievements in a necessary and just war.

Carrington felt strongly that his generation of young soldiers was being mis-understood and misrepresented. They had not gone to war gaily in 1914 in the spirit of Rupert Brooke, only to lose their faith amid the horrors of the trenches and to return in a mood of anger and despair. On the contrary, though loath to speak of their experience and to do so – if at all – with a sort of rough cynicism, they were not disenchanted. War could indeed deal terrible blows, but these, he argued, fell more on the group than the individual. Fighting side by side created a sense of being initiated, of a shared inner life. Moreover not only unpleasant emotions had to be borne; courage and comfort could also be fostered by the shared experience of the company. It was also dishonest to deny that war could yield moments of intense happiness. The unluckiest soldiers, whose leave was always stopped, who never had a 'blighty wound', still spent only a comparatively few days in combat of the most horrible kind. These intense episodes sharpened the senses and made the intervals correspondingly delightful. Young men, he pointed out, like adventures and could experience the thrill of excitement even amid the dangers at the front. There was above all the special bond of comrade-ship, 'richer, stronger in war than we have ever known since'.[5]

Which authors, in Carrington's opinion, had introduced the legend of 'dis-enchantment'? C. E. Montague with his 'charming' book of that title, published in 1922, had clearly popularized the key term but Henri Barbusse's *Under Fire* (1916) had already set the agenda with his unremittingly bleak account of meaningless suffering 'which would not allow any redeeming features in a soldier's life'. Lastly he briefly mentions Erich Maria Remarque, whose hugely popular best-seller *All Quiet on the Western Front* had only appeared in English translation a few months earlier in March 1929. He described Remarque's characters as 'disgusting and contemptible', but accepted that other German authors had faced the unpleasant facts of war without losing all sense of decency.[6]

Carrington reserved his sharpest criticisms for H. G. Wells, whose topical novel *Mr Britling sees it Through* (1916) ought, he wrote, to have been called 'Mr Wells does not see it through'. The anti-hero, Mr Britling, had welcomed the advent of war in a heroic spirit but had lost his nerve in the calamities of 1916 and became a flabby, verbose defeatist. Carrington suggested that Britling's loss of confidence and change of stance reflected H. G. Wells' own *volte face*.[7]

He was clearly very angry with writers who denounced war on account of the discomfort of the trenches, who 'gloat over the mud and the cold, the filth and the disease, making them the principal charges against the decency of a soldier's life'. War's trinity of horrors – discomfort, fear and death – had to be endured: 'those who bear the greatest suffering survive, and it is this which supplies the heroic element even in modern war'. He became rather shrill in denouncing comfortable folk who hate war because it shakes them out of their routine and who can only imagine its negative aspects of suffering and destruction.[8]

Although he does not name him in this context, he clearly had C. E. Montague and similar idealists in mind when rebutting the charge of disenchantment on the soldiers' part. At the outset he and his comrades knew that they had a simple duty and a Herculean task. At the end the game seemed to have been hard and the prize small. 'No golden age of virtue triumphant and vice defeated rewarded our toil, but then I do not remember that we ever expected such results.' At the lowest ebb in 1917 British soldiers were not disillusioned but simply 'fed up'. As they grew war-weary so their doggedness hardened, and there was no widespread loss of belief in the cause. He rightly predicted that if a similar challenge arose in the future, as indeed it would a decade later, the great majority of British citizens would fight and endure all over again.[9]

Perhaps the most important point in this epilogue was his perception that 1919 was 'the maddest year of all': the real moment of disenchantment. The spell which had bound him and his comrades for such a long time was suddenly broken; an illusion came crashing down about their ears and left them in an unfamiliar world. Millions of soldiers keyed up to an unnatural pitch of determination found the tension relaxed so suddenly as to throw them off balance. Because the future was so uncertain, soldiers had learnt to live for the present, grasping avidly at any transient pleasure. Suddenly they were living 'after the war' with a very uncertain future; friends had dispersed and they had to earn a living in a world where a huge gulf was opening up between wartime hopes inflated by propaganda and the harsh realities of life on 'civvy street'. Hundreds of thousands of young men like Carrington had suffered hardships and borne responsibilities scarcely imaginable to non-combatants, but they had known no other adult life. Consequently, he concluded, 'Disillusion came in with peace, not with war, peace at first was the futile state.' In war there had been a clear, overriding objective, but peace seemed to lead nowhere: it was anticlimax. He concluded with a rhetorical question: if the war had been such a disastrous and, ultimately, a futile event why had he and his fellows been such fools as to take part in it? His answer, simple enough at the time, though not so obvious in retrospect, was because there was absolutely no other course open to a plain, honest man.[10]

After demobilization in 1919 Carrington spent two years studying history at Christ Church, Oxford before becoming an assistant master at Haileybury, a minor public school whose imperial associations suited him well. He had the necessary intellectual and personal qualities to have made a permanent career in secondary education. He was a commanding and inspiring figure, strikingly handsome in a military style but also charming, approachable and a sparkling conversationalist. However, in 1929 he was appointed educational secretary to the Cambridge University Press where he remained, with a break for war service, until 1954, travelling widely and developing his deep interest in the history of the Dominions. In the Second World War, attaining the rank of lieutenant-colonel, he served as the Army's senior liaison officer at Bomber Command, publishing an interesting account of this experience in 1987.[11] Between 1954 and 1962 he at last achieved the academic status for which his earlier experience of teaching had prepared him, as Professor of Commonwealth Relations at Chatham House.

As mentioned earlier, Carrington was fortunate to serve for nearly six months in a comparatively quiet sector of the Somme line opposite Gommecourt after arriving in France at the very end of 1915. He sets the scene and movingly describes the disastrous attack there on 1 July 1916 in *Soldier from the Wars Returning*. The Germans had created a virtually impregnable position, at the northern end of the British line, behind the château and wooded village of Gommecourt, heavily entrenched and with a hundred guns in dead ground commanding both flanks with clear views of open downland. Above all there were three thick belts of wire, much more formidable than any other such entanglements the author saw elsewhere in either world war.

On 1 July 1916 Carrington's division (the 48th South Midland, composed of pre-war territorials) was given a supporting role on the south face of the Gommecourt salient, with the task of creating a cloud of smoke and gas which would blind a section of the German line and so prevent the two halves from supporting each other. This they did efficiently but still failed to prevent the disaster that befell the two attacking divisions, the 46th on the northern flank and the 56th on the southern.

An hour after ferocious bombardments had been fired by both sides, Carrington saw a battalion of the London Scottish running forward into the smoke. Although there were about 10,000 men within the normal range of vision, not one living soldier could be seen. There was a tremendous noise of battle yet nothing could be seen even when the smoke cleared. In mid-morning the London Scottish reported that they had penetrated the enemy defences and taken some prisoners.

About noon, in better visibility, large groups of Germans could be seen in the open preparing a counter-attack but no British bombardment was forthcoming. The German counter-attack was accompanied by a crushing bombardment all along the British line and then an eerie silence prevailed through the tranquil, sunny afternoon. At about 7.30 p.m. Carrington heard that the surviving London Scottish were all back in their own trenches, though pitiful cries from the wounded continued to echo across No Man's Land. Post-war reports revealed that the Germans, though considerably outnumbered, had conducted a model defensive battle. Their single defending regiment lost about 445 officers and men out of 1,900 whereas 46th Division lost 69 officers and 1,283 men; and 56th Division lost 114 officers and 3,181 other ranks out of a strength of about 5,000. This was as horrific a disaster as any that occurred on this fateful day, and the Gommecourt strongpoint was never captured throughout the campaign.[12]

In mid-July, as part of the second phase of Rawlinson's offensive, 48th Division was given the difficult task of attacking the fortified hill-top village of Ovillers, held by a crack regiment of the Prussian Guard. Setting out from La Boisselle, where the initial offensive had failed, Carrington saw the grassy slope strewn with corpses, but only later discovered that these were his former friends from the 9th York and Lancaster Battalion. On the night of 15–16 July Carrington was in the leading wave of a flank attack which, without a preliminary bombardment, crossed 1,000 yards of open ground to occupy trenches behind the enemy garrison. He led the assault and helped to defend the furthest point reached against enemy bombing attacks. This was a battle conditioned by chalk dust, not mud, and in fierce summer heat. Consequently, the Warwicks' greatest ordeal was shortage of water, particularly for the wounded, who could not be evacuated until the relief took place. The outcome was a minor but encouraging tactical success: the Ovillers garrison surrendered on the afternoon of 16 July.[13]

On 18 August, the Warwickshire Brigade accomplished a spectacular feat of arms by capturing the Leipzig Redoubt, on the eastern end of the Thiepval ridge, by a sudden attack with a limited objective and shielded by the first creeping barrage (of 18 batteries) they had witnessed.

> The Germans were overrun before they had time to man their defences, so that many were killed and 400 were forced to surrender with nine officers, a high proportion. Better still, their reserves put in a counter-attack, over the top, which we shot to pieces with rifle-fire.[14]

The attack on Ovillers was Carrington's first full experience of leading his company in battle and in *A Subaltern's War* he was remarkably frank about his personal reactions. As he marched up to the front line from Albert he, and his comrades, experienced 'the first exaltation of battle'. He felt uplifted in spirit and could 'almost gloat over the warlike preparations around'. He had already discovered that in combat he could kill without qualms of conscience, but this was a new kind of challenge. During the battle the high tension caused a strange sense of dual personality: a realistic, cynical side aware of dangers; and against this 'a romantic ardour for the battle that was almost joyful'.[15]

In the chaos of the advance he briefly behaved heroically, scrambling 'over the top' and urging his men to follow. In a curious sense of detachment the cynical and cowardly part of his nature looked down at the capering little figure posing and shouting encouragingly at the frightened men in the trench below. When the men at last followed his lead and they found the next bay empty there was a moment of intense relief and joy; it was 'good fun like playing the soldier in the garden at home'. However, in the crisis of the enemy counter-attack, with dead and wounded around him and all desperate for lack of water, fear began to get the better of him. With shell fragments falling in the trench and hearing the panic-stricken cry 'Allemans, they're coming', he lost his nerve and was about to order pulling back when he was gently rebuked by a calm, pipe-smoking sergeant saying, 'What's that, sir, go back? No, sir, let's go forward' as he strolled along the trench alone. When a bomb burst at his feet, Carrington suffered only a minor wound to the hand, but all the nerve was blasted out of him. Ordered by his captain to gather the men and make a counter-attack he replied 'I'm damned if I will, I'm done for'. He lay panting in the trench without an ounce of grit left in him. Another officer retrieved his abandoned revolver (a serious offence) and led the counter-attack. Carrington meekly followed his captain and soon regained his nerve. He was considerably calmed and encouraged by the presence of his battalion commander (Lt. Col. G. C. Sladen) in the trench, but had to endure another night of terror unrelieved and punctuated by panic cries of 'Stand to! They're coming!' which haunted his dreams long afterwards. He candidly admits that he began discussing with a sergeant whether they would be justified in surrendering if rushed by a large force, but managed to get a grip of himself. When they eventually stumbled back to their start line, desperately tired and thirsty, Carrington confesses that he failed to stop to aid a badly wounded signaller and also abandoned two Lewis guns in a shell-hole.[16]

In concluding this narrative of the attack on Ovillers, the author succinctly and vividly describes most of the 'horrors' of combat including the utter confusion and uncertainty about what to do; false alarms and panic-stricken retreats; comrades – and most poignantly his servant – killed instantly by his side and – far worse – a soldier taking hours to die in agony; the struggle to hold one's nerve and not openly to break down; and the desperate need for water. Carrington had come through this ordeal with some credit but on the whole, as he admitted in print with remarkable candour, he had behaved far from coolly or heroically. The successful action had cost the battalion 129 casualties killed and wounded, about a quarter of those who took part.[17]

From a diary which the author kept during the year 1916 he was able to calculate the typical experience shared by hundreds of thousands of infantrymen during the middle period of the war.

In the course of 1916 he spent 101 days under fire in the front line or in close support trenches. A further 120 days were passed in reserve positions near enough to march up to the front for the day when work or fighting required, and 73 days were behind the lines in rest. The remaining days were spent in schools of instruction, in hospital, on leave or tediously moving from one place to another – he packed up and moved about 80 times during the year. The 101 days under fire contained 12 spells in the trenches varying in length from one to 13 days. He was in action with the battalion four times during the 12 tours; namely one direct attack, two bombing actions and once to hold the line from which other troops advanced. This, and other careful analyses, unfortunately failed to shatter the still widespread popular delusion that soldiers spent long continuous periods in the front trenches, until either killed or wounded.[18]

In November and December the 5th Warwicks endured appalling conditions in the front line at Le Sars and in support near Contalmaison in the middle of the devastated area of the Somme battlefield from which the enemy had been driven in September. On the commanding ridge there was a clear all-round view for four or five miles entirely composed of mud of a particularly glutinous quality, even worse than in Flanders. It looked as if a tidal wave had flowed over the whole area. The sites of a dozen villages could just be descried, but not one with a house or even a barn still standing. The acrid smell of the mud and the stench of rotting corpses was always with them. Some 200,000 had been killed in the area since 1 July and a vast number of them lay unburied or hastily buried and blown out of their shallow graves again.

In the line at Le Sars the British had entered a new 'valley of humiliation' dominated by the enemy-held Butte de Warlencourt.[19] In daylight movement was impossible while even at night machine-guns raked the British trenches. 'In your funk-hole, with no room to move, no hot food ... there was nothing worse to suffer than a steady drizzle of wintry rain and a temperature just above freezing point.' 'Life was entirely numbed; you could do nothing.' When out of the line, digging and road making in the comfortless terrain near to the dreary huts at Contalmaison was the only alternative and not to be called a period of 'rest' without bitter irony. Even without a battle, the battalion lost a third of its strength as a consequence of sickness and stray shelling on the approach routes to the front. Carrington admitted that his morale sunk to its lowest ebb in these weeks. Exhausted and dispirited, he even wrote to his mother that he was 'heartily sick of the whole affair' – the nearest he ever came to an expression of defeatism. He had been cold and frightened and could no longer delude himself that it had been great fun.[20]

However, better times were soon to follow. In the Spring of 1917 the 48th Division briefly took over French trenches south of the Somme near Biaches and then later, between May and August, where the battalion recuperated in a quiet sector of the line looking across green fields to the barbed wire in front of the Hindenburg line. In an amusing aside, Carrington relates that he had sent home for something suitable to read and his brother at Cambridge selected Robert Browning's long poem *The Ring and the Book*, for which he was at first derided by fellow officers but some of whom then became keenly interested, even competing for their turn to read it. When the Third Battle of Ypres began at the end of July Carrington was on leave and then posted to a course, but became bored and irritable, hating the war but longing to be back with the battalion – exactly the same contradictory feelings which Siegfried Sassoon experienced at about the same time.

Although he regretted his absence from the battalion during the opening month or so of the Third Battle of Ypres, he was fortunate to avoid the 'frittering away' of the 48th Division in which, in three small actions in August 1917, his battalion lost the colonel, seven officers and 300 men. With the exception of a dry, hot spell in September the weather was notoriously and abnormally wet, to the extent that parts of the battle area were churned into an almost impassable morass of shell-holes, flooded ditches and mud. As Carrington recalled later, on the western side of the Ypres–Comines Canal you were in recognizable Flanders; 'across the canal you marched straight into hell; a place that offered you nothing but crater-fields and ruins and danger'. Placed in overall command for the later stages of the campaign, General Plumer launched three successive blows on 26 September, 4 and 12 October with limited objectives. The first offensive was helped by good weather but the latter two were badly affected by the return of heavy rains which subsequently – in the name of the final phase, Passchendaele – came to represent the whole campaign in popular memory. Carrington commanded a company in the first assaulting wave on 4 October (known as the Battle of Broodseinde), and described his experiences in detail in *A Subaltern's War*. Some historians later associated it with Messines (7 June 1917) as a tactical masterpiece but for him it was just 'all-in wrestling in the mud'.[21]

At dawn on 4th October B Company, 5th Royal Warwicks left their start line just beyond St Julien with their objective, 'Winchester Farm', a small concrete blockhouse about 1,000 yards away. A barrage of far greater weight and intensity than any experienced on the Somme fell on the objective, while a creeping barrage of shrapnel moved forward just ahead of the infantry. Two factors speedily disrupted the well-laid plans: the lunar landscape of water-filled, sludgy craters made it almost impossible to identify one's position, and formations were promptly broken up as sections straggled round the rims of the shell-holes. Carrington's first ordeal, having lagged behind the creeping barrage, was to be trapped in a shell-hole under close enemy sniper fire with two dead comrades and another dying horribly beside him. When he saw a crowd of 'Boches' running towards them he and his comrades poured rapid fire into them, and, after noticing that they had their hands up to surrender, continued to empty their magazines at them. With only a handful of men Carrington crossed the Stroombeck and found his objective – the ruined pillbox which was held by another company. He therefore pulled back to the stream to 'consolidate his position' but casualties and missing men effectively put an end to his command. He had lost two officers, all four platoon sergeants and 11 out of 12 section commanders. Only 27 men could be assembled out of 109 who had started. Late that night reinforcements arrived, permitting him to return to report to battalion headquarters. After a few hours' sleep he returned to the line on 5 October to find far worse conditions. Heavy, persistent rain turned the Stroombeck into a lake and German heavy artillery systematically searched their positions with the continuous shell-fire roaring like a hurricane. He endured these nightmare conditions for two full days before being allowed to withdraw into reserve near the start line where there was some makeshift shelter from the weather but not from the shelling.[22]

In his more detailed account in *A Subaltern's War* Carrington described an ordeal which he omitted from the later version. In attempting to guide a small group to another company in the dark near the Stroombeck he became completely lost and bogged down in the endless swamp of puddles, mud and chaos. Worse was to follow as he found himself alone in No Man's Land disoriented, and under bombardment from both sides. He was 'helpless for some unmeasured time, wet through, cold and paddling through seas of slime in absolute blackness, broken only by the occasional gleam of a high bursting shell'. Eventually he was able to re-orient himself by a glimpse of the Pole Star and, by amazing good fortune, found his way back to battalion headquarters.[23]

Vivid and dramatic as is the author's description of the chaotic battle, in which the battalion took all its objectives but at a very high cost, his candid analysis of his emotional and mental state is even more interesting. After reconnoitring the area over which his company would advance he was 'quite demoralised'.

> Next day I was miserable beyond belief, description or cure. A sort of blank numbness, such as seems to envelop criminals in the condemned cell, settled on my spirits, suggesting to me in many ways which I rationally knew to be impossible that the Valley of the Shadow might be avoided. There was much routine work to be done, which I did in an unreal mood as if it were a game, a piece of play-acting. My true self had been filled with the presentiment that this was the end, that I was marked to die or be crushed in the military machine; I thought the human spirit could endure no longer postponement of the terror.

He had become nervous and (his own word) schizophrenic, withdrawing into himself and leaving a 'Zombie' in command of his company, a Zombie who did the job efficiently except when the real persona took over in a state of panic. Carrington tried to appear calm and courageous, but he was convinced he would not survive the next battle. Under relentless shelling on the second and third days 'the Zombie withdrew to his own place, leaving behind him a tired and frightened young man', wet through and short of sleep, his mind so numbed and body so exhausted that he was utterly useless.[24]

These later recollections may seem harrowing in self-analysis, but in *A Subaltern's War*, published when he was only 32 and with a career still in the making, he had been even more ruthlessly honest in describing in detail how close he had come to a humiliating breakdown. Throughout 'the most wretched day of his life' Carrington, with two other subalterns, whom he calls Wolfe and Thorburn, were isolated in full view of the enemy in a circular pit five feet in diameter. All day under constant shelling, which grew in accuracy and intensity, they were forced to sit it out trying to maintain a conversation without giving any sign of fear, and playing ritual mind-games to ward off what seemed almost certain death. Thorburn remained calm and steadfast while Wolfe repeated like a mantra his conviction that he would not be hit. Carrington had endured worse times than the others but had never come to terms with shell-fire and got into a thoroughly neurotic state. In the afternoon he was on the point of breaking down; his self-deluding talisman failed; and when a shell burst near enough to shower clods and whining splinters about their heads he swore and lost control of his features. 'Steady,' said Thorburn putting a hand on my arm'. The crisis passed and he recovered his nerve, helped by an encounter with an officer in a much worse state of funk than himself, but it had been a close call and a moment that most writers would have chosen either to suppress or remember with advantage that they had behaved courageously.

At the end of the battle he was awarded the Military Cross and promoted captain but, so far from feeling a hero, he had expected a court martial, presumably for losing touch with his troops and returning to headquarters by himself. The battalion had suffered heavily; ten officers out of 16 and 252 other ranks killed or wounded, that is about half of those who took part in the battle. In his company only one officer (himself), two NCOs and 44 men survived unhurt.[25]

Shortly after 48th Division's ordeal in October 1917 the Italian Army was routed at Caporetto and it formed part of Plumer's Second Arm sent out to shore up the line. This it did, but saw little combat and Carrington served only briefly there before returning to England as an instructor for the reserve (35th) battalion at a dreary training camp in Northumberland. While he would have relished the task of training new recruits he was under-worked and increasingly bored by routine administration. He made determined efforts to rejoin his battalion in Italy but only succeeded in doing so shortly before the Armistice. He was demobilized in March 1919 and decided to become a student at Oxford because, he wrote rather flippantly, 'it would be amusing to read some good books'. He did indeed read widely, but found the two years spent reading history disappointing. His mistake had been to think of himself not so much as a scholar, but as a soldier on a course. Carrington found himself to be 'a kind of survivor' inhabiting two scarcely connected worlds; that of conformist, practical, everyday life and an inner imaginative world inspired by war experiences. Even during the war, when on leave in London, he had felt strongly impelled to share the experiences of ordinary people, and on three separate occasions had gone through an elaborate process to change his identity by donning a private's uniform and staying in cheap lodgings in the East End. This fulfilled his secret longing to escape from the world of officers and society girls (then known unflatteringly as 'flappers') into the life of cockney London where he could associate with his true comrades on equal terms. He had no difficulty in making friends and spent his leave in fish and chip shops, public bars and music-hall galleries, keeping the company that he found most congenial.[26]

In the 1920s he still felt 'an inner glow of sensibility' when in the company of ex-soldiers. They shared a nostalgic view of the war years as their own special world and theirs alone. They might criticize the generals and the conduct of the war, but woe betide an outsider who took the liberty of doing so, an attitude which I recall the author still displaying towards a student audience in the 1980s. Through the 1920s he experienced a widening gulf – though less extreme and less overtly political than in other nations such as Germany – between those who had experienced front-line combat and knew what the war had really been like and all the rest who had not. Carrington could admit in the 1960s that even ten years after the First World War ended he was still immature and adolescent. He could not escape from the comradeship of the trenches which had become a sort of mental internment camp or a soldiers' home. With countless thousands of other ex-soldiers he eventually found release in the drastically changed public atmosphere created by the great economic depression. In the harsh economic and political climate of the early 1930s ex-soldiers at last felt free to speak 'and out came tumbling the flood of wartime reminiscences in every country which had sent soldiers to the war'.[27]

Carrington concluded *Soldier from the Wars Returning* with an epilogue which, though less polemical than his earlier 'essay on militarism', was nevertheless bold and opinionated. He reminded his readers that the national mood in Britain in August 1914 had been exhilarating and idealistic because strategic necessity and the highest principles of combat pointed the same way: 'For once in life the plain practical issue coincided with the moral issue.' There was no doubt about what ought to be done and – to his generation – the prospect of danger and discomfort gave an additional spur. Neither the government nor the people had wanted war with Germany but the latter's barbarous conduct had been critical. Consequently 'in Britain the decision for war was wholly moral, and it was taken by the people'. But in taking on the character of a crusade, British conduct of the war had assumed another characteristic of the original Crusades as 'a squalid series of confused episodes' in which it was hard to perceive that one side's conduct was more virtuous than the other's.[28]

The intransigence of the German High Command had ruled out a negotiated peace so Britain had had no alternative to fighting on until victory was eventually won. The author admits that in 1919 he held political views which many would find indefensible at the time of writing (but which find considerable endorsement from historians now); namely that so far from being too harsh on Germany, the terms of the Treaty of Versailles had been too mild. In particular, her war leaders should have been prosecuted and publicly humiliated as were their successors after the Second World War at Nuremberg. He and his friends realized at the time, that is in 1919, that Germany's military defeat had not been sufficiently emphasized and that the 'stab in the back' myth was already being fostered.

Carrington also made an important distinction between winning the war and disappointment with its political legacy that is still not generally understood, or not accepted, to this day. The British war effort had, in essentials, achieved the original political objectives: Belgium and the occupied provinces of France had been liberated; Germany's military tyranny removed and the threat to Britain and her empire apparently ended. If Europe in general was in a worse state after 1918 than before that was not the fault of the British forces and people who had won the war. Anti-war and pacifist reactions in Britain were, he suggested, ethical not political, based on the conviction that the cost in blood and suffering had been too high.

This way of thinking widened the gap between soldiers and civilians.

> The war was something rejected, forgotten, by the civilians who saw it only as a disaster from which a new world was painfully emerging; and by the soldiers who saw it as an achievement, finished and tidied away. The civilians wanted to hear no more of it; the soldiers kept it to themselves to be discussed in private, like a masonic secret.[29]

Carrington believed that the rift between ex-soldiers and civilians had been further widened by the boom in 'war books' prompted by Erich Maria Remarque's phenomenal best-seller *All Quiet on the Western Front*. While Remarque had vividly depicted scenes and incidents in the rear areas and in Germany, the nearer he approached the front line combat the more doubtful did it seem to knowledgeable readers that he had ever been there. Publicity had transformed this defective account of soldiering into a huge best-seller but had only been able to do this because the reading public was ready to hear about nasty and negative aspects of the war. Thus book after book retailed a succession of disasters and discomforts while playing down or ignoring the positive aspects which Carrington valued. 'Every battle a defeat, every officer a nincompoop, every soldier a coward.' The authors seemed obsessed with the desire to show how unhappy they had been in the Army.[30]

He allowed that there were honest accounts on the German side by writers such as Otto Braun, Rudolf Binding and Ernst Jünger, and largely absolved the best-known British trio of memoir-writers, Sassoon, Graves and Blunden from criticism. In his eyes Graves and Sassoon had shown their true colours in their passionate devotion to their regiment, the Royal Welch Fusiliers, which they elevated above all others, attributing to it virtues it could not have possessed.

In short, they hated the Army and despised their seniors but loved the comradeship they had found in the regiment. As he rightly perceived, much of Sassoon's bitterest verse had been directed at shirkers and ignorant militarists at home. He added that Graves had been as unsuccessful as himself in attempting to say 'Goodbye to All That'. Blunden he placed in a different, much higher category: *Undertones of War* was an outstanding work of literature which would deserve to be remembered, whatever the circumstances in which it had been written. The craze for war books died down in the early 1930s, though many authors belatedly jumped on the bandwagon, and by the time a revival occurred well after the Second World War Carrington and his contemporaries were 'so far removed from current modes of thought as to be mere relics of antiquity, buried beneath many historical strata'.[31]

These two eloquent, reflective and elegiac volumes do indeed reveal Charles Carrington to have been very much a man of his time: born into a devoutly Christian family and temperamentally more a scholar than a career soldier, he was also an unashamed patriot and imperialist. He remained proud of his military service in both world wars and convinced that Britain had had no honourable alternative but to enter them and keep fighting, until victories, however flawed, were achieved. For a generation which may not share his values, or even have much imaginative empathy with them, Carrington's military memoirs nevertheless deserve to be read by anyone wishing to understand the character of the British Army in the First World War and the profound, positive influences which it exerted on a generation of volunteer civilians in uniform. Carrington was a truer representative of that generation, particularly in his grasp of the wider historical perspective, than some better-known authors of 'disenchanted' memoirs and harrowing war poetry.

3

Survivors of a kind: Guy Chapman and Edmund Blunden

Guy Chapman and Edmund Blunden both served on the Western Front as junior officers in New Army infantry battalions and both survived without serious physical injuries, but psychologically they were profoundly affected by their experience. The title of Guy Chapman's posthumously published memoir *A Kind of Survivor* neatly captures the ambivalence of their attitudes to the war in which so many close friends and comrades had been killed. Though alike in several ways, two important differences need to be stressed.

Chapman was born in 1889, so by 1914 he had graduated from Oxford, married, and embarked on a career; 25 was comparatively old to begin military service. Blunden was born in 1896 and volunteered straight from school at the age of 18. Second, though Chapman was deeply interested in literature and history he was not a poet, whereas Blunden was already convinced before the war that that was his vocation.

While they both loathed war for its random destructiveness, squalor and suffering, they were also remarkably honest in acknowledging its overpowering attraction which held them in thrall for the rest of their long lives. Thus Chapman confessed, around 1970, that apart from meeting his second wife, the writer Margaret Storm Jameson, 'the battalion is the only wholly good thing in my life. To the years between 1914 and 1918 I owe everything of lasting value in my make-up. For any cost I paid in mental and physical vigour they gave me back a supreme fulfilment I should never otherwise have had.' Similarly in 1973 Blunden wrote that 'My experiences in the First World War have haunted me all my life and for many days I have, it seemed, lived in that world rather than this'.[1]

Chapman's family, particularly on his mother's side, had been very wealthy, but after two recent bankruptcies of both Guy's grandfathers his parents were living in straitened circumstances. After education at Westminster School and Christ Church, Oxford, Guy's father had been called to the bar but at the age of 40 he accepted a Receivership in the Bankruptcy Court. Marrying late 'he began now penuriously to save'.[2] He insisted that Guy study law rather than his true interest, history, with the result that he graduated, also from Christ Church, with only a third-class degree in 1911. He still managed to qualify for the Bar but his father's early death permitted him to switch to begin learning the publishing business just before the outbreak of war in 1914. In that year he also married

but this did not work out and there is no hint in his war memoirs that he had
a wife. Soon after the war he divorced and remarried, this time very happily, in
1926. He enlisted in the 13th Battalion Royal Fusiliers on the outbreak of war, was
promptly commissioned and served on the Western Front from July 1915 until
the end. During the inter-war decades he was a successful publisher, travelled
widely and wrote several scholarly books. Returning to university as a mature
student, he achieved a first in History at the LSE; interrupted a new scholarly
career to serve in the Royal Army Education Corps; and between 1945 and 1953,
was a 'maverick professor' of History at Leeds University. His lifelong interest in
French history, literature and culture was manifested in three important works
on the Dreyfus Affair, the early years of the Third Republic, and the Republic's
catastrophic end in 1940 (*Why France Collapsed*, 1968).

Chapman's outstanding First World War memoirs *A Passionate Prodigality*
had an unfortunate publishing history but have recently become better known.
The somewhat macabre title is drawn from Sir Thomas Browne's *Urn Burial*
(1658), a treatise which considers the various historical modes for the disposal
of the dead and the question of immortality or oblivion. The epigraph reads 'to
drink of the ashes of dead relations, a passionate prodigality. He that hath the
ashes of his friend, hath an everlasting treasure.'

Chapman, again like Blunden, took about ten years to gain enough detachment to separate himself from the life of the battalion. His own life was involved
inextricably with those of other men, 'a few living, some dead'. The book is
dedicated to certain comrades and to his then surviving ex-commanding officer,
Colonel R. A. Smith.[3]

In the immediate post-war years Chapman was afraid to put his war memoirs
on paper because it had been such an overwhelming emotional experience, but
once he began writing he felt inspired, almost as though the story told itself. 'The
incidents of those years, the faces of the men with whom I had shared them, were
closer to me than my hands or my breathing. I had only to stare, I had only to
listen.' In the act of writing he recaptured the 'unsought sharpening of awareness'
experienced in the trenches. 'Familiarity did not blunt it. I shall never see or hear
so clearly again.'[4]

The draft was completed in 1930 but the boom in war books was already over
and Chapman found difficulty in getting his account published. When it did
appear in 1933 the limited edition sold out in a day. Further editions were delayed
by shortage of paper, then the publisher died, the firm collapsed and the book
went out of print. Only in 1965 was the book republished (and for the first time
in the United States), and to very enthusiastic reviews, but the author admits to
a feeling of regret at the long interval.[5]

Chapman lacked the warrior spirit. He had no romantic illusions and was
loath to go to war; he was afraid and more afraid of showing his fear. He was

terrified of the German heavier shells, above all as he experienced them at Ypres in 1917 where on impact 'there spouted a fountain of smoke and blackened earth and (one could hear) the agonizing split of the steel case beneath the pressure of exploding ammonal'. 'This would fill me with terror in which my body seemed to dissolve and my spirit beat panic-stricken as a bird.' After 12 months on the Western Front he admitted that he had none of that active energy which makes your true fighting man cry 'I adore war!' The sight of dead bodies, recently so full of life, 'made me shudder and stirred in me a hatred of existence'. It took a tremendous act of will to break free of lethargic suspense under heavy shelling. He was deeply moved when in 1960 at an Old Comrades Reunion, a former soldier in his platoon remarked 'I know you. You was told to do something. You was afraid. I knew that. All the same you went to do it, and that taught me something.'[6]

Chapman's battalion enjoyed a comparatively quiet introduction to trench warfare from late July 1915 through to the opening phase of the battle of the Somme a year later. Located first in the Bailleul area south of Ypres and later at Hannescamps, which would lie behind the northern end of the Somme battle area, they experienced the monotony of trench life, often in bleak conditions, with endless fatigues by night and day, hazardous patrols, and in constant danger from machine-guns and more sporadically from enemy bombardment. There were no large-scale attacks; indeed the enemy was seldom seen. 'Sometimes in the valley on the right, a grey shadow would stand for a few seconds, and then slide from the light, like a water-rat into his hole.' These were also relatively carefree days marked by raucous singing on the march and in transport lorries. They had learned the routines of static trench warfare and how stoically to endure shelling and trench mortar fire. Casualties had been light so their spirits remained buoyant and the illusion of imminent victory, 'bred of propaganda', still prevailed. It was in the ruined village of Hannescamps that the battalion's corporate identity was formed. 'To have been at Hannescamps made you free of the battalion.'[7]

The battalion was in the thick of the battle in the first phase of the Somme – La Boisselle, Montauban, Pozières and High Wood – and again in the final phase, in appalling weather, at Beaumont Hamel and Beaucourt. The battalion suffered heavy losses but also came of age as a fighting unit. 'Each company now had a hard core of veterans, and the battalion was welded into a homogeneous unit.' They had forged their own tradition and knew 'the right way' in combat irrespective of the regular 1st Battalion and other Royal Fusilier units. Chapman conveys an almost mystical sense of the battalion as a living entity on the march, 'moving as one man; very strong, very steady, with a sway in the shoulders and a lilt on the feet'.[8]

But the even more intensive, more mechanized combat experiences in the Arras battles in the spring of 1917 and, by far the worst of all, Third Ypres in the late summer and autumn, took a heavy toll both in casualties and in morale. A few familiar faces remained in the ranks and more among the senior NCOs and storemen, but the last flickers of idealism had died. The men, though still docile and willing, were tired beyond hope; and no longer 'decoyed by the vociferous patriotism of the newspapers'. The best they could hope for was a 'blighty wound' to take them home for a year or so. Moreover, very few of the pre-Somme officers remained and of those some had been wounded and rejoined. The newcomers were either very young or veterans promoted from the ranks. Irritation and fear were now harder to conceal; speech was coarser and humour often sardonic and cruel. They were suffering the effects of launching frustrated attack after attack along a 50-mile tract of man-made desolation.[9]

By the end of the Third Ypres campaign only a handful of Chapman's company remained alive and fit for further combat. The battalion was reduced to a shred, able to muster only 113 for an advance to the forward edge of Shrewsbury Forest south of the Menin Road. The dead of many different units lay unburied here because it was simply not worth risking further casualties to approach them. In the Salient, where battalions might suffer up to 80 per cent casualties; where even holding the line was not much easier; and where ration carriers and digging parties were frequently knocked out before they could even reach the forward area, the overwhelming concern was to husband lives. Hence the resort to sending tired officers and men on training courses which were mainly designed to provide periods of rest. Going by lorry to rest at the end the Third Ypres campaign, Chapman remarked to his Colonel, R. A. Smith, that the battalion had changed drastically since they were last there (at Campagne) two and a half years ago. Chapman realized that he was reflecting on people 'who had grown old and altered so much that it was hard to distinguish between a dream and reality'.[10]

Even in what proved to be the final victorious advance, beginning on 8 August 1918, the battalion's casualty figures remained very high after each attack, perhaps as many as six officers and 100 men. 'We are now only a shredded rug', he noted. When the exacting divisional commander praised the battalion as the backbone of the brigade which had never failed him or let him down, Chapman had to fight back his tears – though he knew that in this case the rhetoric was true and the praise hard-earned.[11]

With a few notable exceptions Chapman deeply admired, and even revered, most of his commanding officers and fellow subalterns: Blake and Cuthbertson in the former category, and Fairburn, Whitehead, Vanneck, George Knappett and many more in the latter. Gwinnell won his special praise because, having gone home wounded and become a training instructor, he deserted his inspection committee on a tour of the battle zone to rejoin the battalion. But, as the dedication of the book proclaims, R. A. Smith, first his company and then battalion commander, was Chapman's model of the fearless, tough but fundamentally decent leader. Smith so impressed Chapman by his calm determination in a terrifying advance across the Ypres morass: in holes of stinking water, roots clutching at their feet, shells bursting on the footbridge they had to cross, that henceforth the colonel became a kind of talisman which could soothe his nerves and give him new strength. Another gruesome vignette shows Smith, pipe in mouth, hopping like a carrion crow from body to body, to salvage items of equipment. Smith seemed quite fearless and as interested in corpses as living bodies. Chapman's stomach revolted and he begged to be excused when Smith tried to interest him in a blood-flecked jaw without skull or cervical. We also see Smith dealing brusquely with two dud officers, one a coward and the other incompetent: on Smith's report the divisional commander stripped them of their commissions and reduced them to the ranks.[12]

Senior NCOs loom large in Chapman's narrative like mythical heroes. There was the aptly-named RSM Armour and CMS Dell, who had been an innocuous company clerk at the outbreak of war but two years later, sporting the ribbons of a DCM, became the key figure in No. 1 Company. Though the antithesis of the swaggering regular sergeant major, he could handle men and conveyed a formidable sense of authority. In their smartness and deportment these men, in Chapman's opinion, with two other sergeants, Brown and Baker, were pretty well up to the standard of the Brigade of Guards. Finally mention should be made of J. S. Hefford, another winner of the DCM, an original member of No. 1 Company who was wounded but returned in the summer of 1918. This long, lank figure was noted for his good temper, patience and sardonic humour. 'Only a very rash and stupid man would have dared to try to outface him.' These men, Chapman believed to the end of his life, were 'the salt of the earth, the backbone of the human race, men to whom duty is an inalienable part of their nature'.[13]

Looking at an old platoon roll late in his life with its names, numbers, trades, next-of-kin and so on, Chapman could conjure up faces, habits, nicknames and their aitch-less way of speaking: 'Was you ever at 'at field? Ah, that's a fine 'ouse', but frankly admits that he could never really penetrate their disguise. So they remain in his memory: a line of bowed heads and humped shoulders, sitting wearily in the rain by a roadside still essentially unknown. Chapman believed passionately that it was these ordinary soldiers – not the generals – who had won the war. Watching them trudge wearily out of the line he was most impressed by their sincerity. Though they grumbled incessantly, most 'behaved with a sense of duty completely divorced from their private ambitions and desires'. He remembers them with affection, perhaps even with love.[14]

When I met Guy Chapman in Cambridge shortly before his death in 1972 we talked mainly about the defeat of France in 1940, but I vividly recall his animation when we touched on the subject of First World War generals. He made an exception for Haig, but raged against the incompetence of corps commanders such as Haking and Hunter-Weston. His poor opinion of senior staff officers and commanders had been reinforced by brief attachments to divisional and corps headquarters. He blamed General Sir Richard Haking, then commanding XI Corps, for the sacrifice of the two newly-arrived, inadequately trained and exhausted Kitchener divisions (21st and 24th) at Loos. By 1916 he believed that the senior commanders were too far away from the front line. Divisional commanders might be as far as 17 miles away and corps commanders at least 20, so it was impossible for them to control attacks. Moreover the troops knew the score and tended to become cynical. Even General Sir Ivor Maxse, the successful commander of 18th Division on the Somme and promoted to command XVIII Corps, made a bad impression on Chapman as a platitudinous windbag. His sharpest criticisms, however, were reserved for ultra-patriotic spokesmen at home such as Lord Northcliffe, Horatio Bottomley and Mr Punch whose shrill voices, he felt, drowned out more moderate peace-seekers such as Lord Lansdowne.[15]

Chapman does not sensationalize the horrific aspects of war and he deplored more polemical writers who did, such as Henri Barbusse. But in both his war books he deftly conveys the hellish nature of modern mechanized warfare dominated by long-range artillery. He quotes the description by R. H. Tawney, later his friend and mentor at the LSE, of the Allied barrage on the morning of 1 July 1916 as not so much a noise as a symphony: 'It did not move, but hung over us. It was as though the air was full of a vast and agonised passion, bursting now into groans and sighs, now into shrill screams and pitiful whimpers.' Then there was the ghastly detritus of the battle zone: 'the slimy grass, the dirty food cans … the offal, the rusty bits of metal, the stench, and the rats … which devoured the bodies in no man's land'.[16]

In what seemed an unending battle crisis near Beaumont in November 1916, Chapman, isolated in a shell-hole, tried to read *Jude the Obscure* but found its theme 'extravagantly mawkish beside the long crucifixion of the men in the front line'.

> Above our heads five tanks petered out and stuck immovable in the mud. Their presence induced an extra ration of shells from the distance. When the battle sank to stagnation, we explored trenches and derelict shafts. Dead lay everywhere, three British to one German. One magnificent Boche lay on the lip of a trench, a blond moustache and imperial still jutting in defiance. In front of him lay three English soldiers, killed by his bayonet … On all sides lay a blasted waste, a barren frozen sea, pink, golden, and cream in the afternoon sun, with the austere beauty of a dying planet. Nothing moved on it, except that now and then the black cloud of a 5.9 blossomed and faded. From the river rose the sobbing of water hurrying through the black iron-bound marshes.

Towards the end of the Third Battle of Ypres in 1917 Chapman's battalion was exposed to continuous, relentless shelling in an exposed position on Observatory Ridge.

Day and night, hour after hour, heavy explosions rocked our neighbourhood. Northward ran a trench. It was choked with dead. From the marks on the shoulders and collars, three divisions at least must have been here. They lay slung carelessly on top of each other, sprawled in obscene attitudes. As I walked along the edge with Smith, my eye caught something white and shining. I stooped. It was the last five joints of a spine. There was nothing else, no body, no flesh. This apparition overcame me. I turned away and choked back a sudden nausea.

Shortly afterwards their position was overrun by the enemy employing flame-throwers:

Then the defenders suddenly saw advancing towards them a wave of fire. The enemies were attacking under cover of flammenwerfer, hose pipes leading to petrol tanks carried on the backs of men. When the nozzles were lighted, they threw out a roaring, hissing flame twenty to thirty feet long, swelling at the end to a whirling oily rose, six feet in diameter. Under the protection of these hideous weapons, the enemy surrounded the advance pill-box, stormed it and killed the garrison.[17]

On 4 October 1936 Chapman was reminded of the day exactly 19 years before when the battalion left the front at the nightmarish location of Tower Hamlets only 80 strong.

I can still see the ghastly skeleton of the wood across the Bassevillebeek and the mist silvery in the moonlight, the two long lines of men, exhausted but moving with a terrible urgency to leave behind them the dreadful acreage where we had been destroyed. [18]

Although Chapman gives little space to atrocities two disturbing incidents are mentioned. At the start of the Somme offensive Colonel Terence Blake tells him of a sergeant who accepted field-glasses from a German officer trying to surrender and immediately shot him in the head. Chapman's advice was to do nothing because 'If you start a man killing, you can't turn him off again like an engine'. On another occasion a corporal had taken the valuables of a German officer he was escorting to the prisoner of war cage and then shot him in cold blood. On this occasion rough justice was done because the murderer was killed by a shell later on the same day.[19]

In March 1918 Chapman was entitled to put in for leave, having served two years or more in France, but decided that he did not want to go to England at all. Whereas a year earlier he would have welcomed a chance to escape from the Salient, now he felt he had identified himself completely with the battalion. 'It had become my home and nothing short of its disbandment would induce me to leave it.' As the last days of the war approached in November 1918, watching the Fusiliers march into billets, he felt even more strongly that this body of men had become so much a part of himself that its disintegration would be devastating for him. When eventually obliged to make the choice between staying on or being demobilized he chose the former: England was said to be fit only for profiteers; it was an island they no longer understood.[20]

In later reflection on the war's paradoxical effect on him, he confessed to a strange combination of shrivelling fear and vile attraction. While he could not hope to emulate Colonel R. A. Smith's enjoyment of war, even in its most terrifying aspects, he *did* understand the compelling fascination. This he distilled in a remarkable paragraph on the bewitching power of war:

> Once you have lain in her arms you can admit no other mistress. You may loathe, you may execrate, but you cannot deny her. No lover can offer you defter caresses, more exquisite tortures, such breaking delights. No wine gives fiercer intoxication, no drug more vivid exaltation. Every writer of imagination who has set down in honesty his experience has confessed it. Even those who hate her most are prisoners to her spell. They rise from her embraces, pillaged, soiled, it may be ashamed; but they are still hers.[21]

'You survived the 1914 war', someone remarked to Guy Chapman towards the end of his life, and when he died in 1972, leaving his memoirs incomplete and in barely legible handwriting, the phrase provided his wife, the prolific novelist Margaret Storm Jameson, with a perfect title. Guy Chapman had indeed escaped death and wounds but his war experiences continued to haunt him; he was indeed 'a kind of survivor'.

As his many-faceted career suggests, he had an intense delight in living, wide and passionate interests, a talent for friendship and a genius for happiness. Yet 'nothing before or after that war gave him as keen a sensual and spiritual satisfaction. Nothing'. His widow confirmed what he had so clearly suggested in *A Passionate Prodigality*: 'When he lost the companions of the trenches he lost an integral part of himself.'[22]

In these posthumously published memoirs he is even more emotional in acknowledging his love of the battalion and its personnel than in *A Passionate Prodigality*. He and his comrades started as amateurs but in due course became professionals. When the Armistice was declared the battalion had lost 758 NCOs and men killed in action and perhaps another 1,500 wounded; 32 officers killed and another 59 wounded. This was equivalent to considerably more than the total establishment of an infantry battalion. Chapman continued to attend the battalion's annual reunion at the Tower of London, though by the time of his death fewer than 50 old comrades remained. In meditating on the meaning of the love he felt for some of the men he served with between 1914 and 1918, he found the most satisfying answer in a book by Jacques Meyer: 'La guerre, mon vieux, c'est notre jeunesse, ensevelie et secrète' (War, my old friend, is our youth, shrouded and secret).

He admitted to his wife that he made a mistake in returning to the army in

1940 when over 50. His hope of renewing the earlier experience was doomed to disappointment; it was, as a friend warned him, bound to be 'smaller and drier than the ashes of those early years'. Chapman concluded his manuscript with a moving tribute to some of his closest comrades who were killed in the war, and others more recently dead, such as his revered colonels Cuthbertson and Smith, but added a characteristically sharp postscript: 'I am never grateful for comment, however sensible, on that war, from men who were not in it.' Musing on the friend's remark that he was a survivor of the 1914 war, he remarked that at his age (over 80) he was a survivor in any number of senses of the word, but essentially 'on the deepest level of my being, I am a survivor of the 13th Battalion of the Royal Fusiliers'.[23]

Undertones of War is a work of astonishing maturity in its detachment and literary sophistication. Edmund Blunden had experienced two and a half years of intensive combat yet was only just 22 when the war ended and was only 32 when the book was published in 1928.

He was the eldest of nine children of two London schoolteachers who moved to Yalding in Kent when he was four. In his love for the Kent countryside and for cricket he had much in common with Siegfried Sassoon – and both knew themselves to be poets from an early age. But whereas the wealthy Sassoon was a country gentleman and a keen 'foxhunting man', the impecunious Blunden was still at school on the outbreak of war. In 1909 he had won a scholarship to Christ's Hospital, Horsham, an ancient foundation for the education of poor but intellectually promising boys, and there became a senior classics scholar or Grecian. He won a scholarship to Queen's College, Oxford but joined the army straight from school and did not go up until October 1919. Unlike Robert Graves, Sassoon and some other writers about the war, Blunden was proud of his school and remained devoted to it throughout his life.[24]

Blunden wrote *Undertones of War* while teaching in Tokyo in the mid-1920s. He had a meticulously-kept diary and maps to aid his recollections, but no sources to check or former comrades to consult. This resulted in some minor errors but was not a serious flaw in what was essentially a work of literary imagination. Indeed it was probably a double advantage to write, nostalgically, at a great distance from the battlefields and from England in a strikingly different landscape and culture. The book was immediately a success and remains, deservedly, a best-seller. The first printing sold out on the day of publication; there were seven impressions by the end of 1929; a revised edition in 1930, twice reprinted, and paperback editions in 1962 and 1982. Its appeal is easily understood. It is beautifully written and rich in literary references. More significantly, it is a lament for the destruction of the French and Belgian countryside, and by implication, the threat to natural peace and beauty everywhere by the savage, impersonal menace of war. As Paul Fussell has perceptively written, for Blunden the countryside was not merely beautiful; it was as magical and as precious to him as English literature: 'For it to be brutally torn up by shells is a scandal close to murder'.[25] It is essentially in this poignant sense of natural destruction and needless waste (including the loss of animals and old buildings as well as people) that Blunden could be construed as 'anti-war'. He had little sense of political causation or strategic factors, seeing the conflict rather in terms of a natural disaster such as an earthquake or the effects of a drastic climate change.

Second Lieutenant Blunden, 11th Battalion Royal Sussex Regiment, arrived in France in May 1916 and spent the summer months in the Béthune-Festubert area. This had been the scene of costly British offensives the previous year, culminating at Loos, but in 1916 was comparatively quiet because the great offensive on the Somme was in preparation. Blunden's main duties were to check the company's defences at dawn and dusk and organize nightly digging fatigues to improve the communication trenches. Although he describes some nasty incidents in retrospect, he actively enjoyed this early period in France, delighting in the beauty of the area – albeit badly scarred by war – and the companionship of his fellow Sussex soldiers.

Between August and December 1916, the battalion was based near the Somme, just north of Albert in the Aveluy-Mesnil area, and suffered three horrendous experiences. First the battalion was ripped to pieces in the failed offensive at Hamel, on the Ancre, on 3 September. Second, for several days from 21 October it was engaged in the terrible struggle to capture Stuff Trench and the Schwaben Redoubt after the fortified village of Thiepval had at last been taken. Although Blunden was at Company headquarters and did not take part in the initial attack on 21 October, his awful experiences gave him nightmares for the rest of his life. He sheltered in a shell-hole previously used as a latrine and harbouring two German corpses. He was under aerial observation and constant shelling. The Sussex men in Stuff Trench could not be reached in daylight but on the next night Blunden led a relief party through a trench only 3 feet (91 cm) deep, with corpses under foot and on the parapet. He conducted the exhausted survivors back to the safety of Aveluy Wood. It was the first time the battalion had taken ground from the Germans but the cost was enormous.[26]

Third, on 13 November the last major British offensive of the Somme campaign was launched in ghastly wet and muddy conditions. The main combat area lay on the far bank of the Ancre where the villages of Beaumont Hamel and Beaucourt were captured, but Blunden's battalion was still on the high ground beyond Thiepval. Blunden and a runner were sent on a reconnaissance mission in preparation for an advance towards Grandcourt. Finding himself at the centre of a tremendous bombardment, he bravely pressed on, lost his way and eventually made contact with the German front line. His commander had given him up for lost and was astonished that he had come through the barrage unscathed.

For this enterprise and his conduct throughout the offensive he was awarded the Military Cross, but characteristically does not mention the award in his memoirs.[27]

If Blunden's experiences on the Somme had been severe enough, in terms of nerve-shattering bombardments, grisly incidents and heavy casualties, far worse was to follow in 1917 when the battalion served in or close behind the notorious Ypres salient. Blunden was already depressed before the great Third Ypres offensive began on 31 July, writing to a friend on 22 June that the shelling had been far worse than anything experienced before, except in actual attacks. 'Anyway I loathe the war and the army too.'[28]

His experiences in the first three days of the offensive would haunt him for the rest of his life. He admitted in his diary that he had never before been 'so hideously apprehensive'. He recorded several horrific incidents such as a young runner shot dead and frozen in position with a message clutched in an outstretched hand; and noted the third day as 'the most wicked twenty-four hours I have ever been through'. Heavy, persistent rain and incessant shelling by both sides soon created the hellish conditions for which the offensive became notorious. In mud 18 inches (46 cm) deep the ground became littered with corpses, dead animals and the detritus of battle. Blunden was lucky to escape for a few weeks on a signals course but from late August until the end in mid-November he witnessed some of the worst conditions in the final phase. First, in a battalion attack in September he directed signallers in a dreaded area near Gheluvelt known as Tower Hamlets. Blunden was isolated in a captured pillbox which was insufferably hot by day (contrary to popular belief September was a hot and sunny month in the Salient), and freezing cold at night. A particularly horrific incident occurred when a shell penetrated the door of the neighbouring pillbox, blasting to pieces the battalion doctor and all the occupants. Blunden's servant, sent over to check, returned strained and wild-eyed, urging 'Don't go over sir, it's awful.' After a brief idyllic spell of rest in pastoral conditions west of Mount Kemmel, he spent the last phase of the offensive controlling accommodation in the noisome and claustrophobic Hedge Street Tunnels. He escaped physical injury but was badly gassed on 1 November – his 21st birthday. Sent on another signalling course which was mainly intended to give him a rest, he expressed a sense of guilt that he had escaped while others, who had suffered more, went on in the 'mud and the muck'.[29]

Blunden's final period of active service, between January and March 1918, was spent with the battalion in an essentially defensive role at Gouzeaucourt in the Cambrai salient. Amid gruesome reminders of the previous November's fighting, Blunden's role was to supervise the signallers and observers. With the battalion now less of a coherent fighting force and his relations with some senior officers strained, Blunden felt some relief on being ordered home on a six months' training course, but it was also a melancholy occasion of saying farewells to old friends, probably for the last time.

In the eloquent and moving conclusion to his memoirs, Blunden suggests that as he traversed the already recovering countryside beyond Albert there was no sense of the imminent enemy offensive which would again devastate the area after 21 March. In later years he would bitterly regret that he had abandoned the battalion only weeks before it was plunged into a crisis as bad as any he had experienced.[30]

Undertones of War is a brilliant literary construction which does not seek to be a complete autobiography. Blunden is, for example, remarkably reticent in not mentioning his award of the MC or the fact that, as an asthmatic, even a slight amount of gassing could be life-threatening. Nor does he refer to his regular letters home, particularly to his mother but also to friends such as Hector Buck. In a short account of home leave he only refers briefly to the 'decay of lively bright love of country'; to the dull civilian hatred of the enemy; to the delusion that German air raids had now rendered London the sole battle front; and, above all, to the objections to rationing.[31]

Blunden was a small, hyperactive young officer whose appearance and movements struck many as bird-like, but he was also nicknamed 'Rabbit' by his commanding officer. While he experienced a fair amount of front-line combat his survival unwounded clearly owed much to the fact that his sharp intelligence and enthusiasm were rewarded with signalling, mapping and other courses which, in effect, removed him from the almost certainly fatal role of leading platoon and company attacks. Since his commanding officer, Colonel George H. Harrison, also knew that he was a published poet and admired him for it, he may also have been deliberately shielded to a certain extent.

Blunden was a typical amateur temporary officer insofar as his military horizon terminated at brigade level, while his daily life revolved around company and battalion routines. A brief attachment to a higher headquarters ended abruptly when he told the general that the war was 'useless and inhuman'.

Then, when asked why he wasn't fighting for the Germans, he boldly replied that it was only due to having been born in England rather than Germany. After this exchange he returned with relief to his battalion and thereafter, apart from the standard criticisms of inept staff work and remote commanders, expressed little concern with political and strategic aspects of the war. In this respect he differs markedly from Siegfried Sassoon who was older, more combative in temperament, and more open to influence from dissident opinions at home. Indeed Blunden makes a contrary case that as an imaginative writer even minor but vividly recalled incidents are as significant as the recorded movements of vast armies in coloured inks on the grand maps at Montreuil or in Whitehall.[32] Consequently Blunden's title is highly appropriate because these are carefully orchestrated, ironic reflections by a writer, first and foremost a pastoral poet, more interested in evoking the deeper significance of the war than describing its more obvious military and political 'overtones'.

In his original but uneven analysis *The Great War and Modern Memory*, Paul Fussell discovers irony everywhere in the literature of the war. Sometimes this emphasis seems exaggerated or even mistaken, but in the case of Blunden he is entirely convincing. Thus he describes *Undertones* as 'an extended pastoral elegy in prose', a perception enhanced by the addition of 32 poems which develop the theme of natural beauty and tranquillity ravaged by the destructive savagery of war. The forms of traditional English literary pastoralism are cleverly exploited for ironic effect. Take, for example, the bravura passage on the 'sullen sorcery and mad lineaments of Cuinchy':

> Over Coldstream Lane, the chief communication trench, deep red poppies, blue and white cornflowers, and darnel thronged the way to destruction; the yellow cabbage-flowers thickened here and there in sickening brilliance. Giant teazels made a thicket beyond. Then the ground became torn and vile, the poisonous breath of fresh explosions skulked all about, and the mud which choked the narrow passages stank as one pulled through it.[33]

Similarly at Hamel, where bloodstained equipment lay in the roadway, 'I heard an evening robin in a hawthorn and in trampled gardens, among the refuse of war, there was the fairy, affectionate immortality of the yellow rose and blue-grey crocus'.[34]

At Ypres, especially, the hopelessness induced by the 'befouled fragments' of the ruined city and its ghastly lake could be contrasted with the peaceful scene just a few miles beyond the lines: 'farther off against the sunset one saw the little hills beyond Mount Kemmel, and the simple message of nature's health and human worthiness again beckoned in the windmills resting there. There – and here!' The eloquent concluding passage, as the poet leaves the Front, suggests, ironically, that the ravages of war are nearly over. Near Albert the fields have again been tilled, young crops are growing, and even at Hamel he hopes that the apple trees will put forth their blossoms. In a desperate moment he had found reassurance in the poetry of John Clare and in Edward Young's *Night Thoughts*.[35]

As Fussell justly comments, Blunden's extensive use of pastoral irony sometimes teeters on the brink of sentimentality, and some literary invocations seem over-elaborate and forced. To recall a cottage where he had spent a comfortable night in terms of 'Peaceful little one, standest thou yet?' is to strike a false note. Finding beauty even in the devastation of Hamel, he urges the traveller to 'turn Amarylis, turn – this way the tourist's privacy is preserved by ruins and fruitful branches'. Still he hears the slouching feet of troops wearily crossing the Ancre where 'a guard of trees dripping with the darkness of autumn, had nothing to say but sempiternal syllables'. As for literary conceits, would many readers have picked up the reference (stimulated by a ruined chateau near Ypres) that 'Chatterton might have refused to leave the muniment room of St Mary Redcliff (in Bristol) whether five-nines were occasionally whooping past or not'?[36]

These comments merely suggest that in both prose and poetry Blunden took risks which did not always come off. Prosaically one might question whether the landscape around Albert or Ypres had ever been as beautiful as the poet imagined it before the advent of war; whether anyone but a poet would dwell on these contrasts; and whether some of these pastoral conceits may only have occurred to him in retrospect. As Fussell perceptively sums up, 'The constant allusion and quotation reveal a mind playing over a past felt to be not at all military or political but only literary.' But he goes on to argue persuasively that Blunden is not employing archaic literary language and the vision of an idealized, pre-industrial landscape as a means of escaping into the past, but is rather in his own modest, indirect way, launching 'an assault on the war and on the world which chose to conduct and continue it'. Though his frequent resort to Arcadian or pastoral contrasts occasionally seems indulgent, overall we may feel that the risk-taking succeeds, even including the final anachronistic self-description as 'a harmless young shepherd in a soldier's coat'.[37]

A naturally gregarious man, the nervous young officer found a deeply reassuring 'home' in the battalion, and the comradeship which he treasured was made almost unbearably poignant by the death of most of his friends. Blunden, markedly heterosexual, did not seek close acquaintance with the rank and file, but he expressed his profound sympathy for their hardships. Although officers like himself had a rough time when, for example, serving near the Cuinchy brickstacks, they could at least retire to a fairly dry and secure dug-out, whereas the men 'must hunch and huddle on the fire-step, their legs pushed aside every two minutes by passers, the sky above perhaps drizzling or pouring, and nothing but hope and a mackintosh sheet between them and the descent of *minenwerfer* shells'. In an ecstatic passage he evokes the 'warm fraternity' of the battalion on the march, and lauds the spirit of the ordinary soldier:

> Man, ruddy-cheeked under your squat chin-strapped iron helmet, sturdy under your leather jerkin, clapping your hands together as you dropped your burden of burning cold steel, grinning and flinging old-home repartee at your pal passing by, you endured that winter of winters, as it seems to me, in the best way of manliness ... It is time to hint to a new age what your value, what your love was; your Ypres is gone, and you are gone; we were lucky to see you 'in the pink' against white-ribbed socket-eyed despair.[38]

In a similar vein he commemorates the sergeants, whose cosy dinners and drinking parties were given extra pleasure by defying the rules forbidding social relations between officers and other ranks. There was no higher honour to come, he thought, than these fleeting convivial moments. 'Do you remember me yet?' he rhetorically asked of eight named sergeants. 'I should know you among ten thousand. Your voices are heard and each man longed for, beyond the maze of mutability.' Indeed one of these sergeants, Frank Worley, DCM, a Worthing man, remained a friend until his death in 1954 when Blunden wrote a commemorative poem in his honour. Another lifelong friendship, forged in the trenches, was with Blunden's original battalion commander Colonel (later Brigadier-General) George Hyde Harrison, who after the war retired to Guildford and died in 1965. As with Worley, his great influence on Blunden's life was marked on his passing by a poetic salute, 'On the Portrait of a Colonel'.[39]

Among Blunden's many officer friendships special mention must be made of his former Christ's Hospital contemporaries W. J. Collyer, Horace Amon, Ernest Tice and Arnold Vidler. Collyer and Tice were both killed on the first day of the Third Ypres offensive; Vidler committed suicide soon after the war; Amon and Blunden survived. Blunden wrote commemorative poems to both his school fellows killed in action.[40]

In 1933 Blunden was persuaded by the Southdown Battalions Association to write a brief history of his own battalion, the 11th Royal Sussex Regiment, in the war between 1916 and 1918. Only a few stalwarts are named, but the battalion's ceaseless movements, its ordeals and triumphs are briefly and eloquently chronicled. Blunden movingly contrasts the battalion's spirit of innocence and enthusiasm when he first joined it in France with the weariness and loss of elan evident by the time he left early in 1918. He attributed this decline in morale to the growth of destructive weapons, but more particularly to its experiences in the terrible Ypres offensive in 1917. By the final year of the conflict he was also depressed by his discovery that the civilian population knew virtually nothing about the realities of war. Like Chapman, Blunden found consolation in imbuing his battalion with almost mystical qualities of comradeship and an unchanging identity which he knew to be at odds with the bitter reality due to heavy casualties. Nevertheless he cherished this idealized memory for the rest of his life.[41]

Blunden's tone, both in his prose and his poetry, is generally elegiac and gently ironic rather than bitter or savage. He was critical of some aspects, such as the enthusiasm of some commanders for trench raids, and empathized with the daily hardships of the ordinary soldiers. Above all, he could not understand why the war was allowed to drag on. He regarded the conflict as a natural disaster, equally destructive and pointless for all combatants, and felt no bitterness towards German soldiers, or, indeed, towards Germany. This humane but politically naive attitude would cause problems for him in the later 1930s as another war against Germany became more likely. Seeing himself as a cultural ambassador he made several visits to Germany, where he managed to overlook the ugly manifestations of Nazism in the interests of preserving peace. As in the case of several more senior ex-officers, including Sir Ian Hamilton, he continued to hope that their shared experiences of the trenches would make another war between Britain and Germany unthinkable. He supported the Munich agreement, and even after the outbreak of war continued to hope that there would be negotiations with Hitler, naively regarding Mosley as a possible intermediary. Some unwise public pronouncements caused him to be placed under police surveillance as a Nazi sympathizer until, in mid-1940, he donned uniform and became an instructor in map-reading in the Oxford University Officers Training Corps.[42]

So far from making an effort to say 'Goodbye to All That' or to exorcise the spectres of war, Blunden remained obsessed by his war experiences, frequently recalling vivid incidents in broad daylight and regularly disturbed by ghastly visions at night. In his biographer's words 'He felt a kind of schizophrenia, as though one identity was left in the war and a second, peacetime identity had to be discovered'. When suffering from depression in Hong Kong in the 1950s he revisited the trenches almost nightly in dreams from which he awoke shrieking and shaking. He never lost his sense of guilt about leaving the battalion shortly before the German March 1918 offensive, and more deeply, guilt that he had survived when so many of his close friends and comrades had died. As he wrote in his poem 'Reunion in War':

> Why slept not I in Flanders clay
> With all the murdered men?[43]

Consequently, the preservation of the memory of dead comrades was felt to be a lifelong trust and duty which he deliberately cultivated and kept fresh by visiting the battlefields, attending the annual reunions and recording anniversaries in letters and diaries. Above all, he continued to compose commemorative poems to mark the deaths of former comrades, NCOs as well as officers. In contrast, for example, to Robert Graves, who made a determined effort to exclude the war from his later publications, Blunden's *Poems 1930–1940* included more than twenty new poems about the war and he was still returning to this obsession in poems in the mid-1960s. On a visit to Ypres with other veterans for the 50th anniversary of the Armistice in 1968, he wrote with remarkable frankness of the war's 'imprisoning power' and the 'torturing' effects of his dreams and fantasies. From the magnificent viewpoint on Mount Kemmel he gave a short historical address about the formerly devastated battle zone stretching below and now restored to its pre-1914 peace and beauty. Now, he hoped, at last escape from his awful memories would be granted, but he immediately realized that release was impossible. 'I know, now I am an old man, that I take with me something that will never yield to the restoratives of time.'[44]

Guy Chapman and Edmund Blunden have been selected to represent the innumerable young officers who survived the war physically, yet psychologically remained permanently in thrall to its overwhelming influences. As Blunden wrote later, 'Some of us were driven back by the world of peace and its puzzles to the company of the years of terror.'[45] Well-educated, cultured young men, they looked forward to careers in literature and poetry, publishing, history and teaching at university. Though not naturally brave or imbued with the warrior spirit, both would win the Military Cross but made no fuss about it. They experienced abominable conditions, nerve-shattering periods of combat and the deaths or disablement of most of their friends and contemporaries, but neither was tempted to make a public protest. In their memoirs they recapture the full range of the war's impressions, both positive and negative, not least important its strange powers of attraction and the abiding sense of merging their individual identity in the corporate spirit of the battalion. Both remained under this strange spell of the war for the rest of their lives, survivors whose honest attempts to explain that bewitchment still have the power to move us profoundly.

4

Fire-Eaters: Alfred Pollard, VC and John Reith

'Fire-Eater' – one who is fond of fighting or who seeks occasion to fight – may not have been a politically correct title for First World War memoirs published in 1932, but in Alfred Pollard's case it was entirely appropriate. As a private, NCO and junior officer in the Honourable Artillery Company (HAC) Pollard had been awarded the Distinguished Conduct Medal, Military Cross and Bar, and the Victoria Cross between September 1915 and April 1917.

Pollard had only turned to authorship in the late 1920s after various disappointments and failures and had already published three fiction thrillers before his memoirs appeared. In a writing career lasting till his death in 1960 he published no fewer than 56 titles, but it seems likely that *Fire-Eater* is the only one still worth reading. In his entry in the *New DNB* the book is described as a 'minor classic' written in a 'schoolboy's own' style. While *Fire-Eater* does not rank highly as a work of literature, it is nevertheless interesting as the frank portrait of a British warrior whose outlook could hardly be more different from the 'disenchanted' trench memoirs which are now believed to have been more typical at the time. Pollard recaptures his experiences in remarkable detail, freshness and honesty, presumably drawing on his regular letters to his mother. What inspired his fierce patriotism, love of combat and beliefs which are now, to say the least, unfashionable?

Alf Pollard was born in Wallington, Surrey in 1893, educated at Merchant Taylors' School, and followed his father into the Alliance Assurance Company. Bored with his job as an insurance clerk, like thousands of other young men, he rushed to join up on the outbreak of war. He managed to join the ancient Honourable Artillery Company (established in 1537) in which his elder brother James had already been a member for seven years, and sailed to France with his company ('C' Company, 1st Battalion) as early as 18 September 1914. The battalion consisted of some 800 volunteers, mostly public schoolboys, a natural source of future officers had they not been mostly killed or disabled in the first year of service.

Alf was eager to see action but his brother James was even more impatient, absenting himself from the HAC before embarkation and joining the Grenadier Guards under the name of Frank Thomson. After Alf had been commissioned in 1916 he persuaded his colonel to forgive his brother, re-admit him to the HAC and offer him a commission. Tragically James was killed at Ginchy, in the battle of the Somme, a week before he was due to return home.

As a private soldier Alf experienced terrible conditions in the winter of 1914 in trenches at Kemmel near Ypres. Sanitation was poor, corpses were lying about unburied and dug-outs were almost unknown. Yet life had a strong vein of romance for him; in long nights spent in the open air and the development of strong bonds of comradeship.[1]

Alf experienced a relatively comfortable period as an officer's servant but became restless once he had experienced the thrill of a night patrol in No Man's Land. These excursions with Captain Boyle were everything to him. 'The danger acted like a drug quickening my pulses. At last I was doing something worth while.'

Near Wytschaete in 1915 he witnessed the massacre of a detachment of the Wiltshires haplessly sent across open ground in the face of concentrated machine-gun fire. So far from experiencing fear 'my blood raced through my arteries and veins, and I was filled with such a rage as I had never experienced in my life before. The Hun became my enemy then. He was mowing down my countrymen who were helpless to retaliate.' Only iron self-discipline narrowly restrained him from yielding to the 'blood lust' in his heart.[2]

Promoted to lance corporal and then full corporal in 1915, Pollard by accident found a role that ideally suited his thirst for extreme danger in small-group actions: he became a bombing specialist, earning the nickname 'Bombo'. In June 1915 his battalion, now part of the 3rd Division, was given the daunting task of pushing out the extreme tip of the Ypres salient at Hooge. He was terribly disappointed to find that his battalion would form part of the second wave and might therefore miss the fun. He had no morbid thoughts but looked forward to adventure much as he looked forward to a rugger match before the war. 'I wanted to distinguish myself and I was determined to seize on any chance that came my way. I also wanted to christen my bayonet.' Ordered, to his delight, to take part in the initial charge, Pollard claims he went 'over the top' without fear. This was due, he says, to an extraordinary feeling of being exempt from danger: 'I never once dreamed or considered that I myself should be hit' – a confidence that would grow even stronger when he later became an officer.[3]

After a spell at the Grenade School near Cassel to learn all about bombs, Pollard returned to the Salient in September 1915 and was given the 'herculean task' of constructing 14 bomb-proof shelters for reserve supplies of bombs for the major offensive scheduled for 25 September. This task lay far beyond the capacity of his scattered bombing platoon, but by approaching a colonel at headquarters he acquired the necessary help and got the job done. He and his bombing team were relieved after five days and nights without sleep. He was promoted sergeant.

On 30 September 1915 Pollard took part in a dramatic episode in Sanctuary Wood, in the Ypres salient, which added to his daredevil, glory-seeking reputation, but also showed that he was human and vulnerable. Overnight the enemy had blown a mine under a Middlesex battalion, killing 90 men, and had occupied the crater. With one officer, Pollard's mission, employing only his specialist bombing platoon, was to eject the enemy from his trenches. 'These were great tidings. It was the biggest opportunity I had had in the whole war to show what I could do.' Typically Pollard described the challenge as a game: he was determined to clear his side of the crater before the officer's squad on the other side. Unfortunately for him, the Germans had erected two barriers across the approach trench which defied even Pollard's heroic efforts. Only seven of the 21 soldiers engaged escaped death or wounds. Pollard was severely wounded by a bullet which lodged in his shoulder. He carried on giving orders until he fainted from loss of blood and after coming to he insisted on walking to the Clearing Station.

For his gallant conduct in rallying his shaken men against far superior numbers Pollard was awarded the DCM, an award particularly prized as available only to the other ranks and carrying with it a financial reward. Pollard convalesced from his wounds in England, chafing at his absence from the battalion, until early in 1916 when he returned to France as a commissioned officer.[4]

What inspired this formidable 'fire-eater' in his determination to 'kill Huns' and achieve glory? Part of the answer lies in a somewhat naive patriotism linked to a highly competitive spirit. Comrades do not always admire such compulsive risk-takers and medal hunters, and indeed some of his comrades thought Pollard was mad. This he half-admitted, arguing that 'I wanted to kill, not because I hated the enemy [though at times he clearly did], but because the primitive instinct was strong in me to fight'. Elsewhere he wrote that he 'hated the whole German nation, for no other reason than that they were our enemies'.[5]

Pollard, however, was driven by a more personal passion which reveals his rather pathetic naivety during the war and his courage in writing so frankly about it afterwards. He was hopelessly in love with a young woman (idealized in chivalrous terms as 'My Lady'), who in 1914 knew nothing of his infatuation and later treated him with cold indifference. Pollard glories in the hackneyed and sentimental expression of his love. 'I was a knight going to a crusade. She was my ever gentle lady. I carried her favour in the form of a lace-handkerchief of hers which I had stolen.' To develop the conceit of a crusade, Pollard clearly believed that the more medals he could win the better prospect he would have of storming the lady's resistance or citadel, and winning her hand. On leave in August 1915 Pollard's infatuation intensified. He saw himself as a knight fighting for her protection and as a doormat for her feet. Had she wished, he admitted, he would have crossed No Man's Land alone in broad daylight. More prosaically he sensed that his chances would be improved if he became an officer; indeed she may even have hinted as much.[6]

On returning to France he made a serious mistake in writing to ask if she would marry him after the war. He was rejected in devastating terms. Mary Ainsley, for that was her unromantic name, replied that she was amazed by his presumption that she felt any affection for him: he just happened to be a friend of the family. If she ever married he would be just about the last man she would consider. This rebuff, unfortunately for the lovelorn Pollard, was not the 'end of the affair'. He now felt that he was no longer a knight fighting for his lady but 'merely a soldier doing a routine job for his country'. He thus entered Sanctuary Wood more determined than ever to 'kill Huns'.[7]

The death of Pollard's elder brother James in the summer of 1916, a week before he was due to return home to be commissioned in the HAC, strengthened Alf's determination to seek revenge. 'I felt that never again would I pity any of the enemy.' He missed the main Somme battles that summer because the HAC was stationed in a relatively quiet sector north of Vimy, first at Souchez and then at Calonne. A knee injury, followed by compassionate leave to visit his mother, also caused Pollard to miss the HAC's intensive fighting in mid-November as part of the Royal Naval Division in the battle of the Ancre at Beaucourt in truly appalling conditions. Improbable though it seems, Pollard on his return was severely reprimanded by his commanding officer, Colonel Boyle, for getting special leave to visit his bereaved mother when battalion action was possible. 'Soldiers don't have mothers', said the colonel harshly. 'Your action was the action of a coward.' Pollard resolved never to miss any future battalion combat for any reason such as leave or training courses.

In January and February 1917 Pollard, now an officer, commanded small bombing and reconnaissance parties in even more dreadful winter weather in the Grandcourt area on the Ancre. In a rare reflective passage in the memoirs he noted how he had changed mentally since he first saw a trench full of corpses in June 1915. Now he viewed corpses without any sensation: 'I was just a machine carrying out my appointed work to the best of my ability.' In February 1917 he was awarded the Military Cross for a hazardous mission across the flooded Ancre resulting in several days of intense fighting in which he commanded a company. Describing the battle in a letter to his mother he wrote, 'I was the first man over the Hun parapet and landed right on top of two Huns who tried to do me in, but fortunately I managed to finish them off with my jolly old revolver. Hand to hand fighting was rather fun but we soon cleared them out.'[8]

In April 1917 he writes again to his mother to tell her he has been awarded a Bar to his MC. His patrol was the only one which had penetrated the enemy's wire and precisely located his lines. Again commanding a company he got into an enemy trench thinking it was unoccupied but discovered it was full of Huns so had to beat a hasty retreat. He ended this letter: 'By the way, I have killed another Hun. Hurrah.' Perhaps realizing that this letter to his mother might strike her as odd and that readers would suspect him of having a kink in his nature he adds that he has thought deeply about his love of combat since the war and believes it was simply due to a keen desire to win.[9]

Later in the same month, April 1917, Pollard experienced his apotheosis as a fire-eater by winning the VC in the battle for Gavrelle. He was positioned on the extreme left of the sector held by the Royal Naval Division and witnessed a sudden, panic retreat on his left which, unchecked, would have exposed the whole division to annihilation. Once again he experienced a strange feeling of detachment, of being taken over by a mysterious power outside himself. Not content with stopping the rout, accompanied by only three other men, all expert bombers, he advanced up the enemy trench. Well in advance of any other British troops he killed the first Germans he met and by ferocious bombing forced the rest to retreat. This, he later admitted, was a foolhardy venture, but his blood was up: 'I felt a thrill only comparable to running through the opposition at rugger to score a try.' His tiny squad then fought off an enemy counter-attack and was just about to run out of bombs when reinforcements arrived. A second counter-attack was defeated and Pollard remained in control of the trench throughout the day. His citation for the VC concluded 'By his force of will, dash and splendid example, coupled with an utter contempt for danger, this officer, who has already won the DCM and MC, infused courage into every man who saw him.'[10]

When home on leave before the award of the VC was confirmed, Pollard, left alone late at night with 'His Lady', broke his promise and again begged her to marry him. She replied finally that she did not love him but as he evidently loved her so much it would be a pity to disappoint him. Perhaps frankly impressed by his VC, she eventually wrote to accept him, but there was an ominous indication of future discord when he returned for the investiture at Buckingham Palace. Taking her for a long walk in the country he opted for a short cut back to their hotel but found the way barred by a wide and muddy ditch. What to him was a minor misadventure was to her a monumental act of selfishness on his part. She insisted that they return by the long roundabout road and the tiring trek took place in silence. Pollard later reflected that he should have broken off the engagement there and then since they were incompatible, but he hoped that all would be well once they had married. He was sadly proved wrong and after six unhappy years they were divorced in 1924. The following year Pollard remarried, this time very happily.[11]

After the excitement of winning the VC the remainder of Pollard's war was comparatively uneventful; indeed by his own admission it was boring. He took a course on the Lewis gun at Le Touquet but before he could pass on his enthusiasm to the battalion the HAC was moved to Montreuil to guard Haig's headquarters. Pollard found a temporary outlet for his zeal in helping to train four special platoons to demonstrate British drill and tactical methods to the early arrivals of the American Army. When a second batch of platoons was requested Pollard decided to accompany them and train the Americans directly, but he found them 'Too proud or too pig-headed to let us help them'. In July 1918 he became Adjutant to a Training Camp at Quiberville, but he was depressed by the attitude of 'combed-out' soldiers who wanted to avoid infantry combat if they possibly could. His efforts to rejoin his battalion in time to see action in the final weeks of the war were frustrated by a bout of influenza.[12]

After the war he served briefly in the occupation forces in the Rhineland but left the Army in February 1919. Doubtless he felt some pressure to spend time at home with his recently married 'lady', and in any case it is hard to envisage such a restless fire-eater finding satisfaction in the greatly-reduced and under-funded peacetime army. He did contemplate rejoining the Service a few years later, but was dissuaded by his second wife.

Given his drive for combat and glory Pollard was remarkably lucky to survive the war. Through no fault of his own he had missed all but the final phase of the Somme campaign, the Third Ypres campaign in 1917 and all the battles of 1918. Also, as a specialist bomber leading small groups on specific missions, he had more scope for initiative and calculated risk-taking; indeed at one point in 1916 he demonstrated to his sceptical commanding officer that his bravery was based on careful reconnaissance and calculation rather than recklessness.[13] Despite these considerations it is abundantly clear that Pollard was a natural warrior who again and again displayed outstanding courage and inspired leadership in fluid situations where his bombing skills were most effective.

It is tempting to compare Pollard with Ernst Jünger, author of *Storm of Steel, Copse 125* and a great variety of publications on philosophy, politics and literature, but the comparison should not be pushed too far. Both were staunch patriots, and much decorated front-line heroes who, surprisingly, did not achieve field officer rank. But Pollard was conspicuously lacking in Jünger's wide-ranging scientific interests and his mystical Teutonic approach to philosophy and politics. They were also superficially alike in praising the spirit of comradeship and sense of national unity which the war had produced and which Pollard, in particular, felt to be depressingly lacking in peacetime Britain in the 1920s. But Jünger's ecstatic philosophising in *The War as Inner Experience* (1922) lay entirely beyond Pollard's relatively unsophisticated mental horizons.[14]

For Jünger 'To live meant to kill ... Man would never overcome war, because it was greater than he was; and woe to him if he tried to escape from its grasp, for it was in war that men fulfilled themselves and most completely.' War, for Jünger, was not a cause of man's unhappiness, but an expression of his eternally unchanging nature and at the same time a revelation of things to come. War was a creative force.[15] Perhaps one could sum up by saying that Jünger was an internationally famous writer and militarist whereas Pollard was a simple patriotic fire-eater with only moderate literary ability.

Pollard's career after the war followed the sadly familiar course of the unhappy, unsettled war hero who found it very difficult to adjust to the very different demands of peacetime. He rejected a generous invitation to return to his pre-war job in insurance; his first marriage quickly proved disastrous; and by his own admission he went 'completely off course' for a time. In 1921 he joined the Territorial Reserve as a captain, and in 1924 he was granted a short-service commission in the RAF. After serving briefly with an Army Co-operation squadron he finally resigned at the end of 1926. He became a keen supporter of air power and his publications included a popular history of the Royal Air Force (1934) and several thrillers about air power and espionage.[16]

In the rather bitter epilogue to his memoirs Pollard bewailed the fact that he found little connection between success in war and making good in peacetime. He had had to start again several times from the beginning. In an article entitled 'My useless VC', published in the *London Star* on 24 October 1932, Pollard wrote: 'There is no walk of life where my decorations have given me an advantage over other men'; indeed they were more often viewed as 'tokens of the unsuitability of their wearers'. He tried to pawn his VC but found that pawnshops were not allowed to take them. His obituary in the *Daily Telegraph* on 6 December 1960 mentioned that although he had been proud of his VC 'war decorations have no practical value in life in peace-time. Their possession, instead of being an asset, frequently acts as a definite hindrance in the fight for existence.'[17]

Pollard remained a patriotic imperialist who was fervently anti-Communist but he does not seem to have joined any right-wing party or militarist group. He deplored the 'anti-war' books of the later 1920s because, in his opinion, they dwelt too much on horrors and suffering, portrayed the British soldier in an unattractive light, and failed to bring out the sublime spirit of comradeship.[18]

In conclusion, Pollard was an intelligent, sensitive man, an outstandingly brave soldier and natural leader, and a vigorous, fluent writer with no great literary pretensions. Although he was either very bold or naive to publish war memoirs in 1932 emphasizing the 'fun' of combat and the importance of 'killing Huns', he was not a warmonger. His days as a fire-eater had ended in 1918, but unfortunately he never managed to achieve a really satisfying career in peacetime. His memoirs remain important, however, because of their vivid and honest portrait of a type of patriotic warrior spirit which was not so rare among both volunteers and regular soldiers in the era of the two world wars as it is now very difficult to believe in the radically different circumstances of the early twenty-first century.

John Reith wrote *Wearing Spurs* in the course of a few weeks in 1937 but did not publish the book until 1966, giving as the reason for the long delay an unwillingness to provide ammunition for his enemies. He had showed the typescript to a number of senior colleagues and friends, who all felt that he would be unwise to publish such a frank account of his early life at that time.

The Chairman of the BBC, Ronald Norman, found it 'intensely interesting' but advised that publication would do Reith a lot of harm. The Very Reverend Frederic Iremonger, head of religious broadcasting, said he had not been able to put it down: 'It was the most complete personal revelation since the Confessions of Augustine.' Sir Warren Fisher, Head of the Civil Service, was thrilled by it, but did not consider it seemly that Reith should bare his soul in public. Reith uncharacteristically accepted their advice without protest but was disappointed on two counts: it would have been great fun and he would miss the royalties – he had expected to make £10,000.[19] Meanwhile in 1949 he had published *Into the Wind*, which contained a succinct account of his time on the Western Front and a dense, rambling aftermath.

Wearing Spurs was very well received by the reviewers. Malcolm Muggeridge, for example, attempting to pin down the book's unique appeal, focused on its truthfulness: 'People lie habitually about war, as they do about sex and about money.' This was fair comment as regards Reith's later view of his brief period of active service, but Muggeridge had unwittingly touched on a huge omission. In 1914 the 24-year-old Reith was engaged in a passionate, obsessive affair with a 17-year-old schoolboy, Charlie Bowser, which would continue until a tragi-comic break-up in 1922 after they had both married. Reith's biographer, Ian McIntyre, shows that Reith wrote incessantly to Bowser, suffered pangs of jealousy, and made frantic efforts for them to be united. For the best part of ten years this relationship was the most important thing in Reith's life.[20]

In contrast to Pollard and his idealized lady, there is no evidence that Reith was hoping to impress Charlie and 'win his hand' by valiant deeds. Rather Reith had believed from an early age that he was destined to make a great mark in the world and in 1914 war seemed to offer a splendid opportunity for distinction.

John Reith was born in 1889, the youngest of seven children to parents who were both in their 40s. His father, the Reverend Dr George Reith, was a distinguished Presbyterian minister who was chaplain at Glasgow College Church. John's home life was comfortable but unhappy. He was not close to his much older brothers and sisters and saw little of his parents, who were both preoccupied with religious duties. His father, of whom he was in awe, seems to have been a remote and forbidding figure who forced his son into a long, uncongenial engineering apprenticeship, poured cold water on his scholarly aspirations, and signally failed to offer any encouragement or positive advice throughout his school and college days and early manhood. When, for example, John decided to seek a better-paid job in London his father was 'amply destructive', remarking 'You'll come back with your tail between your legs.' This was, to say the least, imperceptive and insensitive since John was now a trained tradesman fitter, 6'6" tall and burly, and brimming with the self-confident belief that he could do almost anything.[21]

Which came first in the shaping of his personality it is hard to be sure, but loneliness and frustration had surely contributed to Reith's obduracy, priggishness and awkwardness in personal relations. By his own admission he was not a good mixer; 'friendship eluded him' and he seemed to invite disputation and quarrels. He was regarded as unruly and bad-tempered at Gresham's School, Holt where he clashed with the headmaster; he had no social graces and – an enduring problem – could not laugh at himself. But he also knew that he was a born leader: it was only a question of finding a stage on which he could fulfil his ambitions.

Reith had been looking forward to the possibility of war from an early age and for purely personal reasons was delighted when his chance came in 1914. In 1901 he had joined the cadet corps at Glasgow Academy when it was first formed, and at Gresham's he became a corps sergeant, developing a strong word of command and skill as a marksman. Back in Glasgow, he joined the University Officers Training Corps and was commissioned with the 5th Scottish Rifles, a Territorial Army battalion, in 1911. This was not a happy time, partly because his working day stretched from 4.45 a.m. to 11.30 p.m., but also because he was irritated by 'artificialities in the officers' position'.[22]

On mobilization Reith, though an inexperienced and ungainly horseman, was made transport officer, thus enabling him to fulfil his ambition to wear spurs and, later, to realize his dream of arriving home unexpectedly in uniform and march up the aisle of his father's church to the jingle of spurs – a somewhat juvenile achievement to boast about for an officer in his mid-20s who had then seen very little action.

The 5th Scottish Rifles sailed to France in October 1914, among the first Territorial units to do so, and Reith found himself in comfortable billets near St Omer. He enjoyed serving on the Western Front from the moment of his arrival and was relieved to discover that under fire he experienced no nerves or fear. He would write later that 'there was no question of being brave or not brave. Some men are lucky, others unlucky in their make-up'. As transport officer he was by no means out of danger; during the enemy artillery's 'evening hates' ration dumps were especially dangerous as were the slow movements to and from the front line. But he preferred these dangers to 'the ghastly boredom and discomfort of trench life'.[23]

As his war memoirs show, Reith became notorious for unnecessary risk-taking and *sangfroid*: walking along the tops of trenches in daylight, calmly reading in a field frequently shelled, and even walking into No Man's Land to answer a call of nature. A curious incident in these early weeks in France indicates something of Reith's eccentric character and his lack of embarrassment in writing about it later. A casual female acquaintance sent him her signed photograph but, after solemn consideration, he burnt it, 'in almost sacramental style', in case he was killed and the photo should compromise the girl's reputation. This may strike the modern reader as ironic, if not simply daft, because Reith retained his treasured photo of Charlie, a schoolboy to whom he was not related. It must be stressed that there was nothing furtive, and probably nothing overtly sexual, about his friendship with Charlie; he wrote frankly to his own and Charlie's parents about it and even tried, vainly, to get Charlie into his battalion.[24]

Reith's complete abstinence from alcohol and his daily religious observances, kneeling to say prayers by his bed and reading passages from the Bible, must have struck some fellow officers as odd, but he was unselfconscious about religious matters. Indeed, he exhorted his soldiers in the Transport section to read their Bibles daily and encouraged Presbyterians among them to acknowledge their faith by taking holy communion. Not only did he persuade 22 'lapsed' co-religionists to take communion at Easter 1915, he also proudly informed his father of this success and later listed all their names in *Wearing Spurs*.[25]

Although Reith was not in the same class as Alf Pollard as a medal hunter, he too wished he was better placed to win decorations. At lunch in the Hotel de France at Bailleul he was upset to be sitting next to a major with the VC ribbon because his commanding officer had repeatedly declined to 'let us go out and do stunts of one kind or another'. He was also irritated 'by crowds of brass-hatted Olympians' (i.e. General Sir John French's staff) because he felt he could do their job at least as well as they and in retrospect he was sure of it.[26] He longed for front-line service, though not in the infantry. His wish would soon be granted.

After weeks of frustrating delay, in spring 1915 Reith secured a transfer to the Royal Engineers. This resulted from a war of attrition which he had waged with the Commanding Officer (Colonel Douglas) and the Adjutant of 5th Scottish Rifles, Major Croft. While Reith was evidently a super-efficient and manically energetic transport officer, he was also an autocratic and tactless empire-builder, always on the lookout to enhance his responsibilities and deflect any intervention which might cramp his style. In some instances Reith was understandably incensed at the petty obstacles caused by military bureaucracy and procedures, but in the long run he was fighting a battle he could not win. In an early contretemps Reith was unjustly accused of neglecting to groom two horses. The adjutant admitted his mistake and came to apologize but Reith lacked the social grace to accept his antagonist's humility in good part and further antagonized this influential officer. On another minor matter Reith erred in transferring a sergeant whom he deemed inefficient without first seeking higher approval.[27]

Reith was also convinced, erroneously, that the adjutant was a shirker deliberately avoiding the trenches so, on a rare visit by the latter, he quietly but venomously asked him if he would like to 'go out in front'. He immediately accepted but understandably preferred to walk along the trench and scramble through barbed wire obstacles whereas Reith ostentatiously walked upright along the parapet. By the time the adjutant had crawled back through the trench obstacles Reith had slipped off, thereby showing his contempt. Later he admitted it was a 'silly bit of bravado' and he had taken an undue risk. He compounded this tactlessness by spurning the adjutant's conciliatory gestures.[28]

Reith's rage against his former CO and adjutant persisted after he had left France and indeed into the inter-war years. Later during the war Reith encountered his former commanding officer in the street in Glasgow. The latter approached smiling and friendly but Reith cut him dead, remarking in *Wearing Spurs*: 'Is memory so short? Are people so forgiving or so oblivious of the need of being forgiven that they expect the same in others?' Hearing in 1916 that Colonel Douglas had been killed, Reith noted cynically that this was hard to believe 'unless it was by a shell some way back'. This was unjust: Douglas had been shot by a sniper. His enduring enmity towards the adjutant was equally unjustified. His father had gently advised him not to persist openly in this feud, and he learnt later that the adjutant had ended the war with the DSO and three bars. Seeing Reith's comments about him before they were published in *Into the Wind* the former adjutant told him that 'I [Reith] had suffered from an overweening sense of my own importance; and that I had little idea of team spirit and discipline if it did not suit me'.[29]

There was another aspect of Reith's unorthodox approach to the military rank-structure and traditions which would surely have landed him in trouble had he stayed longer in the battalion. Reith's pre-war experience with the Glasgow workforce had, we may think commendably, made him feel more comfortable with the other ranks than with officers, but fraternization across the gulf of rank was frowned upon if not downright forbidden. Reith hosted a party on Christmas night 1914 in the cellar of his billet for his transport soldiers which went on into the small hours; a breach, he admitted, of King's Regulations 'as prejudicial to good orders and military discipline'.[30] Nor was this an isolated incident. He habitually invited NCOs in turn to dine and take a hot bath in his comfortable billet, and sometimes even allowed them to sleep there. This would cause any adjutant some misgivings, regardless of the subaltern's humane and spiritual concerns for his men.

Reith had only been with the Royal Engineers for three weeks near Cuinchy north of Loos, and shortly after the disastrous battle there in September 1915, when fate at last caught up with him. He had already impressed his new major by his fearless work in the trenches.

On 7 October, not expecting to visit the front that day, he had put on his best tunic and a conspicuous light-coloured shirt. At short notice he volunteered to accompany his major to examine a new mine crater which had damaged the defences and required urgent attention. As usual he walked part of the way above ground, but had just entered the trench ahead of the major when he was shot in the face at close range by a sniper. His first thought was that the spouting blood would ruin his uniform; the second was that he would soon know the truth about life after death. Impatient that his great height and bulk were hampering the stretcher-bearers in the narrow trenches, he insisted, to their amazement, on walking half a mile till he reached a mobile trolley. The wound in his face measured five inches by three inches and another bullet had hit his shoulder. He would endure a long and very painful recovery and would not see active service again.[31]

At the moment of his injury, expecting to die, he had asked for a scrap of paper and in a shaky hand had scrawled his mother's name and address and the message 'I'm all right'. With this dramatic incident he brings *Wearing Spurs* to an abrupt end, but he had been economical with the truth. As he lay in the trench expecting to die he had also written to Charlie 'Cheer up, dear old boy'. As it happened Charlie was the first to hear that he had been seriously wounded and sent two messages to Reith's parents before they heard anything from the War Office. Moreover the official telegram was cautiously phrased 'degree [of wound] not stated', whereas Charlie's second telegram reported 'Safe field hospital, not serious, doctor pleased'. After the break-up with Charlie in 1922 Reith had increasingly seen him to be the prime cause of his, Reith's, emotional turmoil and misery and ruthlessly cut him out of his memoirs.[32]

Many soldiers would have been delighted to receive Reith's honourable 'Blighty' wound but he was frustrated and angry that his active military career had ended just as he was beginning to enjoy himself. After recuperation he spent 18 very happy months in the United States, mainly at the Remington Works, in charge of munitions production; and at the end of the war his role was reversed in arranging the liquidation of ordnance and engineering contracts for the Ministry of Munitions. In 1922 he was appointed the General Manager of the BBC and elevated to Managing Director the following year. Between 1927 and 1938 he achieved what most people would regard as the apex of his career in terms of power, prestige and influence as the Director-General of the BBC. Other important appointments followed including Minister of Information and Minister of Transport in 1940, and Minister of Works and Buildings between 1940 and 1942, but none of these later jobs brought him the satisfaction of his tremendous achievements at the BBC.

Reith had undeniably achieved the fame he had coveted as a young man, but at an enormous cost to his nervous system. Like so many public figures with distinguished careers he died, in 1971, disappointed that he had not fulfilled his potential. Despite a succession of demanding appointments he believed that he had never been given a job which would stretch his abilities to the limit. A gigantic figure both in mental and physical terms, Reith had the exaggerated virtues and faults of a tragic hero. Writing his biography, as Ian McIntyre candidly remarks, sometimes brought him close to tears: 'I did not dream when I began to read John Reith's diaries that I would encounter so much raw pain.'[33]

Wearing Spurs would surely be more widely recognized as an outstanding memoir of the First World War had it not been published so long after the event, and by an author then indelibly associated in the public mind with the origins of the BBC and the development of television in the 1930s. Reith was truly a 'fire-eater' in being remarkably free from fear in combat and brave to the point of exhibitionism. Reviewers praised his book for its conciseness, literary distinction, and above all truthfulness, in avoiding exaggeration either in exalting war or in revulsion against it. He came as near as was humanly possible to conveying what it was really like to be a young Territorial officer serving in the trenches in France in 1914 and 1915. Whatever Lord Reith's sense of frustration and failure in later life he should have taken some consolation from these brilliant memoirs, describing with 'true artistry, charm and fidelity, an experience deeply felt, and the response to it of his own highly complex and idiosyncratic character'.[34]

5

Grandeur and misery: the Guards

According to Samuel Johnson, 'Every man thinks meanly of himself for not having been a soldier …' For those who concur with this sentiment one might go further and add 'particularly a Guardsman'. The British Guards regiments – Grenadiers, Coldstream, Scots and, more recent twentieth-century creations, Irish and Welsh – have traditionally set the highest standards in drill, appearance and battlefield performance. In his eloquent tribute to the Guards in his *Memoirs*, Oliver Lyttelton (Lord Chandos) remarks that of the many institutions he had known in a long career 'the best human organisation, the most efficient and the most closely knit … is the Brigade of Guards'. A battalion 'well turned out, the men with their heads up … in step and in some awe of their officers and NCOs, will stand the strain of battle better than bodies which follow looser rules'. From the standpoint of 1962 he admitted that 'some flexibility, some initiative can easily be lost'.[1] But the Brigade had always set a standard which, though sometimes equalled, was never surpassed. When he joined the 2nd Battalion Grenadier Guards in 1915 the discipline was extremely strict and its firepower unbelievable. The 15 rounds of rapid, aimed fire often made the Germans believe they were opposed by a machine-gun battalion.

Stuart Cloete, who transferred to the Coldstream Guards late in the war, noted with pride that to see the Guards marching up to the line brought even the peasants, bored with the war, to the roadside to watch. There was a great feeling of brotherhood and solidarity (as well as fierce rivalry) between all the battalions of the Guards Division. They were without fear because they had absolute confidence in each other. 'They could not fail. They could only be destroyed.'[2]

Sir Charles Wilson (Lord Moran), who had served as a regimental doctor in the First World War, believed that the Guards' superb efficiency was due to their privileged position as well as their own high standards in drill and discipline. No half-trained troops were sent out to them in France, and if Guardsmen were wounded and recovered they would return to their own battalion. While Moran accepted that drill was an important ingredient of morale, he put more emphasis than did martinets, like Lord Gort, VC, on intangible factors such as devotion to the Brigade. Polished buttons, erect carriage and things of that kind were not the cause of excellence but its effect.[3] Aristocrats set the tone and their untitled colleagues were, at the least, well-to-do. Etonians were numerous and

Harrow was also well represented. As a well-defined, semi-independent elite, the Guards successfully resisted large-scale expansion towards a 'people's army'. Many 'hostilities only' gentlemen were admitted as officers, but dilution in both the officer corps and the ranks was strictly limited: the Grenadier Guards were doubled in size from two battalions to four in 1915 but the expansion stopped there. Lyttelton and his friend Robert ('Bobbety') Cranborne had both been in the Eton College cadet corps, but when it seemed they would be stuck at home in the Bedfordshire Regiment the latter's father, Lord Salisbury, easily effected their transfer, as officers, to the Grenadier Guards.[4]

Lyttelton describes some of the characters who strongly influenced the ethos of the 2nd Battalion when he joined it early in 1915. The second-in-command was Major G. D. (later General Lord) Jeffreys, always known as 'Ma' because when he joined in 1897 a notorious *maison de rendezvous* was kept by a Mrs Jeffreys, referred to as 'Ma'. Jeffreys had impressed the battalion by striding into No Man's Land in broad daylight and in full view of the enemy to rescue an isolated platoon; but he would have damned any subaltern who halted his troop on the wrong foot on the parade ground. The oddest thing about him, perhaps, was that he had kept a pet lion while on active service in France.[5]

Another outstanding company commander, 'Copper' Seymour (Major Lord Seymour), had been serving in Africa at the beginning of the war, self-exiled by gambling debts, and had been badly wounded while in command of native levies. He was really unfit for active service but had evaded a medical board to get to France and, due to his wounds, had to be dressed by subalterns. 'He had red hair, brilliant blue eyes, and was a strict disciplinarian.'

Another veteran company commander, Claude 'Crawley' de Crespigny, had been one of the best-known gentleman jockeys of his day. He was racked with pain by a stomach disorder but would not report sick and sometimes lay groaning in the trench for the best part of the night. Yet he somehow found relief next day with a glass or two of port and kept going. His chief interests were hunting, steeplechasing, gambling and fighting. Macmillan never saw him read a book or even refer to one. He had no respect for the higher command (i.e. beyond the brigade), and ignored repeated orders to desist from wearing gold spurs.

Another eccentric character was 'Boy' Brooke, a brigade-major and later commander of the 3rd Battalion Grenadier Guards, who never spoke before lunch and nonplussed his subordinates by intimidating silences. Until he had lunched and drunk a glass of port his indigestion 'clothed the world in a bilious haze', but after lunch he could be 'charming, helpful and humorous', though still capable of a cutting rebuke to any junior officer whom he considered unsuited to the regiment.[6]

Although they were treated sociably and with a remarkable degree of equality (all officers except the CO were referred to by Christian names and seniority was not stressed when out of action), Lyttelton and other young officers found that the slightest deviation from regimental standards was 'visited by reprimand or punishment, and I cannot recall that we were often praised'. Even when marching back from front-line duty a battalion commander could be criticized for poor discipline. When a man had been seen without his haversack and the rear section of a platoon was out of step, 'then there was hell to pay'. At least these ultra-strict standards were applied at all times and irrespective of rank. Lyttelton heard his divisional commander, Major-General Lord Cavan, being ticked off by the corps commander for wearing the gold spurs of a guardsman. 'You are no longer a regimental officer, please remember that, "Fatty"'.[7]

In contrast to these exceedingly high standards when on duty, guards officers (with a few exceptions like Lord Gort) sought comfort, relaxation and enjoyment when at leisure. When in reserve, for example, officers were allowed into Amiens on 48-hour passes. These were wonderful days, Sir Allan Adair recalled, because the city was full of delicious food and amusements. It was a luxury to have a hot bath and sleep in sheets. Whether in the front line or not, all did their utmost to be comfortable. Each company headquarters had its own little officers' mess in a dug-out where the standard of cuisine was high, and there was usually plenty of whisky and port. On special occasions caviare and asparagus would appear, even when close to the front line. Mail reached everyone within a week, as did periodicals like *Country Life* and the *Burlington Magazine*. On longer leave richer Guards officers like the American, Carroll Carstairs, had a wonderful, carefree time in Paris. He had a room at the Ritz overlooking the garden and in the evening, 'all who were in Paris foregathered at the Crillon Bar. What a sight it was, that changing handful of men in the uniform of three armies. Will I ever recapture that atmosphere of fleeting revelry? ... And then a gala night. Ten of us dined at the Cafe de Paris ... Orpen (the artist) was one of us ... We went on to the Folies Bergere ... an indescribable scene ... We danced to a gramophone ... and drank champagne until early morning.'[8]

Within the pervading spirit of paternalism, as Gary Sheffield has shown, officer–other rank relations were generally good. Officers were inculcated with the ideal of looking after their soldiers' interests and welfare to the best of their ability and at all times. For their part the other ranks required battalion officers to earn their respect, notably by courageous leadership in battle and doing their best for them when out of it. There is ample evidence that most officers developed real affection for their men, while soldiers were often profoundly upset by the deaths of their respected company officers.[9] But it was extremely difficult for friendships to flourish across the gulf between officers and other ranks. In the Guards this social gulf was markedly wider, and more strictly maintained, than in less elitist line regiments. Obvious differences in class background, wealth, education and the rigorous standards of dress and discipline rendered informal relations all but impossible. In general it seems likely that this gulf was accepted as a fact of life on both sides of the divide, but a few better-educated rankers from professional or socially respectable backgrounds found these constraints unnatural and irksome.

One Scots guardsman who wrote perceptively about this and other aspects of life in the Guards was the remarkable traveller and writer, Stephen Graham, who published *A Private in the Guards* as early as October 1919. Graham, who was born in 1884 and served in the 2nd Battalion Scots Guards in 1917–18, was already a well-known journalist and author before 1914. His energetic globe-trotting, which would continue throughout his long life (he died in 1975), was inspired by the writer's humane desire to experience life with ordinary people. Thus in Russia he had lived rough with peasants and students, visiting the Caucasus, the Urals and the far north. He had sailed steerage to North America and tramped to the remote western states to work on farms. In 1914 and 1915 he had travelled in Central Asia, Egypt, Bulgaria and Romania; and in 1916 he had revisited northern Europe, getting as far as Murmansk. Clearly, Graham was a suitable officer-candidate, but he preferred to experience life in the ranks with a view to writing about it immediately after the war had ended.[10]

Graham quickly perceived that the officers 'are not really near the men; a great gulf divides them socially, and must do so, but the men would not follow so well an officer who was too free with them'. Then the officer, 'being presumably rich and of the class of masters, is seen to suffer as much or more on the field of battle, and Tommy realises that we are all in it together and have only devised the rules of discipline for the greatest good of all'. He was particularly conscious of class and rank problems when on ceremonial duties in London since he lived a 'double life' as a private in uniform and as a member of polite society when in civilian clothes. Some officers behaved cordially towards him in society, but others remained cold and distant, even refusing to shake hands. While lip-service was paid to the value of the common soldier they were seen to lack power and might be treated almost as slaves. As a deeply religious man, Graham's credo was that the life of the poor could not be understood by the better-off except by immersion among them. Consequently he contended that young clergymen and other well-wishers should follow his example and immerse themselves in the life of the masses. He accepted that war was a brutalizer: all rankers soon realized that the uniform betokened hard duty and bondage, a durance such as that of slave or prisoner. Ordinary soldiers were confined to a largely passive role, whereas NCOs were extremely active and drove the privates to do what was required. 'I noticed that men who were not in themselves brutal cultivated brutality to set the army tone'.[11]

Norman D. Cliff was a Devonian journalist from a conventional puritanical background who lost his job with the *Torquay Times* on the outbreak of war and naively volunteered for the Grenadier Guards. His memoirs, evocatively entitled *To Hell and Back with the Guards*, appear to have been written near the end of his life (he died in 1977) and were not published until 1988 with a dedication 'To all who strive for world peace and an end to wars'. Cliff's war experience made him a pacifist and in later life he was an active member of the Labour Party. The late compilation of the memoirs, with frequent references to authors popular in the 1970s, such as A. J. P. Taylor, and its polemical tone render the book a dubious source for attitudes and opinions held in the era of the First World War. Nevertheless Cliff's frank comments and criticisms are worth considering. He did after all win the Military Medal and his opinions probably did represent what many better-educated and sensitive ex-rankers felt retrospectively about life in the Guards.

Cliff concluded that although there was a great sense of *esprit de corps* and pride in regimental traditions there was little respect for most of the officers, their gallantry in action notwithstanding.

> The sharp division maintained between officers and men allowed no opportunity for mutual confidence to develop, and it was only in the heat of action that the prowess of outstanding leaders inspired confidence and admiration. How wide was the gulf is shown by the fact that never once throughout the war did I have a man-to-man conversation with an officer. Were we not brothers in arms facing death side by side? No, we were members of different species with no habit of communication, separated by the impenetrable barrier of class.[12]

During the war, however, it seems likely that the great majority of guardsmen accepted the almost Prussian approach to discipline and rigid class divisions as an unalterable fact of life.

From the officers' viewpoint Lyttelton recalled that many 'weedy and narrow-chested recruits' were swept into the army by unemployment and starvation; and deserved better treatment than they received after the war. Macmillan also made considerable play in his political career of the fact that his concern for working men had been inspired by his experience in the war.[13]

Graham and Cliff both successfully endured the draconian treatment handed out by harsh and sometimes even sadistic NCOs at the Guards Training Depot at Caterham, aptly nicknamed 'Little Sparta', but their later reactions, though both in some respects critical, differed considerably. This was due mainly to the fact that Graham was an older man, widely travelled, knowledgeable about the grim underside of life, and seeking, as an established journalist, to turn his experience into print. By contrast Cliff, though also a journalist, was younger (born in 1893), inexperienced and priggish by his own admission, and quite unprepared for the obscene language, brutality and sickening injustice that he would encounter at Caterham.

Stephen Graham devoted 60 pages to describing the severe training regime at 'Little Sparta' Barracks, including vivid character studies of the sergeants who dominated the recruits' lives. He was fortunate in having a strong brigade sergeant major who was kind to the recruits but a terror to the NCOs, particularly in stopping them from striking men on the drill square. Graham accepted that tough measures were necessary to break down a recruit's pride and make him amenable to army discipline, but he thought the physical brutality, humiliation and obscenity were excessive.

Graham found many similarities between his comrades and the historical Spartans, especially their courage in battle where they simply would not yield. This outstanding military virtue redeemed the Guardsmen's many shortcomings: ignorance, scorn for all other regiments, vulgarity and coarse bodies. 'We were proved later in the battle-line, and it was seen that we knew how to die.' He paid an eloquent tribute to the spirit of the battalion:

> The regiment has left its memorials in every place where it has been. There are its crosses in every military acre of God; there are its dead, its lonely soldiers, buried in No Man's Land; there are its lost dead too. He [the new recruit] comes to new faces, hard eyes, set lips, patient jaws, faces that have *seen*, the faces of those who have killed many and lust to kill more, the lined faces of those who have been wounded and are still in the fighting ranks. The battalion gives him its style, its stamp and impression, and as he breathes the regimental air he swears the regimental oaths. The spirit, however is born of many sufferings and endless patience.[14]

By contrast, Cliff drew grimly negative conclusions from his time at Caterham. He conceded that the more a soldier reverts to the savage the better killer he is likely to become. 'Mercy, kindliness and chivalry have to be replaced by brutality, hatred and ruthlessness.' But in inculcating instant, unthinking obedience to orders, he believed that the core qualities of personality and initiative ought to be preserved. By giving priority to smartness and almost mechanical precision on parade the Guards Command tended to dull the mind and kill initiative and responsibility. Indeed he believed that the Guards hierarchy pursued incredibly stupid methods: 'the effect of the whole system of drill was not to inculcate self-respect and to fire enthusiasm, but to humiliate and rob a man of his dignity, thus instilling hatred of and contempt for those in authority.'[15]

Cliff illustrates his opinions about learning contempt for authority by several critical remarks about officers. Whereas the soldiers' hair was routinely cropped, officers' *coiffeurs* flourished as elegantly as ever. He uses Winston Churchill's brief sojourn with the Guards for a diatribe against the use of soldiers nominally at rest to lug boxes of silver and crates of liquor for delivery to the officers' mess. While supposedly fighting for freedom and democracy the Army appeared to be 'the most class-ridden and least democratic of all our institutions'. He also resented the fact that a number of officers had been allowed home leave to recuperate from war-weariness after two years or more of active service, whereas no similar concession was made for the other ranks.[16]

Cliff retained an undying anger and bitterness against his former company commander Captain (Viscount) Lascelles. He resented the peer's over-elegant appearance (Lascelles' stylish uniform brought an 'atmosphere of Mayfair in the grimy trenches'); his pronounced lisp ('Call the woll! Pawade, thande at eathe'); and above all the belief that he got a sentry killed unnecessarily by ordering him to look over the top of the trench. Yet he had to admit that Lascelles was a gallant leader in combat, which was true of some other officers whose manner was resented.[17]

Cliff's inclination towards pacifism was already posing problems for him in the trenches. Reflecting that any German he might kill would probably have a wife and children, he experienced a wave of revulsion against the madness of war: 'I would not use my rifle unless there was no alternative', and even then he would try to wound and not to kill. Later he attended a Lewis gun course and admitted it would now be harder to keep his resolution not to shoot to kill. At least he was consistent about his hostile feelings towards officers; though recommended for a commission three times he always declined.[18]

Ceremonial drill and 'bull' inevitably loomed large in Guardsmen's lives in peacetime but there was understandable resentment at the extent to which these routines continued to be drastically enforced on active service. Shortly after emerging from the nightmare of Loos, Cliff's battalion was obliged to drill as though for a royal birthday on Horse Guards Parade for a visit by King George V. This was cancelled because he had been thrown from his horse (i.e. the horse Haig had lent him), but many later parades *did* take place, often after long periods of waiting and 'usually on a plateau swept by bitter winds'.

This grouse may seem excessive since every soldier has undergone similar chores and boredom in preparation for special parades. A much more reasonable complaint was directed at the Guards' obsession with perfect turn-out and immaculate drill even in the immediate aftermath of battle. Cliff gives an example on leaving the dreary trenches at Laventie late in 1915:

> Collapsing in the usual barn, we set about cleaning ourselves, our uniforms and equipment, and longed for nothing more than to rest and recuperate. But no, we were Guards. Parades and drill there had to be, with every man polished as though for 'Buck Guard'. Woe betide anyone on whose boots the Sergeant-Major could detect the slightest speck of mud. This seemed beyond reason and we resented being harried when relaxation would have put us in a better mood for the next round.[19]

On another occasion 14 days of 'rest' were occupied with endless drill and inspections in which defaulters were punished for the tiniest speck of mud. Far from raising morale, persistent drill made the soldiers 'fed up, disgruntled and resentful'. In comparison with this purgatory even route marches were a pleasant diversion. Nor were officers immune from the misuse of hard-won periods of rest. In mid-September 1916 Carroll Carstairs' battalion was relieved after four days of intensive combat (and in his case seven days without taking his clothes off). But the 'rest' was only from fighting because 'drills, parade and training went on with greater intensity than existed in Chelsea Barracks ... I honestly believe that our Commanding Officer looked upon trench duty as a period of idleness to be drastically remedied immediately the Battalion was behind the lines'.[20]

Stuart Cloete, later a Coldstream Guards officer, but earlier serving with the King's Own Yorkshire Light Infantry, provides a graphic example where a brigadier's obsession with inspections to ensure readiness for action passed the bounds of reason and humanity. Cloete's company had been in action for two days and taken all their objectives. The men were lying exhausted on the fire steps and floor of the trench when the brigadier ordered an immediate rifle inspection. Cloete protested that the men were all-in, but he had inspected their rifles and they could stand-to at once if the enemy attacked. Cloete was threatened with court-martial but refused to budge without a written order. The Brigadier retreated, no charge was brought, and Cloete may even have been praised for his spirited defiance of authority in protecting his men.[21]

As we have already noted, the Guards' regimental traditions and brutal training allowed little scope for chivalry. Germans attempting to surrender were sometimes allowed to do so but at other times they were killed. More reprehensible, Germans whose surrender had been accepted quite often did not survive to reach the comparative safety of the prisoner cages. Sometimes there was an excuse for the latter practice, i.e. killing men who had already surrendered. Carstairs cites the 'terrible experience' of a fellow officer who, with about seven men, took prisoner a party of about 30 Germans. The latter were told to make their own way down the trench but, on turning a corner, their officer produced a hand grenade and threw it at his captors. No one was hurt but after this duplicity the whole group was killed. 'Some squealed like pigs but what else could be done?' Regarding the unwillingness to take prisoners, Wilfrid Ewart records casually that in September 1918 his Scots Guards Battalion 'had killed a lot of Bosches, the order being "No prisoners", so they did in everybody, including the blokes who put up their hands'.[22]

Stephen Graham has a long, reflective section on the Guards' ruthless, unchivalrous attitude to the enemy which, he claims, was enforced by officers and NCOs. 'The regimental tone absolutely forbade admiration of anything in connection with Germans ... The idea of taking prisoners had become very unpopular among the men. A good soldier was one who would not take a prisoner.' If called on to escort prisoners to the cage it could always be said they had been shot trying to escape. There were stories about sergeants and even officers who had become regimental heroes for killing prisoners, or soldiers trying to surrender. Dug-outs might be cleared by lobbing in a Mills bomb with the sardonic remark 'Share that among you, bastards!' Some officers were appalled by such behaviour and attitudes; not only was killing prisoners illegal but it was dangerous in encouraging similar treatment for British captives, especially Guardsmen, whose fearsome reputation went before them. As Graham reflected, 'Out of cruelty comes cruelty. Out of mercy comes mercy.' He recounts the chilling story of a German who had been wrongly accused of sniping at civilians. Already wounded, he was shot and left to die, slowly on a dunghill. Later Graham heard this disgraceful episode cited as an example of German wickedness. Only when the British Army entered Germany as an occupying force and witnessed the privation of enemy civilians did a more humanitarian spirit prevail.[23]

The Guards were, and still are, not only a social elite, but also a combat elite. Robert Graves admiringly placed them in his top category 'always reliable', and they were frequently used to try to snatch victory from the jaws of failure, as at Loos, or hold threatened sectors when other brigades and divisions had given way, as in the German offensives in March and April 1918. Their unshakeable *esprit de corps* aroused admiration but also envy among less distinguished regiments of the line.

In the summer of 1915 a Guards Division was formed from the battalions sent out from England. Lord Cavan, appointed to command the new division, was opposed to this creation because he feared that if the Grenadiers fought as a brigade they would lose more officers than could be replaced. He insisted that all brigades should contain battalions from several of the five Guards regiments. After Loos in fact the Guards Division usually contained at least a brigade of non-Guards battalions, while Guards brigades might be detached to stiffen other divisions.

The normal routine for each battalion was to spend three days in the front trenches, three days in close reserve and 12 days at rest in billets, though 'rest', as we have noted, tended to be taken up with drills, inspections and fatigues – especially carrying supplies to the front and repairing defences. The most dangerous times at the front were dawn and dusk when units were alerted and stood-to with arms ready in case of an enemy attack. After morning stand-down there would be the delights of breakfast – cooked bacon and cheese with scalding hot tinned milk and coffee – followed by weapon inspection and a relatively easy day, always provided that the trenches were in good repair and the enemy remained inactive. The Guards prided themselves on the excellent condition of their trenches and defences even in the waterlogged conditions often prevalent around Ypres. They were rarely satisfied with the state of the trenches left by their predecessors in the front line.[24]

A few vignettes of some of the Guards' most important battles must suffice to convey a sense of their performance, very often in a dense 'fog of war' resulting from command and staff errors at a higher level.

Such chaotic conditions prevailed, for example, on 17 May 1915 when, several days after the original attack at Festubert had stalled, Second Battalion, Grenadier Guards was ordered to renew the offensive. Appalling wet and windy weather caused the attack to be delayed until the next day. The men lay in their waterlogged holes all day until, at 3.45 p.m., the battalion was ordered to attack at 4.30 p.m. This short notice and inadequate artillery preparation caused the leading company to be virtually wiped out, with only one officer surviving unwounded. 'Ma' Jeffreys ordered the attack to be renewed but the company commander, Percy Clive MP, refused on the grounds that this would be suicidal. Lord Gort, whose courage was never in doubt, came up to investigate and endorsed Clive's objection, proving that common sense could sometimes prevail over the 'do or die' spirit. The battalion had advanced only about 300 yards and was well short of its objective. That night Lyttelton took up a relief company in pitch darkness and heavy rain and did his best to locate and rescue the wounded. It was a gruesome and depressing experience. The feeling among the surviving officers was that the attack had been badly mismanaged by the high command, particularly in ordering a sudden attack in broad daylight against unsubdued machine-guns.[25]

As Simon Ball has commented about a larger and more chaotic battle, 'It is doubtful whether the Guards Division's attack at Loos ever had a chance.' The operation had already been raging for two days (from 25 September), and the Guards' attack had to start from the old German trenches which the enemy artillery could shell with precision. Muddled staff work caused the 4th Grenadiers Battalion to spend the night sitting on a muddy road. Ordered to attack Hill 70 just to the east of Loos, chaos reigned as the battalion was misdirected, split in two, and then shelled and machine-gunned. Half the Grenadiers' battalion, with the Welsh Guards, swept forward and reached the summit of Hill 70, taking heavy casualties in the process. Those Grenadiers who continued over the crest of the hill were annihilated by fire from the next German line. The 4th Grenadier Guards had lost 11 officers and 342 men but were nevertheless proud of their determined attacks in a hopeless cause.[26]

After the debacle at Loos Lyttelton was promoted and transferred as adjutant to the newly-formed 3rd Battalion holding trenches just north of the battle area. It had lost nearly 400 men killed in the battle and its morale was low. Lyttelton at once realized that the main reason was an utterly incompetent commanding officer, Lt. Col. Noel Corry, whose much more professional son had been at Eton and later in the 2nd Battalion with him. He endured a difficult period as Corry tried to blame him for failures, but at the end of 1915 the colonel was sent home.[27]

In the summer of 1916 the Guards Division marched south to the Somme long after the original offensive on 1 July had stalled. Placed on the right flank in Cavan's XIV Corps the Division was ordered to exploit the first employment of tanks to advance, on 15 September, from the village of Ginchy to capture Lesboeufs to the north-east.

The offensive was ill-fated from the first: the artillery on the Guards' right failed to locate the German trenches with the dreadful result that 6th Division suffered 4,000 casualties on the day with no ground gained. The tanks also proved worse than useless on this sector because the lanes left open for their advance created clear fields of fire for the German machine-guns. Deprived of support on their right flank, unable to locate the neatly-drawn Green, Brown and Red lines in a devastated landscape devoid of landmarks, and advancing on too narrow a front, chaos soon prevailed with Grenadiers, Irish and Coldstreams intermingled. Prior and Wilson, so relentlessly critical of British strategy and tactics in the Somme battles, at least allow that the Guards did all they could to redeem the plan by attacking ferociously towards Lesboefs and bayoneting all the terrified Bavarians they encountered. The Guards gained 2,000 yards (1.8 km) on a 1,500-yard (1.4 km) front which was 'quite a feat in the circumstances', but only the first German line had been captured and Lesboeufs remained in enemy hands for a further ten days.[28]

This was the greatest day of Lyttelton's military career to date. When his Grenadiers saw a German company appear just in front of them they rushed the enemy position with 'a hoarse blood cry' and shot or bayoneted most of the defenders, who did not put up their hands until too late. Lyttelton admits that he was fired up and fighting mad. 'After that nothing would have stopped the Grenadiers – nothing.' He had proved himself a 'thruster', secured a large bag of prisoners, and been awarded an immediate DSO. It had been a 'superbly exhilarating' experience. But these meagre territorial gains had been won at huge cost. In this action, of the 22 officers of Lyttelton's battalion, nine (including the Prime Minister's son Raymond Asquith) were killed and nine wounded. In two days' fighting no fewer than 395 other ranks were killed or wounded: more than half the effective strength. On 25 September the other Guards Brigades stormed Lesboeufs and secured the slopes beyond. The division was then relieved and congratulated in the warmest terms by the Corps and Army commanders (Cavan and Rawlinson).[29]

The German March 1918 offensive confronted the BEF with operational problems it had not had to deal with since the opening phase of the war in 1914: namely a hectic retreat in the utmost confusion, opposed by superior numbers and without properly prepared defence lines to fall back on. To add to the confusion, it was widely rumoured that Fifth Army would have to retreat whereas Third Army, in the Arras area, would try to hold firm. In this sector Lyttelton was now brigade-major in the newly-formed 4th Guards Brigade, which was detached from the Guards Division (though deployed next to it) and transferred to the 31st Division. This was glumly seen as a relegation from an elite formation to one of the poorest – the 'thirty worst'.

Already worried about the competence of commanders and staff in 31st Division and VI Corps to which it was assigned when the German offensive began on 21 March, Lyttelton discovered next day that a rout had occurred and panic set in at Corps Headquarters. The enemy had broken through 40th Division on 31st's left and the troops were paralysed with fear. Lyttelton arrested an officer who tried to flee through the Guards who, to add to the confusion, were being shelled by their own artillery. With both their flanks exposed and no clear orders, the 4th Guards Brigade began a three-day retreat. When his brigadier, Lord Ardee, was gassed and went off sick on 26 March, Lyttelton rode over to the Guards Division near Hébuterne to request that the brigade be taken back under its wing. He was reassured to find the senior staff officer, Ned Grigg, playing badminton. Reunion with the Guards Division was not possible in the short term and in the following days confusion was worse confounded as 31st Division issued a false message that the Germans had broken through to the south. Communications then ceased because a staff officer had felled a tree on to the telephone lines. Consequently the 4th Guards Brigade found itself defending the whole divisional front against a German attack. Despite three consecutive nights without sleep, taken up with endless journeys on foot and on horseback to try to establish solid defences on his flanks, Lyttelton kept his nerve and issued clear simple orders which permitted the Brigade to establish a new line with the reasurring support of the Guards Division on its left. In the post-battle conference these orders were held up as a model of professional staff work – issued in the middle of the night but clear, simple and practical. When the brigade was withdrawn from the line on 31 March it had lost 14 officers and 372 men. The Guards were justly proud of their performance but emerged with little confidence in the command or staff of the division which had issued confusing and conflicting orders based on false information (about enemy penetration in the rear) which could easily have been checked. Lyttelton concluded laconically, with a new brigadier in place 'we immediately started on our usual routine of training'.[30]

When, on 9 April 1918, Ludendorff renewed his offensive further north, driving across the River Lys towards Hazebrouck, the Guards performed one of the most heroic defensive operations of the whole war. The 4th Guards Brigade was ordered to de-bus near Merville to plug a huge gap in the line. This was a critical moment because if the rail centre at Hazebrouck was lost the enemy route to the Channel ports would be open. However, if the enemy offensive could be checked he would be left in a vulnerable salient, like the British at Ypres.

On the morning of 12 April the brigade's situation was desperate: there was no defensive line and the enemy, with superior forces, was threatening to envelop both flanks. The staff solution seemed to be a retreat to a better position behind the Bois d'Aval, but the brigadier (L. J. Butler) decided to attack. Seeing fresh troops advancing in immaculate order on a 3,000-yard front, the enemy thought a major counter-attack was developing and withdrew on both the Guards' flanks. With both flanks still open and in almost featureless country the situation remained desperate, against a skilful enemy exploiting every tactical opportunity. At 4.30 p.m. a fierce German attack along the whole front was beaten off but at heavy cost in lives – the Grenadiers lost eight officers and 250 other ranks and the Coldstreams about the same.[31]

The morning of 13 April proved to be the critical point of the battle and for several hours the defenders' position was desperate.

> The enemy were round both our flanks: a fresh column of infantry of about two battalions was seen by an artillery observer from the top window of a farmhouse, debouching from Bleu: the enemy artillery started to fire at us over open sights: the immediate rear areas were under continuous machine-gun fire. We moved Brigade HQ into the firing line: we had no more reserves to speak of.[32]

With the left flank open and no reserves left a Grenadier Guards company, under a most gallant officer, Captain T. T. Pryce, literally fought to the end. When last seen Pryce was charging the enemy at the head of seven men. He was awarded a posthumous VC. A company of Irish Guards displayed equal valour and were almost wiped out, as were Coldstream companies on the right flank. The 4th Guards Brigade were reduced to a number of isolated posts, still refusing to give in and clinging to their positions. Headquarters personnel, including orderlies and signallers, were thrown into the battle, as were stragglers from other divisions. By about 4.00 p.m. both sides had reached the point of exhaustion and the attack slackened; the Germans had failed to take Hazebrouck, from whose station now detrained the magnificent troops of the 1st Australian Division. The day was saved, but at terrible cost. The Grenadiers had lost 15 officers and 504 other ranks, the Coldstreams also lost 15 officers and 490 other ranks and the Irish Guards nine officers and 250 other ranks. Fewer than 400 fighting men remained when the Brigade was withdrawn on 14 April. For the first time in the long history of the Brigade of Guards a composite battalion of Grenadiers and Coldstreams had to be formed. As Lyttelton proudly concluded:

> The iron discipline and long fighting tradition of the Guards regiments stood the strain and won the day. The individual soldier fought to the last, and once more showed that the greatest of military rules is 'Never give in'. We had beaten off and chewed up two divisions of well-led German troops.[33]

In 1962 Oliver Lyttelton, now Lord Chandos and with a very successful business and political career behind him, published his *Memoirs* with its four brilliant chapters on his experience in the First World War. Harold Macmillan, his former companion in the Grenadiers, hailed it as 'the best description of war from the regimental officer's point of view that has been written since Tolstoy', but this was far from being the prevailing perception in the 1960s of Britain's military performance in the First World War. Alan Clark had already published (in 1961) *The Donkeys* with its seductive popular argument that the ordinary soldiers (all perceived as 'lions') had been led to the slaughter by their callous asinine generals. At this time, as Chairman of the National Theatre Board, a venture to which he was passionately devoted, Lyttelton was waging a long, bitter struggle against Kenneth Tynan, who deliberately sought confrontation by attempting to put on two plays which debunked all the values which Lyttelton and his generation had believed in and fought for.[34] Lyttelton succeeded in seeing off Tynan and neither play was staged, but he had also alienated the National Theatre's director Sir Laurence Olivier and his days as chairman were numbered. Far worse was to follow in 1963 with the Theatre Workshop's production of Joan Littlewood's savage, debunking entertainment *Oh! What a Lovely War*. The merciless caricature of British senior officers in the Battle of Loos was too near the knuckle for Lyttelton and Macmillan who had fought there. Their well-informed but restrained criticism of British command failings was replaced by Littlewood's hilarious mockery of the back-stabbing, cowardice, snobbery and incompetence of the whole officer class.[35]

In an attempt to stem this tide of 'anti-war' and 'anti-officer' influence Lyttelton published a greatly expanded volume of memoirs, *From War to Peace* (1968), which drew heavily on wartime letters to his mother and was avowedly intended to counter what he regarded as pernicious myths.[36] His attempt to restore public respect for the traditional military virtues, especially as represented by the Guards, was doomed to fail in the radical, anti-authority climate of opinion in the 1960s and 1970s. A new generation of literary critics, reviewers and television producers, who mostly lacked any first-hand military experience, were generally sympathetic to Littlewood's overriding concern with the experience of ordinary soldiers who had allegedly been betrayed by aristocratic generals epitomized by Sir Douglas Haig. 'Anti-war' poets, especially Siegfried Sassoon and Wilfred Owen, who had hitherto not been widely influential with the general public, were now publicized as the true representatives and spokesmen for a 'lost generation' sacrificed by incompetent military leaders in a futile war.[37] Lyttelton's traditional viewpoint was supported by a few historians, notably the late John Terraine, but they contended in vain against the seemingly inevitable growth of a deeply-rooted popular myth which would find its most brilliant expression in the 1990s in the tragi-comic *Blackadder* television series. With the news media increasingly concerned with the experience of ordinary soldiers and the tracing of lost relatives killed in action it was difficult to mount a persuasive case for a privileged officer caste, many of them old Etonians and saddled with ludicrous nicknames such as 'Porky', 'Fatty', 'Fat Boy', 'Bulgy', 'Ma', 'Boy' and 'Bobbety'.

Nevertheless, now that nearly a century has elapsed since the outbreak of the First World War, and with the military historians now generally taking a much more sympathetic view of the British and imperial war effort at all levels, including military leadership, it should be possible to understand and grasp imaginatively not only the 'misery' experienced by some of the rank and file, but also the 'grandeur' of the Guards' ethos and their substantial contribution to the eventual victory.

6

Voices from the ranks: Frederic Manning and Frank Richards

As long ago as 1978 the late Andrew Rutherford argued persuasively that the literature of the First World War had been presented too selectively and too simplistically as expressing first a naive enthusiasm for war and then, after the shock of a long war of attrition, an overwhelming sense of disillusion, anger and pity. He argued that, in reality, much of the finest literature reflected the complexity and ambivalence of combat experience and, furthermore, that 'much of it also reasserts an heroic ideal, stripped of romantic glamour certainly, but redefined convincingly in terms of grim courage and endurance in the face of almost unendurable suffering and horror'.[1] In a brilliant chapter entitled 'The Common Man as Hero', Rutherford chose as the main illustration of his theme *The Middle Parts Of Fortune* by the somewhat obscure author Frederic Manning.

Manning was briefly a 'gentleman ranker' who had already established something of a literary reputation before 1914 as a poet and essayist, but it is far from certain that he would have published an account of his brief experience in the ranks on the Western Front without considerable pressure from his publisher, Peter Davies. For the ordinary private soldier, lacking Manning's superior education and literary contacts, the obstacles to publication at that time were almost insuperable. Soldiers might write vivid letters to loved ones at home, but it was quite another matter to find the leisure, and the skill, to compose a publishable account of their war experience. Even if they could get this far there remained the daunting problem of finding a publisher. Not least problematic was the unmemorable nature of most rankers' war experience: a combination of long spells of boredom and fatigues in unremembered villages, punctuated by brief episodes of terrifying combat whose chaotic details defied coherent description. These considerations render the publication (in 1933) of Frank Richards' *Old Soldiers Never Die* a remarkable achievement, but it is doubtful if his colourful story would have been printed without the help of his former officer in the Royal Welch Fusiliers, Robert Graves.[2] A comparison of these sharply contrasting authors, Manning and Richards, will enable us to explore two very different but successful ways to depict the experience of life in the ranks on the Western Front.

Frederic Manning was a most unlikely soldier. Born in Sydney, New South Wales in 1882, he was the sixth of eight children of Sir William Patrick Manning, a major figure in the city's financial and political circles. Slight of build, a lifelong sufferer from asthma and poor health generally, he was educated privately and after 1903 lived permanently in England. His principal tutor was the Reverend Arthur Galton, a classical scholar, who became vicar of Edenham in Lincolnshire in 1904. Although there is no suggestion that Manning was homosexual, he lived a quiet, almost reclusive life with Galton until the latter's death in 1921.

Deeply influenced by Galton's knowledge of literature, languages and art, Manning published a volume of poetry in 1907 and two years later established a modest reputation with *Scenes and Portraits* – a series of imaginary conversations between famous historical figures which demonstrated a precocious talent in depicting personality and conversational styles from different periods. Among the admirers of his early work were Ezra Pound and T. E. Lawrence. He had an indolent streak, perhaps encouraged by the possession of private means, and left a major long-term fictional project, *The Golden Coach*, unfinished. He is described before the war as a 'shy, introverted, and at times almost foppish aesthete'.[3]

Given his age and suspect health it is most unlikely that Manning would have been conscripted but in October 1915, perhaps spurred on by Galton's anti-German attitude, he volunteered for service in the ranks of the King's Shropshire Light Infantry, becoming Private 19022. Initially, believing he lacked 'sufficient experience of men' to try for a commission, he opted for life in the ranks, but harsh conditions in barracks soon caused him to change his mind. He undertook an officers' training course but in June 1916 was returned to his unit ('RTUed', a shaming experience) for drunkenness. He then joined the 7th Battalion King's Shropshire Light Infantry in France in August 1916, where he seems to have coped well and to have admired the spirit of his comrades, before being promoted lance corporal and departing in December to try again for a commission. He succeeded at the second attempt and in July 1917 was posted to the Royal Irish Regiment in Dublin. What precisely went wrong with his health and nervous temperament is unclear; perhaps, as he claimed, delayed shell-shock caused nervous depression and insomnia. Within days of joining his unit he was found to be drunk and incapable of fulfilling his duties. He was court-martialled, found guilty, and severely reprimanded. After a month or so of rest and medical treatment he returned to duty but once again took to the bottle. His adjutant reported that 'this officer is in a stupor, quite unfit for any duty, evidently the result of a drinking bout'. He was hospitalized suffering from delirium tremens. His regiment was remarkably sympathetic, taking the view that a second court martial would serve no useful purpose, the report concluding '2nd Lieutenant Manning is a gentleman but apparently has no strength of will and is quite unsuitable as an officer'. Even so the War Office might have insisted on a second court martial and certain public disgrace but it seems that intervention by an influential legal friend prevailed and in February 1918 Manning was allowed to resign his commission and leave the Army without dishonour though the unpublished reason given was for 'ill health brought on by intemperance'.[4]

Two aspects of this somewhat shameful episode are worth further comment. First, Manning's abject failure as an officer was successfully concealed, even from close friends like Sir William Rothenstein, and remained so until the diligent researches of his first biographer, Jonathan Marwil, in the 1970s. Even in 1977, when the unexpurgated version of Manning's book, *The Middle Parts Of Fortune*, was at last made generally available, the dust jacket erroneously stated that he had refused a commission and served throughout the war as a private. Second, Manning's inglorious departure from the Army did not leave any lasting feeling of bitterness towards the service, though he had expressed exasperation with the officers he encountered in Ireland. Quite the contrary, he remained proud of his time with the KSLI and especially of his few months of soldiering in the ranks.

The Middle Parts Of Fortune, first published in an expensive limited edition in 1929, was dedicated to Manning's publisher Peter Davies, 'who made me write it'. This seems to have been literally true in that Davies, already an admirer of Manning's sparkling conversation and elegant writing, despaired of his dilatory methods so, luring him to London, 'shut him up in his flat' and forced him to concentrate for several weeks on his writing. Davies had an additional personal reason for wishing to see Manning's war memoirs published. He and his four brothers had served in turn as the model for J. M. Barrie's Peter Pan. All the orphaned children had been emotionally harmed by Barrie's obsessive attentions. Peter, who had been endlessly teased at Eton, went off to fight on the Somme but returned after only two months suffering from shell-shock. Although he later returned to France and won a Military Cross, his personality had been permanently damaged by unhappy experiences at school and in the army, and he eventually committed suicide.[5] His relationship with Manning, however, was entirely positive; not only did he persuade the reclusive author to finish the book in six months; he published it promptly in 1929 before the boom in war books declined; and excelled in getting publicity and boosting sales. Public interest was stimulated as to the identity of the author, given in both the limited edition *The Middle Parts Of Fortune* and the expurgated edition *Her Privates We* (1930) simply as 'Private 19022'. T. E. Lawrence was among the few perceptive readers who identified the author by his style and allowed his name and high praise of the book to be used to boost sales.

Her Privates We was an instant success, being widely praised as 'the first book to tell the truth from the common soldier's point of view'. In the first four months more than 15,000 copies were sold and negotiations began for foreign translations. The author's name was not openly announced until a new edition was published in 1943, eight years after Manning's death, while the unexpurgated version, *The Middle Parts Of Fortune*, was not published in England until 1977.[6]

These, and more recent editions, have given Manning's outstanding book a 'second life' for readers with a special interest in the literature of the First World War, but it remains undeservedly less well known than the comparable memoirs of Graves, Blunden and Sassoon. This is doubtless due in part to the author's early death and, despite two biographies, lack of much information about his career, which anyway was unexciting.[7]

Since this study focuses on war memoirs some explanation for the inclusion of Manning's book is required. Though often referred to as a novel there are strong reasons for treating it as a thinly disguised memoir. In his 'Prefatory Note' Manning remarks that the work is 'a record of experience on the Somme and the Ancre fronts, with an interval behind the lines, during the latter half of the year 1916; and *the events described in it actually happened* [my emphasis]; the characters are fictitious'. Moreover, he adds that 'in recording the conversations of the men I seemed at times to hear the voices of ghosts'. It is not a novel in the accepted sense in that there is no real plot and very little dramatic action. The narrative begins just after a disastrous battalion attack near Bazentin le Grand on 14 July and culminates in another failed attack and a fateful raid near Serre in November. The core of the book in the months between covers a typical period in the life of a battalion, frequently marching from one dreary village to another and subjected to alternating periods of front-line defensive duties; in reserve just behind the front line; and onerous fatigues with inspections when euphemistically 'at rest'. As Sir Michael Howard pointed out, Manning's book is about soldiering rather than fighting: 'about the scrounging, drilling, yarning, gossiping, drinking and womanizing which has always constituted the great bulk of military experience'.[8]

While Manning clearly used the imaginative writer's licence (as distinct from the historian's strict dependence on evidence) to fashion characters and to embellish or even invent some of the incidents described – such as the trio's evasion of duties by hiding in a loft, or the peasant woman's tirade against manoeuvres encroaching on her clover-field – the narrative has the detail and texture of memory rather than invention. For example, the accuracy of the battalion's movements from the Guillemont area via Mericourt to rest; thence to the front near Mazingarbe with Noeux-les-mines as the rest centre; and back to the Somme near Mesnil, Mailly-Maillet and finally to Bus-les-Artois close to the front behind Courcelles and Colincamps, can all be checked in the regimental history (published in 1925),[9] which Peter Davies did read and probably Manning also. Rather like the movements of David Jones's battalion, on which he constructed the grand edifice of *In Parenthesis*,[10] so Manning used his battalion's peregrinations to provide a firm foundation for his subtle reflections on war, fear of death and human endurance.

Furthermore, as Marwil points out, Manning as narrator and 'Bourne', his central character, are extremely closely connected; indeed it seems clear that the latter is a somewhat idealized depiction of the author.[11] He is educated, speaks French, knows some of the officers from earlier association and is a paragon of soldierly virtue: he is charming, diplomatic, resourceful, gets on equally well with privates, NCOs, company officers and French civilians and, not least, is an accomplished scrounger. True to life also, Bourne is a gargantuan binge drinker who can outdo the most hardened regular soldiers.

A recurrent topic throughout the narrative is the suitability of Bourne for a commission and when he will leave the battalion. Officers and senior NCOs discuss the question with him while his comrades are agog to hear the latest gossip. Bourne expresses reluctance to go on the grounds that he is happy to be an ordinary soldier with his pals and, more specifically, is reluctant to quit the battalion if a 'show' or attack is imminent. These sentiments may accurately reflect what Manning felt at the time, though of course he excludes from the book any hint of his previous failure to gain a commission and his subsequent disgrace. In the book his eventual, calm acceptance of the commanding officer's decision that he must put in for a commission provides a fitting climax in that he is killed during a raid, on the eve of his departure, thanks to the malicious whim of his company commander who 'has it in for him'.

Finally, two clues or 'slips' may be adduced to support the contention that this is a thinly-disguised memoir based on Manning's actual experience as distinct from a work of fiction. First, in relation to swearing, Bourne hints that he is an Aussie; indeed this helps to explain why he is not inhibited by class and rank barriers. Second, the description of Bourne's features closely resembles those of the author: 'His impassive face was thrust forward, and the beaky nose between the feverishly bright eyes, the salient cheek-bones above the drawn cheeks, the thin-lipped mouth, set, but too sensitive not to have a hint of weakness in it, and the obstinate jaw, had a curiously still alertness in its expression.'[12]

Although Andrew Rutherford calls Manning's book a novel he rates it 'one of the masterpieces of war literature in English, uniting art with authenticity, fictional sophistication with documentary and psychological realism, and imposing significant form on the large untidiness of life and death'. For Michael Howard the main moral of the book – that one must not break – makes the work 'as timeless as Aeschylus'.[13]

Bourne's standpoint as a detached observer gives the book a meditative, even a philosophical dimension. Without feeling supercilious, he imagines that the other men were 'probably a little less reflective and less reasonable than himself' and he envies them their 'wanton and violent instincts'. While he has mucked in with them and they have accepted him, he cannot evade the question: what did you do in civil life? They know he is not really one of them and is likely to leave them shortly to become an officer.

Although many of the men would risk their lives for others, Bourne regards these actions as spontaneous and instinctive rather than calculated. Theirs is a comradeship based on necessity rather than true friendship. 'We are all in it up to the neck together, and we know it'. After the action at Guillemont, with which the narrative opens, Shem and Martlow, Bourne's special mates, had met by chance. They had not a single thing in common and yet 'there was no bond stronger than that necessity which had bound them together'. When Shem is slightly wounded in the final attack, Bourne reflects calmly that he was now convalescing and so all right, he had gone his own way, but Martlow's death cannot be so easily consigned to memory. When Bourne himself is killed there is, of necessity, a change of viewpoint and for the only time we see him momentarily through his comrades' eyes. His particular ally, Sergeant Tozer, quietly accepts his death: 'It was finished. He was sorry about Bourne, he thought, more sorry than he could say... there was a bit of a mystery about him; but then, when you come to think of it, there's a bit of a mystery about all of us.'[14]

In his determination to depict a brief period of 'real soldiering' as he had experienced it, Manning was deliberately rejecting the format of some contemporary best-sellers, notably Remarque's *All Quiet On The Western Front*, which created the impression of ceaseless intensive combat and wholesale pointless slaughter. Nor does he seek to portray the troops 'as anonymous cannon-fodder or archetypal victims'. Manning's approach was approved by Cyril Falls in his critical appraisal of *War Books*, who commented that he had depicted 'the authentic British infantrymen'.[15]

Though his pages are never dull, a great deal of Manning's narrative concerns the boring routines of his company when out of action: the nagging anxieties, wearying delays and fatigues, petty disputes, feuds and rumours and, above all, being 'buggered about' by those in authority. Thus, early in the book, Bourne admits to the Padre he is becoming demoralized: 'I begin to look on all officers, NCOs, the military police, and brass-hats, as the natural enemies of deserving men like myself.'[16]

Bourne complains bitterly when, in contravention of regulations, 50 men are paraded in a street and kept there for half an hour until horribly mangled by a shell. In a similar incident a general orders an extra guard-mounting as a punishment and 'Jerry comes over and bombs the lot'. These and other costly errors cause Bourne to reflect: 'The war might be a damned sight more tolerable if it weren't for the bloody army.' Regarding another incident he notes cynically that in the British Army 'the chain of responsibility ... means that all responsibility for the errors of their superior officers, is borne eventually by private soldiers in the ranks'.[17]

Manning's frank use of soldiers' obscenities was thought unacceptable in 1929 and was bowdlerized in *Her Privates We*, but in 1977 the original text was at last made generally available. Although he had an excellent ear for dialogue the longer obscenity-studded speeches are skilfully orchestrated, while staccato expletives ('Ah don't care a fuck') are carefully rationed to avoid the boring monotony of soldiers' argot. Here speaks the eternal private in the form of little Martlow: 'They don't care a fuck 'ow us'ns live. We're just 'umped and bumped an' buggered about all over fucking France.' When told blandly that the enemy will offer little resistance to their attack the lugubrious Weeper Smart retorts 'What fuckin' 'opes we've got!' and when this provokes laughter he cries in vehement rage: 'Laugh, you silly fuckers!… You'll be laughing the other side o' your bloody mouths when you 'ear all Krupp's fuckin iron-foundry comin' over.' Martlow rejects a corporal's accusation that they are 'a miserable lot o' buggers', adding 'Only I'm not fighting for any fuckin' Beljums, see. One o' them buggers wanted to charge me five frong for a loaf o' bread.'[18]

Manning is never sentimental in his artful portrayal of ordinary soldiers. He knows they are mostly ill-educated, coarsely spoken and often crude or brutal in their behaviour; but he also shows that individuals are capable of remarkable delicacy, depth of feeling and compassion. Moreover, though only Martlow's Christian name ('Charlie') is revealed, all are subtly differentiated as individuals and their interaction with each other admirably shown; witness for example the comparison between the gangling, pathetic and terrified (yet ultimately heroic) Weeper Smart and the loathed and despised deserter, Miller. Bourne's two special chums, Shem and Martlow, are more fully delineated. Shem, a somewhat stereotyped Jew, is a stout comrade, champion scrounger and compulsive liar. Martlow is a country lad, not yet 17 and affectionately known to Bourne as 'the kid'. He is foul-mouthed but also vulnerable and clearly, although he affects bravado, in need of comforting before the final, fatal assault. Bourne (and perhaps from memory, Manning) is deeply attached to him and his berserker rage when the youth is killed is entirely credible. 'Bourne's teeth were clenched and bared, the lips snarling back from them in exultation: "Kill the buggers! Kill the bloody fucking swine! Kill them!"' This is how Siegfried Sassoon behaved in March 1916 when his closest friend David Thomas was killed near Fricourt.

Manning depicts the battalion as a beleaguered, closely-knit and interdependent group whose only conceivable release from their grim predicament lies in death or a 'blighty-wound' to effect an escape to England. Consequently, they are suspicious of, or downright hostile towards, all 'outsiders' and the 'enemy' broadly defined. Most of the company officers earn their respect by brave conduct in combat, and even a fierce new commanding officer with his just but merciless face wins approval. But they are made uneasy by rhetoric and fine sentiments: when Mr Rhys 'spoke to them of patriotism, sacrifice and duty, he merely clouded and confused their vision'. As for the identity of the enemy, the Hun is rather taken for granted compared with the more proximate danger posed by senior commanders and staff. Civilians at home are not much respected and actually hated if they showed disrespect to soldiers: 'Take that you fuckin' bastard!' says the brutal Madeley and beats up a man in a pub who had boasted about his high earnings and easy life. The deserter Miller makes periodic appearances in the narrative, universally despised and deserving to be shot out of hand because he has abandoned his comrades whereas others equally frightened, like Weeper Smart, have stuck it out. When Bourne is fatally wounded it is Weeper who insists on staying and trying to save him, repeating 'A'll not leave thee'. He carries back the body, then mixes his account of Bourne's death with 'raving curses'.[19]

As Michael Howard noted, the main theme or moral which the book inculcates is the vital necessity of 'sticking it out' and not breaking. At the very beginning of the book Bourne daringly rebukes an officer who talks of 'moving from one bloody misery to another, until we break'; calling out in the dark 'Don't talk so bloody wet. You'll never break.' Sticking it out in the face of imminent death is a frequent exhortation in moments of tension but there is also the grim realization that the comforts of comradeship can only go so far: in the end each soldier must face death alone.[20]

Bourne reflects that his battalion, recruited mainly from farms and small mining villages, had an advantage over those drawn from London and other cities in that 'The simplicity of their outlook on life gave them a certain dignity, because it was free from irrelevances.'

> These apparently rude and brutal natures comforted, encouraged, and reconciled each other to fate, with a tenderness and tact which was more moving than anything in life. They had nothing; not even their own bodies, which had become mere implements of warfare. They turned from the wreckage and misery of life to an empty heaven, and from an empty heaven to the silence of their own hearts. They had been brought to the last extremity of hope, and yet they put their hands on each other's shoulders and said with a passionate conviction that it would be all right, though they had faith in nothing, but in themselves and in each other.[21]

Manning, through the character of Bourne, was thus prepared to cast his former companions in an heroic light as ordinary men able to survive whatever war and fate could throw at them. In this vein, he goes well beyond the conventions of the standard war memoir to touch on the most fundamental issues of life and death. He concludes, however, without any definite answers: every individual is ultimately alone and mysterious. As the survivors of the raid huddle in a dug-out with shells bumping heavily outside 'They sat there silently; each man keeping his own secret'.

Despite his inglorious exit from the Army and failure to achieve any further notable success after writing *The Middle Parts Of Fortune*, Manning nevertheless believed that his war service in France, however reluctantly undertaken, had

had a curiously liberating effect. He expressed the paradox in a letter to William Rothenstein: 'I found that I felt most free in precisely those conditions when freedom seems to the normal mind least possible – an extraordinary feeling of self-reliance and self-assertion.'[22]

FRANK RICHARDS' *OLD SOLDIERS NEVER DIE*

Frank Richards' memoirs of the First World War, first published in 1933, were very favourably received and have since become a classic, referred to in numerous books about the war and seldom out of print. The author was a genuine ranker, having left school at 12 to become a miner in South Wales and enlisted as a regular soldier five years later in 1901. As Robert Graves would comment in his introduction to a paperback edition in 1964, the book owed its success in part to 'its humorous restraint in describing unparalleled horrors. The style is lucid, economical, never in the least pretentious, and reflects Frank's long training as an Army signaller.'[23]

Although the book was essentially Richards' own work, based on his remarkable memory, it is doubtful if it would have been published without Graves's encouragement and editorial assistance. In 1930 Richards sent the manuscript to Graves, whom he had known when in the Royal Welch Fusiliers. The latter spent a couple of months 'sorting it out'. This involved substantial editorial work on paragraphing and punctuation, the insertion of some officers' names and the incorporation of Frank's answers to numerous questions. Curiously Graves also suggested changes of words and phrases to make the style seem more working class and outspoken. Richards gratefully acknowledged that the already famous author of *Goodbye to All That* 'didn't half lick it into shape, better shape than I had it'. There are also some anecdotes which had already been published in Graves's memoirs, but of course Richards could have witnessed these incidents himself, or heard of them later from Royal Welch cronies. In sum, Graves's involvement was substantial, as is evident from the fact that he accepted one third of the book's earnings (Richards had offered him a half) as he did also for the sequel *Old Soldier Sahib* (1936), but it seems certain that he did not re-write the book.[24]

It is interesting that Dr J. C. Dunn, distinguished medical officer of the Second Battalion Royal Welch Fusiliers for most of the First World War and compiler of the outstanding battalion history *The War The Infantry Knew* felt that *Old Soldiers Never Die* had 'Far too much of the Graves flavour for my liking', but he added justly that 'the portraits of old sweats of our Old Army by one of them is worth having'.[25]

Frank Richards (known to his mates as 'big Dick') was born in 1883 to an unmarried mother and brought up by an uncle and aunt. Excited by the South

African War, he quit the coal mines and enlisted as soon as he was old enough in 1901. He qualified as a signaller and marksman (and also boxed), and served with the Second Battalion, Royal Welch Fusiliers in India and Burma from 1902 to 1909. He then returned to work as a timberman's assistant in the South Wales coalfields but continued as a Reservist and as such was recalled to the battalion in August 1914. His remarkable achievement was to serve with the battalion throughout the war on the Western Front, as a rifleman until June 1915 and then as a signaller, without being seriously wounded, though he did suffer from fevers and other ailments incurred during his earlier period of service. Although battalion signallers were specialists who enjoyed certain privileges, their duties were extremely hazardous, so Richards' astonishing survival cannot be ascribed to holding a 'cushy' rear-area job or to long absences on courses. He mentions that he was ordered to resume the signaller's role in 1915 having several times refused requests to do so. He describes his initial duties as follows:

> Now I was warned and had no option in the matter. There were at this time eighteen signallers to a battalion, with a sergeant in charge; in the front line there were generally three signallers in each company and the remainder in Battalion Headquarters, but sometimes four were posted to a company. Signallers were also runners; in the Royal Welch there were no Battalion runners except signallers until July 1916. Signallers had to do no trench work or patrols and were the only men in the trench that were exempt from stand-to.[26]

He adds that all messages were sent in Morse, which was quicker and more accurate than the spoken word. The telephone lines generally ran down the communication trench from battalion headquarters to the most advanced companies and then along the front-line trench. Even in relatively quiet periods the lines were frequently broken and many signallers died trying to repair them. When out of the line signallers formed a separate unit and were billeted together; and when in the line they usually occupied their own dug-outs.[27]

He describes several signalling innovations or 'stunts' which proved to be a washout when used in attacks.

> The truth was that we were very lucky if Battalion Headquarters could keep up communication with Brigade and always, with the exception of one case, had to depend on runners for taking company messages back from any captured position to Battalion Headquarters. I could never make out why signallers were not issued with revolvers instead of rifles.

Richards describes several attacks, notably that on the 'Red Dragon' mine crater at Givenchy on 5 July 1916, in which the signalling arrangements were shattered within a few minutes and the signallers suffered heavy losses. When the battalion moved to the Somme front seven signallers were killed and six wounded in July and August (1916). Signallers who were part of an attack were expected to fight as infantry until the objective was taken and then, if unwounded, act as runners.

> A runner's job was very dangerous: he might have to travel over ground from where the enemy had just been driven and which was now being heavily shelled. In shell holes here and there might be some of the enemy who had been missed by the mopping-up party or who had been shamming dead; they would pop up and commence sniping at him. I remember one show we were in later on, where extra runners had been detailed off for the day, losing fifteen out of twenty.[28]

As Dr Dunn rightly remarked, Richards' narrative is unrivalled as that of a genuine ranker or 'old sweat' of the pre-1914 Army in a proud regular battalion which had spent long periods on overseas service and retained its high standards and traditions even in the drastically changed environment of the Western Front. Consequently Richards and his pals embody the outlook of Kipling's Private Thomas Atkins: there are no showy heroics, patriotism, fine sentiments or agonizing about the rights and wrongs of the war. Instead there is a fierce pride in the honour of the battalion, displayed, for example, in Richards' scorn for a New Army battalion which had failed to post sentries after an attack, and for French and British units which did not hand over deep, well-drained and tidy trenches when relieved. He also notes that march discipline was strict, preventing soldiers falling out without really serious disabilities. Veterans like himself also found it very difficult to be excused front-line duties on account of sickness (such as fevers or minor wounds); Dr Dunn taking a stern line that old soldiers were essential to set an example to less experienced men.[29]

The positive aspects of soldiering for Richards and his chums included eating, drinking, womanizing, gambling and looting. As regards food, he records that until September 1915 soldiers did not receive cooked meals or hot drinks when in the front line, so that hunger and cold were constant problems. The staple, monotonous rations consisted of bully beef, jam, biscuits and an inadequate amount of bread. When out of the line, Richards and his comrades were adept at catching chickens and even an occasional pig, but the greatest bonanza resulted from the 'liberation' of the rations of dead officers from another battalion, including various tinned stuff, cooked sausages and three loaves of bread, providing – in Richards' usual phrase – 'a good feed'. Soldiers were apt to drink as much booze, principally vin blanc, as their meagre pay could buy on the assumption that any 'beano' might be their last on this 'ball of clay'. The rum ration was deeply appreciated and woe betide the reputation of a 'bun-puncher' or teetotaller such as Major-General R. J. Pinney who abolished it in favour of tea.[30] As regards prostitutes or 'fillies', Richards was evidently wary of contracting venereal disease from the over-worked women near the front line, but he was happy to accept the favours of a 'respectable bit of goods' a little further back. However, he did acknowledge that this was merely a matter of degree (or distance from the front) and not of principle. Richards was an inveterate card-player and – before and after the war – a proverbially unsuccessful gambler on horses. He describes fellow-soldiers coolly playing Pontoon in a shell-hole even during a bombardment. He admitted that looting was universal among the old hands, and all prisoners were made to hand over their valuables. Otherwise, he claimed, they would have been robbed by soldiers in the rear areas before they reached the prisoners' cages. He further claimed that all the loot was sold to non-combatant soldiers in the rear areas and the proceeds were spent on having a good time when out of the line. When reproached on leave for not bringing home German helmets to distribute as souvenirs he raised a laugh by pointing out that these were routinely used in the front line as makeshift chamber pots.[31]

Just a few more of the many interesting aspects of Richards' memoirs may now be mentioned. As a professional soldier it is not surprising that he generally treats the enemy (or 'Jerries') with respect. On the eve of the battle of Loos, for example, he predicts a disaster because the enemy's good intelligence and accurate machine-gun and artillery fire will mow down our troops as soon as they leave the trenches. The enemy generally respects truces when dead and wounded can be brought in from no-man's-land; and he has no complaints about British prisoners being ill-treated. He successfully intervenes to prevent a comrade from killing German prisoners, and cites only one example where he knows this crime to have been committed. The culprit told him 'I done them in about 200 yards back. Two bombs did the trick.' As so often in this narrative, retribution swiftly follows: the man had gone scarcely 20 yards when a shell-splinter went clean through him.[32]

Richards' attitude to all British generals and senior staff officers is unremittingly hostile. Though at odds with later historical evidence and changed perspectives, he was probably reflecting the other ranks' views during the war. He claims that during the whole war he never saw an officer above the rank of brigadier-general in a front-line trench; even his own brigadier had no concept of the conditions they had to endure. He accuses his Corps Commander of being over-optimistic after the battle of Loos in issuing orders from his chateau, or 'abode of luxury', many miles in the rear. When this commander orders all brasses to be polished 'many prayers were offered up for his soul', as they were also for the detested General Pinney for restricting the rum ration. When the regimental history was published later, Richards notes, this deplored aspect was not mentioned. As for staff officers, Richards states that 'we all hated the sight of them and the only damned thing the majority seemed to be any good at was to check men who were out of action for not saluting properly'. He gives an example near the end of the war when he was rebuked by a staff officer for collecting a reel of signal wire from another divisional area. Richards' explanation was brushed aside but when shells exploded nearby the officer took to his heels 'as though in strict training for some important track event'.[33]

Richards paints devastating portraits of his company and platoon commanders in the early months of the war, whom he calls respectively Buffalo Bill (Captain and eventually Brigadier C. I. Stockwell) and Deadwood Dick. The former especially had an alarming habit of pulling out his revolver and 'threatening to blow a man's brains out and threatening one and all for the least trifling thing we done' (sic). At least he never remembered Buffalo Bill having any favourites: 'he treated all men in the same way – like dirt'. Deadwood Dick was a milder version of Buffalo Bill and Richards says he respected him as a decent platoon officer. Buffalo Bill too earned his respect, being 'as cool as a cucumber under fire' – 'he had plenty of guts'. When he was transferred to the First Battalion and promoted Richards described him as 'a great soldier and a great bully'. If he returned for another existence on earth it would be as 'a bloody roaring Bengal tiger'.[34]

Richards embodies what would now be termed politically incorrect notions regarding other nationalities including the French, Portuguese and, above all, Indian soldiers – the latter prejudice doubtless deriving from his service in the subcontinent. At the first battle of Ypres a platoon of Indian native infantry on the right of his battalion had lost their officer and were terrified by enemy shelling. Richards alleges they were firing like mad into the air with their heads below the parapet. The Royal Welch Fusiliers sent 12 soldiers over at night to keep them in order and, finding that cursing them in Hindustani had no effect, began to kick and hit them about and threatened to bayonet or shoot the lot. He rejects the mitigating factor that they were suffering from the cold weather, saying harshly that it was simply cold feet. Then, returning to the same area three years later, they observed 'several half-caste mites playing in the streets and a British veteran rudely remarked that "if the bloody niggers were no good at fighting they were good at something else that sounded much the same"'.[35]

Richards was surely representative of the vast majority of front-line soldiers in detesting 'base-wallahs' who tried to throw their weight about and 'shirkers' at home who complained about their hardships, though they often received better financial rewards and medical treatment than front-line combatants. He gives several examples of outsmarting NCOs and officers well behind the lines who only believed in 'saluting, drill and spit-and-polish parades'; once escaping the charge of 'going sick without a cause' by getting a sympathetic young American doctor to endorse his (fictitious) sick report. Richards was particularly angry at his treatment by Medical Boards after the war. He had suffered from both rheumatism and haemorrhoids during the war but had, through no fault of his own, not received hospital treatment for either. He found that Medical Boards went by what hospital service a man had entered on his medical history sheet and not by his front-line service. Consequently, a man who had served briefly in England and had been admitted to hospital even for a few days would have a better chance of being awarded a disability pension than a man who had done four years in the firing line but had a clean medical sheet. Even at the time of going to press in 1932 he knew of men who had never been in action who were receiving a larger pension than men who had been wounded or disabled in action. Richards told his civilian friends, incredulous about these injustices, that he was thankful that he was not blind or disfigured and was not an inmate in a mental home. But like many old soldiers he understandably felt that he had not had a fair deal.[36]

Richards has a good deal to say about the strictness of military discipline and the vagaries of various crimes and punishments. By his own account he was lucky to escape court martial on several occasions, for example by nearly missing the march-off for an attack due to a drunken spree, and on another occasion for cursing Buffalo Bill over an unmerited reprimand. He and a fellow medal-winner did experience the detested Field Service Punishment Number One – being tied to a cart or gun-carriage for up to two hours a day – for ignoring a curfew when celebrating their award of the Distinguished Conduct Medal (DCM). However, they got off comparatively lightly, receiving only eight days' punishment instead of the usual 28, and being bound only at the wrists and not also at the ankles.

While serving at Houplines early in the war as many as 58 members of the battalion were simultaneously undergoing this humiliating punishment and were tied to railings in the street where they were inspected by the female population, some laughing at them. One prisoner remarked that he didn't mind being tied up but he didn't want a lot of frog-eating bastards gaping at him. Some of these old sweats were hard cases and always in trouble, but often harsh sentences, say five or ten years' imprisonment, were speedily quashed, particularly if the prisoner stayed in the battalion, and they were given a chance to redeem themselves by gallant conduct in battle. Richards recounts the remarkable story of 'Private Jones', who deserted a second time because an inexperienced officer from another battalion withheld his pay after he had completed his punishment. On the second occasion he wandered in the rear areas for three months before becoming bored and giving himself up. He was sentenced to death, but in view of his gallant conduct in the past this was reduced to ten years' imprisonment and he was sent back to England. Within seven months he had not only returned to fight on the Somme but had been promoted to sergeant in a Royal Welch service battalion. Another young soldier ran away after all his colleagues were blown to bits by a shell and was absent for six weeks. His death sentence was also commuted to a prison sentence, though in this case Richards comments that he was either killed or taken prisoner in 1917. He also witnessed incidents of self-inflicted wounds, usually by an individual but sometimes by two or three soldiers who shot each other by mutual agreement so as to make the wounds look more convincing. This crime was punished by imprisonment if detected but on at least one occasion the culprits were discharged as 'honourably wounded'. Richards calls them 'wise birds' and from the very early days of the war was sympathetic towards any soldier fortunate enough to be sent home with a disabling or 'Blighty' wound. He also mentions, without critical comment, a shameless shirker, 'Morris', who pretended to have been badly gassed and managed to deceive the doctors and get sent home.[37]

Richards was a front-line combatant in most of the famous battles from Le Cateau through Ypres, Loos, the Somme, Arras, Third Ypres to the final advance where he found himself, once again, at Le Cateau. These experiences, narrated in a graphic but unemotional style, often understated in a tone of dry humour, make his survival, virtually unscathed, all the more astonishing. To take just one example, at the disastrous battle of Loos his brigade lost 1,500 men, mostly killed, in less than an hour, and the losses would have been even heavier had not the adjutant stopped two companies from going over. All day the survivors, like Richards, had to stand by helpless in their front trench while the wounded cried out in pain.

> From the time I arrived in the front line I had been looking through a trench periscope. Some of the Argyles and Middlesex had very nearly reached the enemy's barbed wire: I don't think any got any further. But if the whole Brigade had reached the enemy's barbed wire without any casualties they would have been skinned alive trying to make their way through it, as hardly any damage had been done to it by our shelling. As the Old Soldier had truly remarked some days before, it was a glorious balls-up from start to finish; and J.C. had not been very kind to our Brigade.[38]

This quotation neatly captures the pervading tone or spirit of the whole narrative: the pessimism and stoical humour of the old soldier who has 'seen it all before' and takes the daily ration of bungled orders, mechanical cock-ups (such as the infamous 'Bangalore Torpedo' which failed to explode) and tactical disasters, without surprise or disillusionment, contenting himself with a non-believer's rebuke to 'JC' and offering up 'prayers' for the speedy removal of detested commanders and their staffs.

A recurrent theme or *leitmotiv* is the randomness of fate, which annihilates individuals in an instant while miraculously sparing the author who, to his own amazement, 'lives to tell the tale'. To give just a few examples, in trenches near High Wood in 1916 Richards declined to move into a fellow signaller's shack because they were both going on a course the next morning. Both shacks were destroyed by shells in the night but Richards' had been built over a shell-hole and he had been 'laying' in it. His friend was killed. In another incident two runners and a signaller were playing pontoon in a shell-hole during a barrage when the runners were ordered to take messages back to brigade. The signaller complained that the game had broken up just when his luck was changing but five minutes later a shack nearby was blown to pieces, killing all those who had remained in it: the card-players and the signaller were unharmed. A married man, just returned from leave and marching next to Richards, was killed by a random shell splinter just after the latter had told him it was a very quiet sector. A nervy sergeant, 'jumpy as a bag of fleas', managed to miss two consecutive attacks by going sick, but the next attack he did not miss 'and he was the first to pass into the next world'. During the German offensive in March 1918 Richards and a pal were searching for water and were told they could fill their cans in a farmyard near a church where shells were falling. Richards suspected the enemy was using the church tower as a marker and risked a taunt that he was 'windy' by going elsewhere. Half an hour later a shell exploded in the farmyard, killing or wounding 20 men who were waiting their turn at the pump.[39]

Whether these and several other similar coincidences occurred precisely as Richards later recalled them is impossible to be sure, but each seems quite plausible.

One story, however, is distinctly weird and as such is in sharp contrast to the author's usual matter-of-fact attitude. Towards the end of 1915 Richards and a fellow-signaller, 'Dann', were in the trenches at Hulloch near Loos when they saw a huge black rat which evaded their attempts to hit it with clods and seemed to be staring at Dann. The latter went pale and said (to a sceptical Richards) the rat made him feel queer and he knew his number was up: 'when I do go West that rat will be close by'. Several months later they were on the Somme, far from Hulloch, when a terrified look came over Dann's face: the same black rat was sitting on the edge of the trench looking fixedly at Dann. Seconds later Dann was killed by a spent bullet which had penetrated his neck and touched his spinal column. Stranger still, the rat had been killed by a shell burst and lay by his side. Richards, who admits he was 'getting the creeps', seized the rat's tail and threw it back into the shell-hole. Richards says he has no doubt that it was the same rat we had seen at Hulloch more than 50 miles away. It was his only uncanny experience during the whole war.[40]

Although Richards received little formal education he clearly had the intelligence, tradesman's qualifications (as a signaller and marksman) and vast military experience to have made an efficient NCO but as he explains, he refused promotions many times. He reasoned that, as a company sergeant or an NCO with the signallers he would have been on parade day and night. As we have seen, the signallers' duties were extremely hazardous but, when out of line Richards enjoyed a certain amount of independence and, when responsible for the tidiness of the billet, he was free to 'go scrounging around' once the daily inspection was over. More generally he seems to have been content to escape responsibility and spend his time with his mates, the majority of whom came from Birmingham. However, he evidently remained on friendly terms with several of his former pals who became NCOs and a few who became officers. This trust and friendship across the ranks was clearly reciprocated, for example by Robert Graves and by 'The Athlete', who confided in him about his fear of being court-martialled for over-reliance when in action on a cowardly sergeant. In this case common sense prevailed: the young officer was not court-martialled and later fought gallantly, winning the Military Cross.[41]

Richards felt strongly that the strict pre-war regulation that an NCO must never be seen in company with a private soldier had rightly been relaxed and overlooked during the war, so he and his old soldier comrades were furious when the acting battalion commander, 'The Peer' (Major de Miremont) attempted to reinstate the pre-war code of practice immediately after the Armistice. The major's exhortation was not needed because nearly all the survivors, including Richards, were preoccupied with early demobilization.

Thus Richards differed sharply from Manning in being a genuine ranker (and also a pre-war regular soldier) who did not wish to become an NCO, let alone an officer. But their narratives are very similar in one respect: namely in showing that – off duty – there could be friendly, social relations between privates and even quite senior NCOs and, to a lesser degree, with junior officers.

At the end of his book Richards admits that he has relied mainly on his memory, which was clearly phenomenal, supplemented by meeting or corresponding with a few former pals including Sealyham, 'the architect' and 'the bank clerk'. He adds that there are no fictitious characters, though in many cases nicknames have been substituted. He allows that that there may be some errors regarding dates and place-names, and a few do indeed seem to have escaped Robert Graves's editing.[42] But, very similar to Graves's *Goodbye to All That*, which had originally prompted Richards to try to write down his own account, these may be seen as picaresque memoirs – a graphic narrative about military rogues, emphasizing vivid incidents and personalities with a spicing of fiction (or at least exaggeration) here and there.

In conclusion, Frank Richards' narrative is conspicuously lacking in Frederic Manning's reflective, philosophical style; its imaginative attempt to portray the ordinary soldier's inner mental life; and the heroic stature accorded to inarticulate men like 'Weeper' Smart. Manning after all was a classical scholar, a poet and a published author. Nevertheless Richards successfully conveys the attitudes, behaviour, prejudices and ordeals of professional soldiers in a regular battalion. Thanks also no doubt to Robert Graves's refining and shaping of Richards' original longhand draft, the narrative has a compelling drive and readability: it is a literary work of considerable quality well beyond what could be expected from an uneducated private soldier. However, despite the occasional suspicion that Graves's inventive genius may be at work, Frank Richards' personal account of his experiences is ultimately convincing. It surely deserves a special accolade as an outstanding depiction of 'the war the infantry knew'.

7

Protesters against the war: the contrasting cases of Siegfried Sassoon and Max Plowman

Military service in the Royal Welch Fusiliers between 1914 and 1918, and particularly his public anti-war protest in 1917, was the pivotal period in Siegfried Sassoon's long life. But the protest and its aftermath remains a confused and controversial episode which Sassoon himself found it hard to come to terms with, mainly because it brought two contrasting sides of his character into sharp conflict; namely the brave and popular battalion officer and the sensitive, homosexual, highly imaginative poet who detested the boredom and gregariousness of soldiering and loathed the horrors of combat. He dealt at length with his service in his partly fictional, but essentially autobiographical, trilogy *The Memoirs of George Sherston* (three volumes 1928–36), and returned to the subject from a later perspective, without the fictional veneer, in *Siegfried's Journey*. So powerful was the grip exerted by his early life and war service that in six volumes of memoirs Sassoon never took his autobiography beyond the year 1920.

Siegfried Sassoon was born in 1886 into a wealthy upper-middle-class Jewish family comfortably housed near Tunbridge Wells in rural Kent, with artistic interests as well as a fortune derived from merchant banking. Although Siegfried's father, Alfred, soon left home and died young, his schooldays, youth and early manhood were superficially happy, even idyllic. He was mainly privately educated before going to Marlborough and on to Clare College, Cambridge where, as an aspiring poet he unwisely read law and came down without a degree. In a life of leisure in beautiful countryside, lovingly evoked in *Memoirs of a Fox-Hunting Man*, Siegfried played cricket, golf, hunted and wrote insipid poetry.

But although he was well-off, handsome, athletic and a published author, his career before 1914 lacked motivation and a clear goal. He was also socially inhibited, mainly because he was aware of his homosexual inclinations, which he had not come to terms with, despite mixing with homosexual artist friends in London. However, the fundamental conflict or bifurcation in his character lay in the tension between his early love of poetry, particularly of a Romantic, introspective kind, and his need to present a confident and manly face to the world of public school, university and the Kentish hunting squirearchy. Siegfried was dissatisfied with his aimless mode of life and eagerly welcomed the prospect of military service in 1914, even volunteering before war was formally declared. Where his autobiographical works were understandably discreet, Siegfried's diaries, unpublished in his lifetime, were refreshingly frank. For example, as a newly commissioned subaltern recently arrived in France he wrote on 3 December 1915:

> I never thought to find such peace. If it were not for Mother and friends I would pray for a speedy death. I want a genuine taste of the horrors, and then – peace. I don't want to go back to the old inane life which always seemed like a prison. I want freedom not comfort.[1]

A fortnight later he recorded how happy he was to have escaped his extended, constricted childhood and to have found peace in conditions he expected to loathe. He realized that experience of real combat would be good for his character and his poetry: 'Anything but a "cushy" wound! That would be an awful disaster.' Adrian Caesar is surely right, therefore, to argue that 'the war promised Sassoon a way of integrating the man of action with the creative artist.'[2] War would not only provide enough experiences to galvanize his poetry, but would also plunge him into an all-male environment where notions of suffering, sacrifice and paternal responsibility for his soldiers would more than offset the boredom, lack of privacy and miseries of life in the Army.

Sassoon was fortunate to experience several months of relative quiet and peaceful soldiering out of the line between the late autumn of 1915 and the following spring. As late as 31 March 1916, for example, he recorded that a night patrol up to the German wire had been 'great fun'. He found it most exhilarating – just like starting for a race. The great thing for him was to experience as many sensations as possible. Even after the deaths of David Thomas, a young Welsh officer whom he had loved, and his younger brother Hamo – fatally wounded at Gallipoli – he could still write to an uncle that the last six months had been the best of his life. He had experienced both beauty and terror and was astonished that he had enjoyed it so much. Thus, even allowing for his emphasis on suffering and sacrifice, his diary entries in late 1915 and early 1916 are on the whole extremely cheerful, with no hint of dissatisfaction about the course of the war.[3]

David Thomas' death did, however, have an immediate effect on Sassoon's attitudes towards combat and the enemy; namely in provoking a reckless determination to exact revenge; even, in his own phrase, 'a lust to kill'. Grieving for 'Tommy', 'a gentle soldier, perfect and without stain' had been beautiful but it also stimulated a hatred for the enemy. He longed for the chance to go over the wire and look for Germans with a bludgeon. His battalion commander wanted prisoners but Sassoon wanted to smash skulls; to have a scrap and get out of the war for a bit, or for ever.[4]

Sassoon earned the nickname of 'Mad Jack' in the battalion for his voluntary night patrols, some in defiance of orders, armed with bombs or a knobkerrie, in what were essentially personal revenge missions. Ironically, however, he won a Military Cross (a crucial asset in his later career) in a rescue attempt after a night raid on an enemy-held crater on 23 May had failed. He made heroic efforts to bring in the dead and wounded, especially the difficult recovery of Corporal Mick O'Brien who, alas, did not survive. As well as stressing his desire to kill and be killed, Sassoon was also determined to show that poets could be warriors. He would show that poets could fight as well as anybody else.[5]

Sassoon and his company were fortunate to be in reserve for the first three days (July 1–3) of the Somme offensive, behind the Fricourt–Mametz sector of the front. Although his division (7th) and Corps (XVth) were among the most successful in the opening phase, he nevertheless witnessed numerous gruesome casualties and appalling destruction in wet and muddy conditions. In an act of reckless gallantry in broad daylight on 4 July, Sassoon single-handedly charged the German-occupied Quadrangle Trench, on the approach to Mametz Wood, scattering its 50 or 60 occupants by throwing bombs and shouting the hunting cry of 'View Halloa!'. Since enemy fire prevented reinforcements from reaching him, Sassoon remained alone in the trench for several hours, ignoring an order from his commanding officer to pull out. He recalled that he definitely wanted to kill someone at close quarters. Unshaken by his battalion's heavy casualties he found combat thrilling: 'addictive, heroically solitary, without introspection or regret'.[6]

If Sassoon expected praise and further decoration for what was clearly a more heroic action than that for which he had received the MC, he was to be bitterly disappointed. He was sharply reprimanded by his company commander for failing to return with the bombing party or report his position, thereby delaying a British bombardment of the front trenches for several hours. This rebuke did not, however, cool his reckless impulse for gallant action with the hope of adding to his much-prized medal.

Sassoon's diary entries frequently juxtapose the dreary scenes of the trenches and rear areas with idyllic memories of summer evenings at home in Kent: 'Sunset above the tall trees and the village streets in the dusk and the clatter of a brake driving home.' But, if he survived, he was determined to 'get right away from the silliness of my old life in Blighty! What a world of idle nothingness the name stands for.' He was very conscious of always acting a part among his unimaginative fellow-officers, who dulled his vivid impressions and made the strangeness commonplace. His assumed persona was that of the 'cheery reckless sportsman – out for a dip at the Boches'.[7]

If most of his fellow-officers were dull and boring, Sassoon's great consolation was the belief that he was loved by his men. To some extent this clearly involved sentimental self-delusion. As Max Egremont remarks, 'throughout his war diaries little grenades of Edwardian snobbery explode with invidious frequency, sometimes loaded with the nasty kick of anti-Semitism'.[8] He also generalizes about working-class soldiers in a condescending way, portraying them in simple categories of heroes and villains. After all, the men with whom he served in 1916 were all volunteers and many, like Frank Richards, were former regulars or 'old sweats'. All were capable of finding various sources of enjoyment on active service while stoically enduring periods of boredom, hardship and suffering. Not least significant many, like Sassoon himself, were killers and not merely passive victims. This blinkered view somewhat distorts the increasingly angry and bitter poems which Sassoon was beginning to pour out.

After a brief spell in the front line beyond Mametz village, Sassoon and the battalion moved into a damp and depressing tented camp, supposedly at rest in the rear area. The poet became unwell and on 23 July was admitted to a base hospital with trench fever. He was soon evacuated to England and remained there, convalescing and then on leave until February 1917, thus missing the remainder of the Somme campaign in increasingly wet, cold and muddy conditions.

During this long absence from the war and the hermetically enclosed atmosphere of the battalion, Sassoon became increasingly angry at the news of disastrous battles and the ceaseless reports of deaths or disfigurements of friends and comrades, including the serious wounds suffered by one of his closest pre-war friends, Bobby Hanmer, to whose sister he had been briefly engaged. His rage at military mismanagement, resulting in seemingly pointless slaughter, began to spread to distrust of the political direction of the war, about which he knew very little. In time, as he acquired more self-knowledge, he realized that when in France with his battalion his mind was so numbed by routine duties, danger, boredom and the all-pervasive conventions observed by his fellow-officers that he had no time or energy to think independently. At home, however, it was an entirely different matter as he was exposed to a wide variety of intellectual discourse with many unorthodox opinions, which came to influence him greatly. By the end of 1916, he noted in his diary, his long absence from the battalion had blotted out his sense of discipline. Now all he wanted to do was to play golf and be independent and alone so that he could write poetry. His Military Cross ('my absurd decoration') was the only thing that still gave him a sense of responsibility to the battalion and to the war.[9]

More specifically, by the end of 1916 he was falling under the influence of certain critics and pacifists who held that Britain's role was unjustified and that conflict could and should be ended swiftly by a negotiated peace settlement. Most significantly in this context, in August 1916 he had been introduced to Lady Ottoline Morrell and her coterie of pacifists and conscientious objectors at Garsington Manor near Oxford. In her cosy, panelled drawing room after dinner he first heard frank, unguarded criticism of the war, as being waged for unworthy motives. These critics urged that it was the duty of a courageous minority to protest against the prevailing public opinion which, they said, was being shaped by Jingoist propaganda.[10]

At this stage the Morrells did not try to draw him out about conditions at the front or ask him to join in a public protest, but many years later he would acknowledge that this marked the start of his disillusionment which resulted in 'a fermentation of confused and inflamed ideas'. By the end of the year he was also deeply depressed by the evident failure of the Somme campaign to deliver the widely expected victory. More specifically, his battalion had lost heavily; few of his friends had survived; and the prospects for his return were grim. His anger and depression were deepened by a letter from Lady Ottoline in which she said that a Cabinet minister, 'Old Birrell', had told her that the Germans had made definite peace proposals, but there seemed a lust in the Government, especially on the part of Lloyd George, for more blood to be shed. According to her, the coming 1917 spring offensive was 'pure devilry' because peace on advantageous terms was available to the Allies.[11]

Even before he returned to France in February 1917 Sassoon was in low spirits, with his leave coming to an end and his return to the dreary battalion depot at Litherland. But at least, he consoled himself, there were no women, he could get away to hunt with the Cheshire hounds, play golf at Formby and eat well at the Adelphi Hotel in Liverpool. In these relatively pleasant conditions his increasing rage against all civilians seems disproportionate. Like many officers home on leave or wounded, he was understandably irritated by the ignorance of most civilians about the harsh realities at the front, and by their foolish type of militarism which was encouraged by ill-informed war-reporting and press propaganda. Even so there is something disturbing about the intensity and range of targets for Sassoon's anger as expressed in his diary and in ferocious satirical poems. His targets included fat business profiteers, officers on leave gorging themselves on delicacies, all generals and staff officers who were callously killing off his friends and, not least amongst the guilty, women who prided themselves on having children by warriors. 'O their glutinous eyes', he wrote, 'I think they love war, for all their lamenting over the sons and lovers.'[12]

As for the bitter verses with their devastating punchlines, while still in England over Christmas in 1916 he had composed 'The March-Past', describing General Rawlinson as 'the corpse-commander', and soon after returning to France he encapsulated his rage against the 'scarlet Majors at the Base', guzzling and gulping at the best hotel while speeding 'glum heroes up the line to death'. Later in 1917 his anti-war poetry would take on a very nasty political tone, notably in 'Fight to a Finish' where he imagines soldiers returning to England and turning their bayonets on the mob, causing the 'Yellow-Pressmen' to grunt and squeal in agony before going on to 'clear those Junkers out of Parliament'.[13]

Consequently Sassoon returned to the battalion in February 1917 in mental turmoil, his belief in the necessity to continue the struggle seriously undermined, yet feeling an overriding urge to do the best for his men while welcoming another opportunity to die a decent death. On this tour of duty he was to serve with the Second Battalion for 36 days before being seriously wounded at the Battle of Arras. Although serving in the front line for only five of these days he again witnessed the full horrors of war and again displayed reckless gallantry well beyond the call of duty. The offensive began promisingly on 8 April with the Canadian capture of Vimy Ridge and a British advance eastward towards Douai. Sassoon's battalion was initially in reserve several miles to the west of Arras, but on 12 April they began to march towards action in snow and bitter cold weather, passing en route many mangled corpses of both sides. After three virtually sleepless nights in miserable conditions and tactical confusion, Sassoon's moment of personal crisis arrived. In the early hours of 16 April he was ordered to take a bombing party of 25 inexperienced soldiers to retrieve the failure of a Cameronian battalion which had retreated in disorder after being driven back from the Hindenburg Line. The Scottish adjutant despatched him with the grim valediction, 'Well, old chap, I suppose you're for it.' After trying to check a panic-stricken group of Cameronians, Sassoon halted his party, sent his sergeant back to collect more Mills bombs, and went on with only a single Scottish corporal. Angered at the sight of the corpse of a fair-haired Cameronian, Sassoon hurled bombs towards the retreating Germans and pressed on with the corporal until they reached their objective. Impulsive as ever, Sassoon looked over the parapet and was shot between the shoulders by a German sniper. Relieved to be still alive and in a very excited state, Sassoon believed himself to be a hero 'capable of the most suicidal exploits', but he was ordered to go back as the attack had failed elsewhere. He had been in action for about four hours, his exhaustion and pain muffled by the surge of adrenalin. After his wound was dressed at a first-aid post he had to march three miles through mud and the detritus of battle before he could board a bus to the casualty clearing station. Reluctant to leave the battalion at this critical time, he protested he would be fit to return to action in a few weeks but instead he was given the 'Blighty ticket' which so many other soldiers longed for.[14]

At the end of April, while convalescing in a London hospital and beset by horrific nightmares of the dead and dying he had left behind, he heard that he had been recommended for a further decoration, probably a DSO or a bar to his MC. Interestingly, he wrote to a friend that had he received either award 'it would have queered [his] criticism of the war' though later he contended that it would have strengthened his position when he started 'playing hell with British smuggery'. In the event the award was withheld, probably because the attack as a whole was reckoned a failure. The only recognition he received for his bravery was a printed card signed by the divisional commander he hated, Major-General

Sir Reginald Pinney. This disappointment apparently freed him from any reservations about loyalty to the Army which would have prevented him from making a public protest.[15]

Irritated and depressed by the unending flow of visitors to his hospital bed, many of them asking inane questions about the war, Sassoon passed sleepless nights, not only troubled by hideous dreams but also tormenting himself about his absence from the battalion which, he had heard, had been sacrificed in a botched attack on 23 April. Four officers had been killed and nine wounded along with about 40 other ranks killed, including some of the best NCOs. Later, in his partly fictionalized memoirs, he would recreate the imagined disaster: 'Of people bombing each other up and down ditches; of a company stumbling across the ground and getting mown down by machine-guns, of the doctor [J. C. Dunn] out in the dark with his stretcher-bearers, getting in the wounded.' He later admitted that he had invented the notion of a genial division commander glibly glossing over the fiasco, but he did know for certain that his friend, Ralph Wilmot, had lost an arm so would never again be able to play the piano.[16] Gradually, through the spring and summer of 1917, his general antagonism to the continuation of the war intensified until he reached the decision to make a personal protest, no matter what the cost to his military reputation and the predictable consternation of relatives and friends.

The flames of his smouldering anger against civilians' incomprehension of the realities of war were fuelled by his convalescence at the delightful country mansion in Sussex of the elderly Lord and Lady Brassey. When, for example, he confessed to Lady Brassey his longing to survive the war she replied airily that 'death is nothing'. She added the spiritualist gloss that 'life is, after all, only the beginning. And those who are killed in the war, they help us from "up there", *they are all helping us to win*.' Perhaps she offended him even more by the snobbish remark that as he was not an only son with a great estate to inherit he was expendable.[17]

Sassoon began to reflect that the facility he had discovered for writing satirical anti-war epigrams, which were appearing in pacifist journals such as *The Cambridge Magazine*, was not enough. His decision to do something 'spectacular and heroic' was influenced by Glyn Philpott's portrait of him at the time, which made him feel 'a bit Byronic'. Lunch with H. W. Massingham, editor of the liberal weekly *The Nation*, on 7 June, gave him a further important push towards open rebellion by being told (misleadingly) that England's war aims were acquisitive and that she had refused to divulge them to the new Russian government.[18]

Three days later he consulted the Morrells about a public protest. Philip Morrell, a Liberal MP and sympathetic in principle, advised him against any such gesture on the practical grounds that it would fail; but Lady Ottoline strongly supported the idea and offered to introduce him to the philosopher Bertrand Russell, a pacifist and opponent of the war who would later lose his fellowship at Cambridge and go to prison for his beliefs. Russell and the writer John Middleton Murry helped the young officer to draft and clarify his statement, giving it their own gloss or 'spin'. Russell also introduced him to H. B. Lees-Smith, a pacifist MP, who would ensure that his statement received publicity by asking a question about it in the House of Commons. The statement, dated 15 June 1917, read as follows:

> I am making this statement as an act of wilful defiance of military authority, because I believe the War is being deliberately prolonged by those who have the power to end it. I am a soldier, convinced that I am acting on behalf of soldiers. I believe that this War, upon which I entered as a war of defence and liberation, has now become a war of aggression and conquest. I believe the purposes for which I and my fellow soldiers entered upon this War should have been so clearly stated as to have made it impossible for them to be changed without our knowledge, and that had this been done, the objects which actuated us would be obtainable by negotiation.
>
> I have seen and endured the sufferings of the troops, and I can no longer be a party to prolonging those sufferings for ends which I believe to be evil and unjust.
>
> I am not protesting against the military conduct of the War, but against the political errors and insincerities for which the fighting men are being sacrificed.
>
> On behalf of those who are suffering now, I make this protest against the deception which is being practised on them. Also I believe that it may help to destroy the callous complacence with which the majority of those at home regard the continuance of the agonies which they do not share, and which they do not have sufficient imagination to realise.[19]

Russell, of course, had immediately grasped the value of Sassoon's intended protest as a publicity coup for the anti-war movement. He was, after all, a decorated officer noted for his bravery and also a published poet well known on the London literary scene. Ruthless regarding his own beliefs and their practical consequences, Russell was not concerned about the outcome for the politically naive and emotionally confused subaltern. At some point Sassoon realized that he was being used: the pacifists were essentially hostile to anyone in uniform but temporarily accepted him expediently as an ally in their cause. He agonized for some time before taking the fateful step; fearing that some of his fellow officers would deem him a disgrace to the battalion; his mother and other relatives would be appalled; while others would write him off as deranged. How many, he wondered, would understand that he was, in effect, sacrificing himself for the sake of the soldiers still unwounded at the front? Much later, in the 1940s, he would speculate about his personal fears at the time; how much had he been influenced by the fact that his protest would almost certainly prevent the Army from sending him to the front again? If, as he had assumed, his protest would result in imprisonment and martyrdom, it would also enable him to escape from his fear that he might break down and disgrace himself in combat.[20]

As Sassoon's most recent biographer, Max Egremont, points out: 'As a political document, the statement is quite startlingly naïve.' And though well-meaning, 'seriously ill-informed'. Germany still occupied Belgium and much of northern France and was well on the way to knocking Russia out of the war. Her submarine threat to Britain's vital supplies was only just being successfully countered and, although Sassoon could not have known this, the French Army was being rocked by widespread mutinies. On the positive side, the United States had recently entered the war but it would be another year before her military effort began to affect the Western Front. The ill-fated Third Ypres campaign, the Italian collapse at Caporetto and the Russian revolution had still to take place. Moreover it is difficult to see how British strategy could be interpreted as one of aggression and conquest. At the time of the protest the Allies would have been negotiating from a position of abject weakness; it was a matter of hanging on grimly in the hope that Germany would be weakened by domestic unrest and America's numerical superiority in trained manpower would begin to tell. Doubtless Massingham and other anti-war activists were impressed by the German Chancellor's call for peace in December 1916 and the vote in the Reichstag in July 1917 in favour of a peace without annexations, but these were deceptive. German policy and strategy were firmly controlled by Generals Hindenburg and Ludendorff, who were determined to defeat Russia and then make an all-out bid for victory on the Western Front. Indeed Sassoon seems to have made his protest from 'a mixture of emotion, compassion, vanity, guilt, and the trauma of his own battle wounds'.[21]

Sassoon suffered an agonizing period of doubt before making his statement public because he knew that his mother, his uncle Hamo, and close friends, such as Bobby Hanmer, Robert Graves and Eddie Marsh would disapprove and try to dissuade him. Once the fateful step had been taken he received strong messages of support from Russell, Lady Ottoline, H. G. Wells and his Cambridge mentor Edward Carpenter. But, as anticipated, Hanmer, Graves and others tried to save him from plunging deeper into trouble. Eddie Marsh wrote in moderate terms to say that he could not accept Sassoon's ideas about British policy being acquisitive 'just at the moment when the Americans have decided that they must come in to safeguard the future of democracy'. Arnold Bennett wrote in sharper tones, telling Sassoon that he was not in a position to judge the situation and was merely voicing a minority opinion that this particular war should be stopped. He accused Sassoon of suffering from spiritual pride. Later the poet would admit his protest was essentially emotional and personal; but even in 1917 an attempt to gather information to defend his anti-war stance 'only served to open up the limitless prairies of my ignorance'.[22]

Having deliberately overstayed his leave, on 4 July 1917 Sassoon received a peremptory telegram to 'Join Litherland immediately'. He then sent a copy of his protest to the adjutant there with an apologetic note saying he knew what he was letting himself in for. Meanwhile some of his friends, especially Eddie Marsh and Robert Graves, were making frantic efforts in Whitehall and at Litherland to persuade the authorities that Sassoon's behaviour was due to war weariness and, as such, should not be regarded as a court martial offence. Graves, who was himself convalescing on the Isle of Wight and close to a nervous breakdown, was angry that the Garsington pacifists had taken advantage of his friend's confused and nervous condition.

These efforts paid off in that when Sassoon arrived at Litherland he was treated kindly in a scene of mutual embarrassment, offered a medical board and went away, in a relieved state, to wait at the Adelphi Hotel in Liverpool. However, his rebellious intent remained strong. He ignored the medical board which had been specifically set up for him and, in a mood of gloom and defiance, threw his MC medal ribbon into the Mersey. This gesture perfectly represented the ambivalent nature of the protest: the possession of the MC was vital to his self-esteem and his status as a war hero, so to have thrown the medal itself into the water would have been tantamount to breaking his strong emotional ties with the battalion. But disposing of the ribbon, though showing his anguish and frustration, was much less serious since it could be, and was, replaced when he returned to soldiering.[23]

Robert Graves was the key actor during his friend's ordeal and, in view of his own health, his behaviour bordered on the heroic. He discharged himself from hospital and travelled to Liverpool on 18 July. En route he met Eddie Marsh in London, who advised him that he must persuade Sassoon that he would not be granted a court martial and, if he persisted in refusing the medical board, would be declared insane and incarcerated in a lunatic asylum. Marsh may have gathered hints to this effect from two sympathetic ministers, W. C. Bridgeman at the Ministry of Labour or Winston Churchill, just appointed Minister of Munitions.[24] It is unlikely, however, that anyone at the time could say what the outcome would have been.

In the event, when warnings of military and social disgrace failed, Graves played his trump card, advising Sassoon 'on the highest authority' that he would never be given a court martial but would be locked up for the duration. This well-intentioned deception was only accepted after Graves had sworn, on an imaginary bible, that he was telling the truth. At the subsequent medical board Graves put on a dramatic performance, bursting into tears three times and stating that Sassoon had suffered hallucinations of corpses strewn along Piccadilly. After questioning Sassoon, the board decided that he was suffering from neurasthenia and referred him for treatment to Craiglockhart Hospital near Edinburgh, where he journeyed on 24 July.[25]

Although Sassoon would later be enraged that Graves had lied to him about being imprisoned without a court martial, he admitted that his acceptance of a medical board had 'lifted an enormous load' from his mind, and also wrote (in *Memoirs of an Infantry Officer*) that he would have done the same for Graves had their positions been reversed. This was a satisfactory compromise for all but the militant pacifists like Bertrand Russell, who were deprived of a public controversy involving a war hero. Sassoon had made his protest, which was published in several newspapers, but had preserved his military reputation – and his freedom. Most importantly, it seems likely that the military authorities were relieved to avoid the bad publicity likely to result from the harsh treatment of a prominent poet and decorated officer. In comparing Sassoon's protest with that of Max Plowman, it may be suggested that the former's possession of a Military Cross gave him a significant advantage; but the latter was more strongly driven by his conscience and was more determined to make a stand against the very notion of war as a human activity.

At Craiglockhart, which he called 'Dottyville', between late July and November 1917, Sassoon became bored by the bleak conditions and irritated at the behaviour of some of the 150 officer-inmates, many of whom really were 'dotty', but on the whole he had a very relaxed and enjoyable break from military horrors while the Third Battle of Ypres raged in Flanders. He was encouraged to take outdoor exercise, especially walking in the hills and playing golf; he entertained a variety of visitors, including Lady Ottoline Morrell and Lady Margaret Sackville; and he frequently visited Edinburgh. Whenever he could find peace and quiet he would write poetry, finding an enthusiastic admirer and disciple in a young fellow-inmate and poet, Wilfred Owen.

However, by far the most important relationship during his stay at Craiglockhart was that established with his doctor, the anthropologist and psychologist W. H. R. Rivers. The latter was comparatively humane and enlightened, at the time, in his approach to the ill-defined and scarcely understood condition broadly categorized as 'shell-shock'. He relied essentially on therapeutic conversations in order to help patients face their fears and anxieties; his aim being to reduce fear and inculcate a sense of duty. Shell-shock he tended to perceive as a failure of nerve which could, in principle, be remedied. He immediately impressed Sassoon as 'a fine man', and as early in his stay as 30 July the latter wrote to Lady Ottoline, 'My doctor is a sensible man who doesn't say anything silly ... but his arguments don't make any impression on me. He doesn't *pretend* that my nerves are wrong, but regards my attitude as abnormal.' Although Rivers' ideas and method of treatment created tension and friction, he and Sassoon became friends and remained so until his early death in 1922.[26]

By October 1917 Sassoon was becoming very restless and miserable at 'Dottyville'. This was partly due to 'degenerates' among the other patients, who created an atmosphere of failure and defeat which Sassoon was reluctant to accept in his own case; but probably had more to do with Rivers' attempts to modify his opinions about the justice of the Allied cause and the need to press on until victory was won. Sassoon experienced terrible mental conflict: on the one hand he remained adamant in his views about the war, but on the other hand he felt increasing guilt about abandoning the men on whose behalf his protest had been made. His nightmares began again and with them the fear that he might be behaving like a coward, particularly as he felt physically fit to return to duty. Consequently, in November, he told Rivers that he was prepared to return to military duty but only on condition that he would be posted to active service. He did not want his protest to peter out in a 'cushy' job at home, such as instructing cadets at Cambridge. After a final display of defiance by deliberately missing a medical board he was severely reprimanded by Rivers and, after attending a reconvened board on 20 November was passed fit, despite telling the panel of officers that he had not changed his views on the war. Revealingly, he wrote to Robert Graves on 7 December that he would be going back to 'the sausage machine' but 'I don't think I'll be any good when I get to the war'. In his diary he wrote that he must try to be 'peaceful-minded' and think as little as possible. 'It is the only way by which I can face the horrors of the front without breaking down completely.'[27]

During the weeks after being invalided home from France, when he was in mental turmoil about whether or not to make a public protest, and the subsequent months spent at Craiglockhart, Sassoon was in a very excitable and nervous condition, but whether he had truly suffered from shell-shock is doubtful. Rivers on the whole thought not, noting that there were no physical signs of disorder of the nervous system, and the patient was able to discuss his actions and their motives in a perfectly intelligent and rational way. He was clearly under stress due to the death of friends and men under his command and due to the apparently endless prolongation of a hopeless war. Perhaps more jocularly, Rivers told his patient that he was suffering from 'an anti-war complex'. Yet on 9 May 1918, when on the way back to combat in France, Sassoon noted in his diary 'I must never forget Rivers. He is the only man who can save me if I break down again.' Evidently Sassoon believed that the stress caused by his combat experience, notably at Arras, his agonized dilemma about the protest, and the psychological pressure exerted on him at Craiglockhart had together constituted a nervous breakdown. He would remain outwardly brave and as reckless as ever but inwardly he felt himself on a nervous edge for the remainder of his military service.[28]

In February 1918 Sassoon was posted to the 25th Battalion Royal Welch Fusiliers, which travelled out to Palestine via Egypt at a leisurely pace. Although he was glad to find he could take 'a wider view of things' than during his protest, he also longed for escape from the war and underlined the ending of one diary entry 'I will not go mad'. He found his fellow officers dull, unthinking and snobbish, but managed to write some poetry; found comfort in 'the simplicity of the men';

and made an impressive list of the birds seen in Judea between 15 March and 11 April. By early May the battalion had arrived in France. He sensed that he was on a pilgrimage leading him deathward; but the nearer to the war he got the more he felt he was working up to a further climax. He wished to experience war's terrors again and learn more of the meaning of them. But he no longer had a desire to kill. Now, as a company commander of keen but completely inexperienced soldiers, Sassoon found the prolonged period of training entirely absorbed his time and energy and concluded, revealingly, 'one cannot be a good soldier and a good poet at the same time'.[29]

When, on 20 June, the company moved up towards the front from comfortable billets west of Arras, Sassoon's old reckless bravado soon showed itself again. On 8 July his company took over trenches in the Saint Floris sector north of Béthune from an East Lancashire Battalion. Two days later he rediscovered the old excitement of action in crawling through a cornfield into a deserted enemy trench and, a few days later, against his brigadier's orders, went on a night patrol to sketch the enemy defences opposite his own trenches. Early on 13 July, again defying orders, and accompanied only by a corporal, he crawled up close to a German machine-gun post, which fired on them, and threw all his grenades at the enemy. His nerve had held and he seemed to have retained the military virtues of the 'Mad Jack' of old. But, in a moment of carelessness or hubris on returning to his own trenches he stood up to look back at the enemy lines and was shot in the head, possibly by one of his own men. He hated leaving the company and called out 'I'll be back' when walking away to get his wound treated, but the injury proved sufficiently serious for him to be evacuated to England and so, in an ironic fashion he had received a 'Blighty' wound from his own side which ended his active career.[30]

In his partly fictionalized autobiographical trilogy *The Memoirs of George Sherston*, Sassoon artfully disguises and rewrites his own early life in the character of the title. The characterization is essentially that of Sassoon the country-loving sportsman as distinguished from Sassoon the introverted, homosexual, aesthete and poet. The missing intellectual dimension is less important in the first volume, *Memoirs of a Fox-Hunting Man*, which brilliantly depicts an idyllic pre-war world, but is less satisfactory for dealing with the author's military experiences in *Memoirs of an Infantry Officer*. To his great credit he was determined to provide a detailed, accurate and unsensational personal account of the war in contrast to E. M. Remarque's *All Quiet on the Western Front*, whose vagueness regarding dates, units and places and exaggeration of horrors he deplored. But Sherston is very different from Sassoon in his simplicity and lack of intellectual and moral concerns and is given no literary imagination. As Adrian Caesar puts it: 'All the passion, all the heights and depths of emotion are erased in that later account, to be replaced by an urbane and ultimately very conservative "understanding".'

The rage expressed in the diaries and satirical poems against generals, journalists, civilians and especially women has been moderated and toned down. Similarly, in dealing with combat, Sherston's reactions are less exultant, reckless or heroic than the author's. Sassoon skilfully manages to combine his genuine anti-war sentiments with the positive message that, thanks mainly to Rivers' help, Sherston's personal pilgrimage has not been futile: his suffering has made him wiser and more mature.[31]

As Sassoon admitted to Lady Ottoline Morrell, he found his protest against the war particularly hard to recreate convincingly through the character of George Sherston: 'a young man who was not a writer and did *not* love books.' In particular, as we have seen, Sassoon's act of rebellion had been prompted and then orchestrated by the 'Garsington Pacifists', with his statement fine-tuned by Bertrand Russell and Middleton Murry. Sherston faces his tribulations with endurance and courage but the moral agonizing and willingness to sacrifice his reputation for a cause seems out of character. The author attempts to bridge this gap in credibility by 'having the narrator look back on his protest as simply the outburst of an angry and impetuous young man', but this is not entirely success-ful. Does the older narrator actually disapprove of the actions of his younger self, believing in hindsight that his protest lacked both insight and wisdom?[32]

Sassoon returned to this pivotal episode in his own persona in *Siegfried's Journey* (1945), affirming from the standpoint of the early 1940s that he had never regretted the course of action, for which there was no alternative. Interestingly he reflects that his mental tension, aggravated by his long convalescence in the spring of 1917, might have found release had he been passed fit for general service at the end of June. He might then have returned to the war in 'a spirit of self-destructive bravado'. While he was now inclined to accept Arnold Bennett's accusation (at the time) that he had suffered from spiritual pride, he pointed out, in self-justification, that the ideas and emotions that led to his protest had been fermenting for almost a year and, furthermore, his behaviour was in accordance with that temperament which had led him to perform reckless exploits in the front line. In almost a throwaway tone he concludes the chapter with the admission: 'I must add that in the light of subsequent events it is difficult to believe that a Peace negotiated in 1917 would have been permanent. I share the general opinion that nothing on earth could have prevented a recurrence of Teutonic aggressiveness.'[33]

As Sassoon's wartime diaries reveal, he was an extremely complex character, troubled by his homosexuality and anxious to prove his manliness in combat and so to earn the respect, perhaps even love, of his men. Also, as a poet first and foremost, he was never at ease with the majority of his fellow officers whom he found boorish, dull and snobbish, hence his delight in meeting other poets and literary men such as Graves, Owen and de Sola Pinto. Both on his own account, and for the reputation of poets, he wanted to prove himself a hero and did so in several gallant actions. But in seeking to protest against what he thought of as the excessive suffering of his men in an unduly prolonged war he allowed himself to be influenced by pacifists who had little respect for men in uniform and were disappointed that he did not provide publicity for their cause by going to prison.

Sassoon experienced only three quite short periods of front line combat, in July 1916, April 1917 and June to July 1918, but he witnessed enough suffering and carnage to be deeply affected, not only in himself but also vicariously for the soldiers in his battalion. Although his satirical poems hit some legitimate targets in shirkers, profiteers, hysterical women and home-front militarists, they are too sweeping, savage and self-centred to carry conviction. Indeed some now seem unnecessarily brutal, telling us more about the poet's troubled mind than about the war on the home or military fronts. Most seriously, at that time Sassoon shows no understanding of the meaning of the conflict in strategic or political terms. Although his protest had been well-intentioned and required great moral courage, it took another world war for him to admit that in 1917 there was no possibility for Britain or her allies to gain acceptable peace terms.

For a more principled and determined protest by a serving officer it is interesting to examine the contrasting fortunes of a less well-known writer and political activist, Max Plowman. Max (christened Mark) was even less of a warrior than Sassoon before the war. Born in 1883, he was the seventh child of Plymouth Brethren, from whose religion he escaped by the age of 20 after bitter domestic conflict. By 1914 he had escaped a dull routine at his father's brickworks, had recently married and was beginning a new career as a writer. Unlike Sassoon, he did not rush to enlist and did not reach France until July 1916 when he was nearly 33. As a dutiful subaltern, troubled by poor health and by qualms of conscience about taking up arms, he developed none of Sassoon's reckless aggression but instead followed 'an erratic journey towards pacifism'.[34]

After being 'educated at various inferior private schools', Plowman began working in the family business at the age of 16. In December 1914 he joined the 4th London Field Ambulance Territorial Force, but after a year of boring duties in England decided he must do his bit in defeating Germany on active service. This was a remarkable change of mind because in January 1915 he had written to his brother John, who was serving in the Royal Army Medical Corps: 'No man properly alive ever kills another whether by machinery or bayonet ... war is ultimately an affair of individuals – and as such is insane and unmitigated filth.' His quirky character is revealed in another letter to his brother in August 1915 where he wrote: 'I don't mind a commission so long as it's in a decent regiment and I can afford it, but unless I can satisfy myself on these two points I'd rather go into the Coldstreams or any first class regiment as a private, than continue to muck about in a second class show.' In December 1915 he was commissioned in the West Yorkshire Regiment and in mid-July 1916 he joined the 10th Battalion, which had suffered the worst casualties of any battalion on the first day of the battle of the Somme – 22 officers and 688 men.[35]

In his six months of active service on various sectors of the Somme front he experienced some intense fighting, often in appalling conditions, but was determined to stick it out till the end. In January 1917, however, he was badly concussed by a shell exploding on the parapet of his trench. He was evacuated to England and never returned to France.

Plowman wrote a careful, unsensational account of his experiences in France in 1924 and under the pseudonym 'Mark Seven' published it in 1927 with the title *A Subaltern on the Somme*. He was delighted that for the front cover the publisher's artist adapted his own sketch of a splayed red body tied to a wheel suggesting Field Punishment No. 1, a practice which Max abhorred and regarded as the perfect symbol of the army's brutality.[36]

Closely based on diaries and letters, the author succeeded in writing a detailed, truthful but understated account of a terrifying yet also rewarding experience. Although he avoids retrospective references to his anti-war protest, signs of his moral agonizing are already evident. As early as 18 October he had written that he wanted to start an International League of individuals sworn never to take up arms. He realized that the widening gulf between his ideals and his active service might prove inexplicable, especially coming from an instructor of bayonet fighting. He was serving in 'mud and blood and all the damned insanity of war' but 'I wouldn't be out of it, *things being as they are*'. He believed that the war would eventually end in mutual exhaustion and, through suffering, the peoples of all belligerents would realize its wickedness.[37]

He was irked by various aspects of military callousness and incompetence: his battalion commander savagely hectoring men who were volunteers; the folly of ordering a patrol out in bright moonlight; and the failure either to equip or properly relieve troops in the front line short of rations and suffering terribly from trench feet. He despaired of the prospects for peace: 'one cannot imagine a future for the kind of government that makes its final arbitrament the placing of vast numbers of men in an area of flying iron.' What makes war so ghastly is that it is dominated by machines. He and his comrades might be blown to bits at any moment by shells fired from guns by 'hearty fellows who would be quite ready to stand you a drink if you met them face to face'. Shortly before he was wounded he was delighted by a present from his wife of six small Medici prints and reflected: 'Art lives by all that war destroys ... war shatters its [life's] very fabric and breeds this desolation that now surrounds me to the horizon.' He is disgusted by the brutal attitude of the firing instructor who tells them always to aim for the head, 'as if human heads were of less account than pheasants'. Although he believed that Germany had to be beaten he shows no animosity towards the enemy and it is unlikely that he ever deliberately killed anyone.

Plowman was evidently an efficient, humane officer whose profound admiration for the ordinary soldier's stoic endurance was not influenced by any homosexual inclination. He failed to report a sentry asleep at his post or to shoot an habitual offender who dared him to do so when he flatly refused to carry rations to the front line. He also put up the best defence he could when acting as 'soldier's friend' for a private plainly guilty of desertion and got him off with a sentence of two years' imprisonment. He depicted his ideal soldier as 'Jackson' (really Lance Corporal L. Barrett) who, though weak and ill, devoted himself tirelessly to helping and cheering his comrades.[38]

In November 1916 Plowman's company endured heavy rain and terrible muddy conditions in a featureless morass between Ginchy and Lesboeufs, an ordeal which forms the most remarkable section of the book. In charge of the nightly rations party, Max records that the journey of 3,000 yards took seven hours. Despite every precaution the men began to suffer badly from frostbite; they had reached 'the very limit of their endurance'. When the battalion was at last relieved half of the men had to be carried off in wagons because they were unable to walk. For his heroic efforts in getting rations up to the front trenches Plowman was recommended for an MC, but in the event none was awarded due to the higher command's erroneous belief that the brigade had not performed well. The colonel and those above him in the chain of command were simply ignorant of conditions at the front which had rendered orders completely impracticable. Plowman expresses his cynicism about the award of medals and even doubts whether he would have accepted an MC. However, given his gritty determination to stick it out, it seems possible – even probable – that had he been awarded the decoration and been given the leave which he desperately wanted he would have continued to serve with the battalion for as long as health permitted. Despite his ideological criticisms of the war, it is unlikely that he was looking for a permanent way out when he was evacuated, badly concussed, in mid-January 1917.[39]

A Subaltern on the Somme received generally favourable reviews and sold well in 1927 and 1928, but the author was modest about his success and uneasy about the reactions of pacifists who had no experience of combat. He found it strange that he was being made the 'mouthpiece of a [pacifist] challenge while ardent pacifists are unheard'. In November 1927 he noted that he had received 25 reviews, all favourable, but no Labour paper had mentioned his book. 'The silly devils who favour peace don't know what's grist to their mill and what isn't.' When he became a 'Conchy' he knew he was joining the fools' party. 'The best men went to the front and died. Now the job is to build *their* bridge into the future – to give a mark to their idealism.' He was bitter towards 'mere protesters against war' who really like war 'so long as their own skins aren't involved or are too flabby to know peace from war'.[40]

To a female admirer who called his book 'great' he replied, 'it is low in tone and thus too pale really for something as lurid as the war. I wrote it to give recurring memories a resting place.' It was, he said, a carefully-done miniature but 'the real, the spiritual wounds are barely hinted at – the agony of the human spirit mauled by the machine'.[41]

Between January and July 1917 Plowman was treated for shell-shock at Bowhill Auxiliary Hospital near Selkirk, a branch of Craiglockhart, where he met Dr Rivers for the first time. Although he found the latter interesting and they discussed Freud's book on dreams, Max did not approve of him because he was 'off poetry'. During these months of convalescence Plowman prepared a small book of poems for publication and also published anonymously a pamphlet entitled *The Right to Live* which was concerned not so much to stop the war as to explain his own complex ideas about how to change the post-war world for the better. His was an idealistic vision, based on romantic socialism, attacking materialism and the tyranny of the machine, and calling for more emphasis on simplicity and spiritual values.[42]

In July 1917, when he was considered fit enough for home service (with the 3rd Battalion, West Yorkshire Regiment), he wrote to a friend that he feared he would be of no further use to the Army; he was too tired of it and its tyranny. But he would have preferred to stick it out until the end because he feared he might be considered guilty of cowardice or at least of vacillation. But over the coming weeks he decided to make a protest by refusing to serve and was quite prepared to go to prison.[43]

At a medical board on 1 January 1918 Plowman was told that after a further month of home service he would be liable for front-line duties in France. Two weeks later he wrote to his commanding officer asking to be relieved of his commission on the grounds of conscientious objection. 'My opinion has gradually deepened into a fixed conviction that organised warfare of any kind is always organised murder. I believe wholly in the doctrine of Incarnation that believes killing man is always killing God.' Clearly, this was a very different kind of protest to that made by Sassoon a few months earlier: Sassoon had called for a change in British policy to end the war in progress whereas Plowman's objection was to the legitimacy of war itself. When Plowman rejected a home posting he was placed under open arrest to await a court martial.

He prepared an elaborate philosophical statement on his reasons for resigning which he read out at his court martial early in April 1918. He argued that 'God is incarnate in every human body, soul and body are one and inseparable, God being the life of both. From which it follows that killing man is killing God.' Later he wrote that 'the designed and intentional killing of any person against

1. Robert Graves.

2. Siegfried Sassoon.

3. Frank Richards.

4. Guy Chapman.

5. Royal Welch Fusiliers Officers at the Litherland Depot. Robert Graves is third from the left in the second row standing.

6. Frederic Manning as a lieutenant in the Royal Irish Regiment, 1917.

7. Captain W. A. 'Billy' Bishop in early 1917 standing by his Nieuport Scout B1566.

Capt. A. O. Pollard, v.c., m.c.,
D.C.M.
1st. H.A.C.

8. A. O. Pollard.

9. Stephen Graham. A photograph taken shortly after the First World War.

whose personal character you can make no charge is murder of the worst possible kind'. He had ceased to believe that the present war, by its very frightfulness, could prevent future wars. Also, he contended, 'doing evil that good may come is apparent folly'. The only way to achieve lasting peace was to establish an international parliament for the making and maintaining of international law. He was dismissed from the Army but spared a prison sentence, presumably because of his obvious, if somewhat tortuous, integrity and honourable record of front-line service.[44]

Plowman's ordeal was, however, only just beginning. Between May and November 1918 he conducted a physically and mentally exhausting struggle to resist being conscripted, resolutely refusing to do any work of national service related to the war. The authorities evidently wished to treat him kindly, as a last resort asking if he would object to reading to the blind at St Dunstan's. He replied that he had no objection in principle but would not do it if it meant obeying an order. As late as 5 November he still expected to be sent to prison, but six days later his ordeal was ended by the Armistice. Never enjoying robust health, these months of resistance to the ceaseless pressures of the civil and military authorities cost him dearly in both nervous and physical strain.[45]

Since he had admired Sassoon's statement against the war in July 1917, Plowman sent him a copy of his own letter of resignation. Sassoon did not reply but simply passed it on to Dr Rivers. The latter wrote sympathetically to Plowman asking if he could help, but pointed out that 'Sassoon has returned to duty and is quite happy in it'. Plowman was not impressed because as Sassoon had acted merely on the question of British war aims he could be persuaded to change his mind: his was 'a queer halfway house, but I daresay it was useful'. In July 1918 Plowman met Rivers again and thought him 'a very clever liberal-minded person' but also a 'fundamental ass' because his line was that in war the individual is bound to be in conflict with society and must show more restraint and willingness to compromise. Rivers' arguments might persuade less morally committed objectors but would not do for someone like himself who had experienced war and now rejected it completely. Plowman also strongly disagreed with Rivers' contention that Germany had to be beaten ('we must eat the German militarists') before there could be peace. They seem to have parted without a reconciliation.[46]

In the inter-war years Plowman pursued his literary interests, writing poetry and publishing a book on William Blake.[47] He joined the staff of *The Adelphi* magazine and was briefly its editor in the late 1930s. But his predominant concern lay in supporting international and domestic peace campaigns. In 1934 he joined Canon Dick Sheppard[48] and Brigadier F. P. Crozier (a most unlikely pairing) in launching the Peace Pledge Union, and in 1937 became its General Secretary. Sassoon was also a fervent supporter until 1937 but then renounced pacifism mainly because of his loathing for Mussolini and the Italian fascists.

Already in poor health and devastated by the sudden death of his son Tim, the outbreak of war in September 1939 came as a terrible blow to Plowman. As a continuation of his work for peace he ran the Langham Voluntary Service on a 70-acre co-operative farm near Colchester to provide a refuge and work on the land for elderly evacuees from London and young conscientious objectors. The effort to combine writing, administration and hard work in the fields proved too much. He died, sick and exhausted, on 3 June 1941.[49]

It is not surprising that Sassoon has become a legendary, almost mythic figure as an anti-war poet, whereas Plowman has been largely forgotten. The former was altogether a more attractive figure, handsome, wealthy, educated at Marlborough and Cambridge and extremely well connected, even before 1914, in literary and political circles. He was also fortunate to belong to that most literary of regiments, the Royal Welch Fusiliers, along with Robert Graves, David Jones and Vivian de Sola Pinto. He also managed to combine the roles of romantic poet and heroic warrior. In literary terms also Sassoon was a more prolific and, at his best, impressive poet, while his six autobiographical volumes, and especially the Sherston trilogy, have deservedly become classics.

By contrast, Plowman was a brooding, difficult character, always wrestling with moral issues and with few of Sassoon's glittering social contacts. Unlike Sassoon, Plowman was a happy family man, devoted to his wife and children. His literary output was limited compared with Sassoon's, and as he said himself about reviews of A Subaltern on the Somme, although they were favourable there was nothing to 'lift it out of the water'.[50] Also, while prepared to go to prison and ruin his health for his pacifist beliefs, he could not abandon his old soldier's viewpoint that only men who had served at the front were fully deserving of respect. This attitude must have made him an awkward colleague for purely civilian pacifists after the war. But he is surely worthy of respect and interest for his great courage in deciding first to sacrifice his moral scruples and join the Army to help defeat Germany; and second for his equally brave decision to change his mind during the war and refuse adamantly to make any further contribution whatever to the conflict. His name should at least be linked with Sassoon's in any discussion of brave regimental officers who protested publicly against the conduct of the First World War while it was still in progress.

8

Martinet, militarist and opponent of war: the strange career of Brigadier-General F. P. Crozier

Frank Percy Crozier is an unusual soldier to be found in these ranks of, mostly, literary subalterns. Although he achieved the rank of Brigadier-General and wrote three books of overlapping memoirs about the First World War, notably *A Brass Hat in No Man's Land* (1930), it would be stretching the term to call him a regular officer since his career was highly irregular.

Crozier was born in 1879 into an Anglo-Irish family with a strong military tradition. His father, who died young, was a major in the Royal Scots Fusiliers, his mother subsequently married a general, and Frank's first wife, whom he married in 1905, was a colonel's daughter. From an early age Frank wanted to be a soldier, but after a promising start at Wellington College he was rejected as being too short and too light (under 9 stones).

After a brief spell as a tea planter in Ceylon, Crozier took a calculated gamble in sailing to South Africa where his mother's great friend (and later second husband) Colonel Thorneycroft was raising a new company of mounted infantry. Although Crozier scarcely knew how to mount a horse, he was promptly promoted corporal and eventually obtained a commission. He took part in, or witnessed, several famous actions including Spion Kop and the dramatic cavalry dash to the relief of Ladysmith. During the next five years (1900–5) he saw a good deal of exciting action in Colonial conflicts in Ashanti, Northern Nigeria and Zululand. These experiences left him with a number of ailments, including malaria, but on the positive side he made many military friends and contacts who would be useful in his later career. These years are fully described in his second book of memoirs *Impressions and Recollections* (also published in 1930).

Initially to dull the effects of malaria, Crozier admits that he doped himself continually with nips of brandy, whisky and other so-called stimulants; in short he became an alcoholic. Further misfortunes followed, notably a sudden reduction in his income when he was placed on half-pay as a consequence of the disbanding of two battalions of his regiment (the Manchester). He then made a disastrous trip to West Africa for a firm of timber merchants, where he and his wife became seriously ill and had to pay their own fares home. As if these were not troubles enough, he was knocked down by a motor car in Plymouth and nearly killed. All these misfortunes together caused Crozier to retire in 1908 in order to join the reserve forces as a captain. The following year he admits he

got into a 'stupid, silly senseless scrape', from the worst consequences of which
he was saved by another friend of his mother's, the then General (later Field
Marshal) Sir Herbert Plumer. He resigned his commission and, after further
medical treatment, sailed to Canada as a soldier-farmer. What he understandably does not spell out is that he had been forced to resign from both the
2nd Manchester Regiment in 1907 and the 3rd Loyal North Lancashire Regiment
in 1909 for dishonouring cheques. Indeed he had issued a dishonoured cheque
as early as 1902 while on a musketry course at Hythe. Fortunately for him this
earlier history was not spotted by the War Office when he was recommissioned
in 1914.[1]

Crozier's roller-coaster experiences continued in Canada, where he helped
to raise a squadron of light horse (which later fought in France); took part in a
trapping expedition in the Hudson Bay area; and laid a telephone line across a
wild and isolated part of Manitoba. He continued to drink heavily and was briefly
imprisoned after a brawl with Americans who had cast aspersions on Britain's
new monarch, George V. St Patrick's Day (17 March) 1912 was, almost literally,
a watershed in Crozier's life because, after suffering from a uniquely painful
hangover, he vowed never to drink alcohol again. In achieving this remarkable
transformation he became a somewhat fanatical convert, holding alcohol responsible for numerous individual and collective military and social shortcomings,
and making it one of his main reforming missions after the war.[2]

In 1913 he returned to Britain expressly to join the Ulster Volunteer Force
because he believed that Ulster had an absolute right to determine whether or
not it wished to remain connected with the British Parliament. He was posted, as
a captain, to raise and train a special force of 300 men in the West Belfast UVF.
In the pre-war months Crozier displayed conspicuous zeal and individualism
in ignoring official 'red tape' while training this group of tough, hard-drinking
Shankhill Road lads, and on the outbreak of war was promoted major and second
in command of what then became the 9th Battalion Royal Irish Rifles in the 36th
Ulster Division.[3]

Although the Ulster Division was to perform heroically on 1 July 1916 in its
first major battle, its disciplinary record, in Ireland, in England and eventually
in France was notoriously bad. This was mainly due to the initial appointment
of elderly, inexperienced and patently incompetent officers at all levels from
companies all the way up to the divisional commander. Sweeping changes had to
be made, particularly after the division arrived in France, to make it reasonably
fit for combat. The new division commander, Major-General Sir Oliver Nugent,
singled out 107th Brigade for a fearsome harangue and Crozier was personally
castigated for bringing an indisciplined mob to France: the faults included
desertions, looting and drunkenness, the last involving a number of senior
NCOs. The Brigade was temporarily transferred to the 4th Division, but Crozier

was mistaken in believing this to be a punishment because Nugent had opposed the move.[4]

In any event it was an unintended favour because the 4th was a good, mainly regular, division which permitted the 107th Brigade to see more front-line duty than it would have done with the 36th. However, a recent historian of the Irish Regiments' discipline and morale concludes, on the basis of courts martial statistics, that attachment to the 4th Division 'appears to have done little to improve discipline in the 107th Brigade'. Indeed, he suggests that the three executions carried out in February 1916 may have done more to check indiscipline than attachment to the 4th Division.[5]

In his memoirs *A Brass Hat in No Man's Land* Crozier spells out the beliefs and methods which gained him the reputation of being a martinet. He believed it was necessary to inculcate a spirit of blood-lust to prepare essentially kindly men for the barbarity of combat. Although he personally doubted the truth of many alleged German atrocities, they were useful to bring out the brute-like savagery which was necessary for victory. Military ferocity could also be fostered by martial music: drums, Irish pipes, bands and marching songs. Crozier would later assert that his militaristic stance was largely a pose: he did not hate the Germans and did not really like to see 'the red blood flow'. He did not have a 'callous disregard for casualties', but said rather that he regretted every loss simply because it weakened his strength. But he was prepared to sacrifice 1,000 men in half an hour provided a position was gained or held. Moreover he would immediately dismiss a colonel for throwing away lives by making a wrong decision, such as renewing a failed attack.[6]

Crozier found the best method of conquering personal fear – the all-important issue – was by means of lectures on *esprit de corps*, and examples of heroic personal sacrifices in the present war. His high ideal was that every officer would only go to a base or staff appointment under protest because his heart would be with the battalion in the firing line. He believed that he had largely succeeded in instilling this attitude in his officers, first in the battalion and later in the brigade. Some had 'fallen by the wayside' due to health and professional failings, but few had shown a desire to quit the war zone for a safer appointment. He also believed he had largely succeeded in transforming civilians, many of them boys, into hardened soldiers who would stick at nothing to carry out his orders. No matter what positive military virtues his soldiers might possess, Crozier always believed that fear of punishment, and especially court martial leading to execution, was essential to ensure 'sticking it out' in a crisis.[7]

In slightly polemical tones in *Brass Hat*, but much more stridently in *The Men I Killed*, Crozier would contend that 'Those who wish to abolish the death sentence for cowardice and desertion in war should aim at a higher mark and strive to abolish war itself'. He was evidently troubled by recollections of one private soldier whom he had sent to his death at Mailly-Maillet in February 1916. Private 'Crocker', whose real name curiously was James Crozier, was found guilty of desertion and, after due process, executed at about the same time as two other privates from the brigade. Crozier describes the execution at length and in rather gruesome detail, including the admission that he authorized the man's being made unconscious with alcohol, and also that another officer had to finish off the dying man with a pistol shot. It may have been the shared name that stuck in his mind, but in reality he had only been a cog in the Army's legal process because it was Major-General Nugent who bore the main responsibility and he had acted out of concern to improve the division's discipline.[8]

Crozier does not reproach himself in a case where he had more reason to do so; namely that of an officer whom he referred to as 'Rochdale' but who was actually Second Lieutenant A. J. Annandale. Crozier had earlier made a case for Annandale to have special leave to get a venereal disease treated, but when he ran away under full view of the men during a bombardment there was no alternative to a court martial. He was sentenced to be dismissed from the Army with a recommendation to mercy on health grounds. Crozier evidently did not press for the death sentence in this case and though he claims he refused to allow Annandale back into the battalion it is not clear if this is so. He was allowed to relinquish his commission in August 1916. His virtual free pardon only days after rifleman Crozier was sentenced to death for a comparable offence was unpopular in the battalion. As Lt. Col. Crozier's batman noted, if the officer did not know what he was doing why had the same discretion not been applied to the private?[9]

Although it eventually had to retire through lack of support, the 36th Ulster Division distinguished itself on 1 July 1916. Attacking from the northern edge of Thiepval Wood, the six leading battalions had the formidable Schwaben Redoubt to their right front and the marshy Ancre valley on their left. They had sensibly been ordered to leave the wood before zero hour and creep up near to the German front line. Immediately when the barrage ceased, and without waiting to form up in waves, the fired-up Ulstermen, by a combination of good tactics and Irish dash, quickly captured most of the enemy front line. Fresh men pressed on to attack the Schwaben Redoubt but there they encountered stubborn resistance. Worse still, the 32nd Division's attack on Thiepval village and chateau failed completely with the result that the garrison's machine-guns could fire straight down the open slopes of No Man's Land against the Ulsters' exposed right flank.[10]

Crozier, now in command of the 9th Royal Irish Rifles, was in the supporting brigade (107th) in Thiepval Wood, where he and his colleague Lt. Col. H. C. Bernard (commanding 10th Battalion RIR) blatantly disobeyed orders against leading their troops up to the start line and beyond. Hence the appropriate title of Crozier's memoirs since 'brasshats' were not supposed to risk their lives in

No Man's Land. Bernard was killed immediately but Crozier behaved gallantly in leading his Ulstermen up to and beyond the Schwaben Redoubt towards the enemy's second line. When, at about 8.00 a.m., Crozier led his troops out of the shelter of the wood and into heavy shell-fire, his worst fears of a disaster on his right at Thiepval were confirmed by the heaps of British dead and dying. With his blood up and in an exalted state as though drugged, Crozier stood in the open to shepherd his companies across No Man's Land and to give them amended orders. Among his own officers killed that day was Major George Gaffikin, whom Crozier had spared from a charge of drunkenness while on duty in the trenches. Crozier himself then returned to his battalion dug-out in the wood, which he found packed with dead and wounded men.[11]

Eventually the surviving Ulstermen not only captured the Schwaben Redoubt but advanced well beyond it to the wire of the enemy's second line, from where they could clearly see Grandcourt village away to their left. But the advance was on too narrow a front and not well supported. The survivors were not only hit by determined counter-attacks but were blasted by their own artillery's barrage. Although the day ended in retreat it had been a magnificent achievement. These were the only troops to reach the enemy's second line anywhere that day and it was the furthest advance by a division. The basic cause of the Ulster Division's failure to hold the ground it had captured lay in the fact that for four miles on either flank there had been no advance to distract the German defenders. As Martin Middlebrook sums up, 'The Ulsters in their first battle had done as much as could be asked of even the most experienced soldiers.' They needed reinforcements but these were not forthcoming. No Man's Land had become virtually impassable and the sunken road, which had earlier provided invaluable shelter, was now packed with corpses.[12]

Crozier details his own and others' efforts to stem the tide of stragglers and exhausted men trying to flee the battle area. His neighbouring battalion opened ferocious fire against an advancing crowd in field grey which turned out to be Germans trying to surrender escorted by British wounded. A young officer successfully checked a panic flight by shooting a British soldier. German counter-attacks succeeded but at a terrible cost. At 10.00 p.m. 'the curtain rings down on hell'. Nature had been supplanted in that Thiepval Wood had disappeared. Was there ever such a day? Not in Crozier's recollection. He went out into No Man's Land and found about 700 dead and wounded in an area a quarter of a mile square (400 m). On the third morning he was allowed to withdraw the remnants of the battalion to Martinsart: 'the net result of the barren, glorious bloody battle of Thiepval' was that over 700 men of his battalion had 'proved their ability to subordinate matter to mind. Intellectual discipline had triumphed'. He recorded gratefully '*My* star is high, even though the sufferings of others are great.'[13]

Crozier had indeed made a very favourable impression amidst the general shambles on 1 July, and despite the Division's relapse into drunken disorders after the battle he was rewarded, in October 1916, by promotion to command a brigade – a remarkable step for a junior lieutenant-colonel who had only been a reservist in 1914. This was probably the most pleasurable moment in his professional career. He generously acknowledged his debt to the battalion, naming not only officers in his memoirs but also ten of the rank and file among those hundreds of 'stout fellows'.[14]

When Crozier arrived to take command of the 119th Brigade in the 40th Division he was astonished to be told by a senior staff officer that his brigade was in a very poor state; indeed it was quite the worst in the division. The men were bantams from the Welsh coal mines who could not even carry packs and whose morale was low. Crozier retorted that there were no bad soldiers, only bad colonels, and he at once set about a purge of officers and senior NCOs, including nearly a dozen commanding officers, several doctors and transport officers. In six months, with the full support of the divisional commander, Major-General Harold Ruggles-Brise, Crozier surmounted appalling weather conditions at the front to produce a highly efficient military machine determined to secure victory. The brigade took over a sector at Rancourt from the French, who had left many of their bodies unburied.

> Trenches there were none. The [troops in the] firing-line, existing in shell-holes, remained four days in the line, carried up rations for two days and could never be reached by day, while no man's land became an impassable obstacle of mud.[15]

The battalions comprising the 119th Brigade were the 19th Royal Welch Fusiliers, the 12th South Wales Borderers and the 17th and 18th Welch Regiment. The SWBs were by far the best when Crozier took over and the only one which kept its headquarters staff unchanged during his time in command. The formerly 'despised little Welshmen' began to demonstrate their fighting skills in the early months of 1917 in forcing their way into the German trenches as the latter began to retreat to the Hindenburg Line. In April, south of Cambrai, they captured 'XV Ravine', Welch Ridge, Borderer Ridge and Fusilier Ridge, while in May they made a successful sortie to La Vacquerie. As many of the troops were ex-miners their trenches were better dug than anybody else's, and they could now carry their packs further than most of the other battalions. Their new commander had proved his point that poor discipline, manifested, for example in large numbers going sick with 'trench feet'; or poor fighting qualities, such as allowing enemy night patrols to penetrate their lines without being immediately expelled, were due to bad officers and would simply not be tolerated. Crozier cites several cases of his sacking battalion commanders on the spot for not being properly informed or not sufficiently aggressive when in the front line. Doubtless there were some injustices but he got results in completely transforming the brigade's reputation.[16]

The brigade's culminating achievement lay in the epic struggle for Bourlon Wood, a key sector in the battle of Cambrai on 23 November 1917 and the following three days. Against pessimistic opinions at GHQ, the Welch Brigade captured the wood on their first morning of the battle (which had begun on 20 November), and continued to hold it against ferocious counter-attacks. Crozier, from his headquarters at Graincourt, decided that with both flanks in the air the brigade must withstand a siege. Accordingly he sent up rations, water and ammunition and ordered that there must be no withdrawal. In what is usually called 'a soldiers' battle' of chaotic close-order combat in the dense and cratered wood, the Welch Brigade suffered heavy losses in officers and men but held on until relieved by the Guards. As usual Crozier stresses that the minority who tried to retreat or run away were ruthlessly shot down: 'a revolver emptied "into the brown" accounts for five; a Lewis gun fired into the panic-stricken mass puts many on the grass and undergrowth.' The brigade had suffered great carnage. 'The little Welshmen are no more', Crozier recorded, 'but those who do remain are to carry on the torch.'[17]

While one would not recommend reading *A Brass Hat in No Man's Land* for details of battles or a discussion of tactical developments, it does remain of great interest for certain themes which the author pursued obsessively. Several striking passages, for example, are devoted to the problems which sex posed for military discipline and for fitness more generally. Crozier seems to have been a devoted family man. He was twice married and had children and there is no suggestion that he had homosexual inclinations. Nevertheless, some references hint at prurient or puritanical attitudes which a more introspective writer, such as Siegfried Sassoon, would have explained more fully. Crozier's discussion of 'the sex question' in the early months of his connection with the 9th Battalion Royal Irish Rifles is sensible and tolerant. While still stationed in Ireland there were few problems, but when the battalion moved to the Brighton area and then to France they increased rapidly. Many soldiers were tempted to 'have a fling' while there was still a chance and, inevitably, 'prostitutes and loose women always followed the big drum'. Crozier says he regarded the matter entirely from the viewpoint of efficiency and would not tolerate 'self-inflicted ailments'. With the co-operation of the battalion medical officer he ensured that all ranks received careful instruction and were given disinfectants after indulging in sexual intercourse. Many girls and women were offered similar facilities free of charge. In an eloquent passage he rebutted the criticism – which would recur in the Second World War – that by such measures he was condoning or even encouraging vice. After several edifying anecdotes about individuals who gave way to temptation in France, he mentions a pleasant visit to four young army officers whom he finds standing stark naked on the banks of the Ancre ready to jump in for a race. He starts them off and realizes that he is in the presence not only of boys versed in war, but men already known to women:

> I think as I watch them ducking each other in the water, and playing like young seals I have so often seen up North, 'What a pity they are not married in order that they might implant their seed'. Alas! The weaklings and shirkers escape and breed like rabbits, while the strong suffer and are wiped out.[18]

After the battle of the Somme, when two young officers were late for a train departure, Crozier made them open their packs to reveal astounding contents including: 'Two pairs of girls' garters and an odd one. Two pairs of silk stockings and a chemise … A pot of vaseline, a candle, two boxes of matches, and an envelope full of astonishing picture post cards.' Perhaps this was a jolly, memorable episode but the author seems to record it in loving detail.

Later still, while stationed near Bailleul, other ranks' casualties from VD caused more concern than losses in the line until the culprit was caught: 'an infected girl who hops from camp to camp and ditch to dyke like the butterfly she is'. The author, rather than appear censorious, blames the war itself and those responsible politically, not soldiers who succumb to temptation in dreary and anxious circumstances.

Towards the end of the war he hears from a young friend, 'Madge', who is a nurse at Boulogne and has a husband serving overseas (later killed), that immorality in that city is as prevalent as death in the line. British girls working there became 'war-mad' and 'sex-mad' and free love was easy. The author makes it as clear as possible that he strongly disapproved of these goings-on and did not himself give way to temptation. Finally, at the end of the war he records, in Brussels, Cologne and other allied-occupied cities, 'orgies of vice', but realizes at this stage there is little to be done beyond warnings of the likely consequences. He seems chiefly concerned that demobilized soldiers will infect their hitherto 'clean' wives and girlfriends at home.[19]

As a reformed alcoholic now strictly teetotal, Crozier makes numerous references to individuals – officers and other ranks – who ruin their careers and, much worse, undermine security and discipline by their inability to stay sober. Drunkenness was a continuing problem for the 9th Battalion Royal Irish Rifles, whether in Ireland, England or France. Major-General Nugent's devastating 'strafe' of the battalion was partly caused by Crozier's attempt to cover up the absence from a parade of four senior NCOs who were lying dead drunk in an *estaminet* due to drinking French fire-water, otherwise adulterated brandy which should not have been sold to them. The case of Major George Gaffikin has already been mentioned in passing. Essentially a good soldier, he had been unnerved by several incidents and, after drinking a bottle of whisky while on front-line duty, had ordered two platoons on a suicide mission to rescue two missing men. Crozier gave him time to sober up and then extracted a promise that he would never again touch alcohol while serving with the battalion. This was a humane alternative to disciplinary punishment which he accepted and honoured, until killed leading his company gallantly on 1 July. On other occasions, however, Crozier showed no mercy and indeed went to great lengths to get colonels who favoured the whisky or brandy bottle removed from their commands. One commander, whom Crozier found issuing unauthorized tots of rum to his men as they passed him in single file, to hold the line for the first time, was dismissed after he got the medical officer to report the man unfit to command.

So strongly did Crozier feel about the evil effects of alcohol not only on the soldiers but also, in the long-term, on their families that he (vainly) tried to get the sale of spirits forbidden to British soldiers serving anywhere in France. In his view profiteers made money out of canteens and clubs behind the lines at the expense of the youth of the nation who, without conscription, would never have learnt the taste of strong drink. Half of the many cases of indiscipline on the part of officers which passed through his hands were, directly or indirectly, attributable to easy access to alcohol.[20]

As the title of this chapter suggests, Crozier's character, as revealed in his autobiographical publications, was a very odd mixture of militarism and anti-war attitudes which fell only just short of outright pacifism. Unfortunately, since all three volumes were written in the later 1920s and 1930s, it is impossible to say for certain whether he was an unthinking militarist during the war who became an anti-war crusader only afterwards. It seems likely that he could not have displayed the single-minded, almost fanatical drive towards military excellence in the quest for victory had he been seriously troubled by doubts about the justice of the war or the vital necessity of beating Germany at almost any cost. One can suggest, however, that anti-war sentiments of a broader kind, such as blaming politicians, church leaders, profiteers and other 'enemies' on the home front were already present in his thoughts during hostilities but only began to obsess him once the war was won. If only his publisher, Jonathan Cape, had insisted on his taking the advice of a stern editor then the post-war reflections could have been winnowed out of *Brass Hat* and treated separately and more succinctly in *The Men I Killed*.

Crozier admits he was happy at the outbreak of war in 1914, but later became chastened because he had seen so much suffering. Many others welcomed the war through ignorance of its nature, as a chance to escape from domestic unhappiness, or with hopes of power and profit. Now he sees the task as to 'guide our youth to the hard battle of peace'. The cataclysmic change has come, he believes, through the rapid development of air power, particularly the ability to bomb enemy cities. In a future war, consequently, everybody will have to be in it. After a sentimental bout of philosophizing with Madge and another war widow, they conclude that wars are a stupid man-made invention without a single redeeming feature, so that 'if we women can't abolish war ourselves we shall deserve the consequences'. Moving on ten years in his narrative, Crozier concludes that 'The great war was the SOS danger signal to civilization. If we ignore that SOS and the lessons of the war, civilization is doomed.'[21]

Before discussing Crozier's later reflections in more detail there is one further critical campaign to cover; namely the final German offensive in the West in March and April 1918, and in particular the 119th Brigade's important role in checking the enemy breakthrough and holding up his advances towards Hazebrouck in the desperate battle of the River Lys.

Crozier had barely begun the daunting task of reconstituting his depleted brigade after the battle of Cambrai when a devastating re-organization took place. In January 1918 all brigades lost one of their four battalions but, worse still for Crozier, he had to relinquish three of his battalions, retaining only the 18th Welch. His two replacement battalions, the 13th East Surreys and the 21st Middlesex, came from different brigades and needed personnel changes and vigorous training to bring them up to anywhere near Crozier's standard.[22] Already it was widely expected that the enemy would launch a last desperate all-out attack in the West early that spring. When the great German offensive began on 21 March, the 119th Brigade was forced to retreat for four days but never lost its cohesion and then counter-attacked to recapture the villages of Ervillers and Mory, a few miles north of Bapaume. From his headquarters at Gomiecourt Crozier heard that the formations on either side of him, including a Guards Brigade commanded by Lord Ardee, were pulling back but, bearing in mind his own principle – derived from the disaster at Spion Kop – never to retreat without an order – he held on until it was received. Characteristically he had destroyed an enormous store of alcohol from the British depot to prevent drunkenness in retreat, but he did allow his men to smoke liberated cigars. Though the brigade's casualties were heavy it had come through the second battle of the Somme better than its commander had dared to hope, given the inadequate training and two inexperienced battalion commanders out of three.[23]

On 7 April the 119th Brigade was moved to a supposedly quiet sector of the front south of the River Lys near Armentières, but Crozier was worried by the unpreparedness of the 2nd Portuguese Division holding a key part of the line on his right, and vainly urged GHQ to replace it at once. He had walked along the Portuguese front without seeing any sentries; many of the soldiers were sleeping without boots or equipment on, while their rifles and ammunition were engrained with rust and grit. He knew that the enemy was concentrating opposite this sector but his appeal was not acted upon in time. Consequently, when the German offensive began at 4.15 a.m. on 9 April in a thick mist the Portuguese division disintegrated and a great gap yawned in the Allied line. Crozier was woken sharply to find that his headquarters was being gassed and bombarded and two of his battalions were at once involved in close-quarter combat.

It is surprising that Crozier does not attempt a coherent description of his brigade's role in the Battle of the Lys between 9 and 11 April 1918, particularly as the excellent 40th Divisional history had been published in 1926. At 4.15 a.m., when the ferocious German bombardment of high-explosive and gas shells plastered the whole sector held by the 2nd Portuguese and the 40th (British) divisions, Crozier's 119th Brigade was in the most dangerous position next to the Portuguese, whose defences had disintegrated in about an hour. The full force of the German attack fell on Crozier's right-hand battalion, the 18th Welch, which resisted heroically until virtually annihilated by 9.00 a.m. No survivors reached battalion headquarters and only two officers and 14 other ranks, all wounded, were taken prisoner. Only the gallant commanding officer and a handful of his headquarters staff survived to withdraw to the Lys. Crozier's other advanced battalion, the 13th East Surreys, escaped the full force of the initial onslaught but by 10.00 a.m. they had been surrounded and only a handful of troops managed to fight their way back to the Lys. Crozier's criticisms of the East Surrey's conduct seem unduly harsh unless he had personal intelligence not passed on to the divisional historian. His remaining battalion, the 21st Middlesex, also fought extremely well in delaying the German advance to the Lys, but by noon it too had been reduced to a remnant. By about 1.00 p.m. the survivors of both the 119th and 120th Brigades had been forced to cross the Lys and continue to defend its bridges from the north bank. Crozier and a scratch force did well to hold the main bridge at Bac St Maur for several hours but at about 2.15 p.m. the bridge was destroyed just as the enemy was approaching it. That evening the 119th Brigade was withdrawn a mile or so to the north of the Lys and in the two following days (10 and 11 April) fought a number of delaying actions as it retreated up the main road towards Strazeele. By the time the 40th Division was relieved on 13 April it had fought itself to a standstill and was incapable of taking any further part in the battle. Crozier's brigade had done very well, with the 18th Welch and 21st Middlesex battalions singled out for special praise. As the divisional historian justly concludes, its losses were so severe that it had virtually ceased to exist:

> In its great effort the Division performed a duty than which there is no nobler in war. It sacrificed itself to retrieve the effect of mishap elsewhere. A considerate tact for the misfortune of an old ally is undoubtedly a good thing; but it is not so good as justice to the Division which had to pour out its blood like water in its splendid endeavour to make things good.[24]

For Crozier personally the battle had been 'a real thriller', but he stressed that the precipitate flight of the Portuguese had not been the only cause of a near disaster. The chaotic retreat had exposed many failings of battalion officers and more senior commanders while staff work had been faulty, particularly in neglecting to shore up the flanks quickly enough. Above all GHQ had been slow to grasp the urgency of the situation, with the consequence that the Portuguese were not replaced in time. He concluded proudly that his battalion commanders, lieutenant-colonels H. C. Metcalfe and W. E. Brown, DSO, MC had saved the day. Later, in *The Men I Killed*, he would boast that he had deliberately ordered the shooting of the stampeding Portuguese by machine-gun and rifle fire on the Strazeele Road, and had shot a subaltern as well as a pursuing German soldier. His drastic action, he claimed, *had* stemmed the tide; it was murder but it was necessary to hold the line. More disturbingly he later admitted that when a staff officer saw his smoking gun and asked if all was well he said 'Yes' and laughed. This was evidently written (in the 1930s) to shock civilian readers as to the barbarity of war, involving split-second decisions which might later look deplorable. He also wrote that had he been present on the morning of 9 April when, he alleged, British commanders and staff officers surrendered without a fight, he would probably have shot them too.[25]

On 1 January 1919 Crozier received a very favourable confidential report from the commander of the 40th Division, Major-General W. B. Peyton: 'Pre-eminently a fighting leader with sound knowledge, energy and determination. The efficiency of his Brigade in all details testifies to his high power of command and organization. It will be a great loss for the Army if he is not retained with rank and position consistent with his age and attainments.'[26] Despite this strong recommendation it seems that Crozier was not offered a commission in the post-war Army.

For a few months in 1919 Crozier, with half-a-dozen British officers he had selected, unwisely attempted to re-organize the newly-formed Lithuanian Army. From the outset, by his own admission, this was a ghastly failure. A tragi-comic three-front war was taking place with the Lithuanians fighting against Germans, Poles and Bolsheviks, but also fighting alongside the Poles against the 'Bolos'. Crozier's responsibility was never properly established and the financial rewards proved less attractive than the original negotiations had promised. Crozier, who had optimistically taken his wife and ten-year-old daughter, was glad to escape back to England, having by then left the Army.[27]

His last active military undertaking, between August 1920 and February 1921, perfectly illustrated the adage 'out of the frying pan and into the fire'. He joined the Auxiliary Division of the Royal Irish Constabulary, composed entirely of ex-officers, and became its commander, perhaps because he was a friend of Major-General Hugh Tudor, who took command of the RIC. The 'Auxies' were to play an inglorious role in the Anglo-Irish War then raging, with appalling atrocities being committed by both sides. Crozier thought the root of British failure lay in the Government's unwillingness to raise regular battalions to enforce martial law. General Sir Nevil Macready's half-measures had disastrous consequences. Crozier quickly found that his motley band, under the guise of policemen, were to carry out organized murder through secret channels. Crozier resigned, but not before his military reputation had been damaged, and for several years he was embroiled in political and legal controversies which militated against his attempts to obtain further public employment. As he recorded in *The Men I Killed*:

> I resigned not so much because I objected to giving the Irish assassins the tit for the tat, but because we were murdering and shooting up innocent people, burning their homes and making new and deadly enemies every day. What was worse, we were swearing to the world that the Irish were murdering each other because they were divided against themselves – or, perhaps for fun![28]

Crozier had enjoyed a remarkably varied, colourful, disreputable and yet militarily successful period since he had inveigled his way into the Army in South Africa in 1900, but when his active career ended in 1921 he was still only 42 years old. In the remaining 16 years of his life he became a political activist in the cause of peace and a prolific, if somewhat repetitive, turgid and polemical writer.

The title of his final book, *The Men I Killed*, was both provocative and distasteful since the victims were mostly British and Allied soldiers. In explaining the title and the at times wild and woolly contents, it may be possible that the author already knew he was seriously ill, since he died in the month the book was published, August 1937. He was also desperately short of money, so he needed to create a sensation. Driven by economic necessity he had published two other books (both in 1932): *Angels on Horseback* about his Boer war experiences, and *Five Years Hard* about his time with the Nigeria Regiment, West African Field Force. He was also a founder member of the Peace Pledge Union in 1934 and clearly idolized its saintly leader, the Reverend 'Dick' Sheppard, who also died, shortly after Crozier, in 1937. Crozier's strange effusion may also be charitably regarded as a desperate attempt to alert the British public to the catastrophic nature of impending war. Whether the author or his publisher chose the title in a calculated attempt to shock may never be known, but an alternative on the lines of 'Never Again' or 'No More War' would have more accurately reflected Crozier's main concern.

The essential steps of this argument, remarkably sustained through nearly 300 rambling, impassioned pages, may be summarized as follows. Only those who have experienced prolonged front-line combat know the true barbarity of warfare and are entitled to warn everyone else who has not. Furthermore, morale and order are only maintained – in the last resort – through fear of punishment, and particularly when in combat, of summary execution by their own officers. Only with this dire threat hanging over them will soldiers be prepared to attack or stick it out in defence in critical situations such as Crozier had experienced on

1 July 1916 at Thiepval, in November 1917 in Bourlon Wood, in March 1918 near Ervillers and in April 1918 on the Lys. At times he writes as though this action, of shooting one's own men, was a grim necessity, only undertaken in extreme circumstances, but at others he seems almost proud and boastful about what he had done. As noted earlier, he said he had laughed after shooting a British officer on the retreat from the Lys, while elsewhere he says that to have sent conscientious objectors to France and then shot them for disobedience would have been 'a splendid way out'. Yet a few pages later he writes that 'there is no escape for me from the memory of the men I killed, my own men, when panic seized them' and he wonders if any of the war widows he sees owe their sad status to him. 'I feel I want to hide as self-accusation invades me, and I sometimes think that they are thinking "Butcher!"'[29]

One suspects that there was an element of fantasy and surely of exaggeration in these references and that he did not habitually prowl around the trenches looking for an excuse to kill. For understandable reasons he is vague about the dates, locations and numbers of these executions. On his own analysis of the foundations of battalion morale and spirit, it is hard to believe that fear of being shot by one's own officers was the reason why men would obey orders to attack or 'stick it out' in defence in grim circumstances. It seems probable that, had Crozier been known to be 'trigger happy' and a frequent murderer of his own men, he would either have been shot by them (or dispatched more gruesomely) or reported and court-martialled. In other words, soldiers in democratic armies have to be motivated by confidence in their officers and loyalty to their commanders rather than by fear that they will be shot if they disobey orders.

Unlike his hero, 'Dick' Sheppard, Crozier wrote that he was 'no Christian pacifist', though after 1918 he had come to respect and admire outright pacifists who would face any punishment rather than compromise their principles. Instead he saw himself as a 'war-resister' 'trying to find a way of preventing another great war which can prove to be nothing but disastrous to both sides'. He believed fervently that a major obstacle to the conversion of the great majority of the British public to the ideals of the Peace Pledge Union was the unholy alliance between Church and State which entailed that the Church's official line must be to support Britain's cause in every war. Where Dick Sheppard was his hero and model therefore, the Archbishop of Canterbury and other overtly patriotic clergymen were depicted as enemies, even as hate figures. One day, he wrote, there may be a real revival of religion in this country, but the Archbishop of Canterbury will not be in it, because before that auspicious day dawns military religion, and all the attendant cant and humbug with it, will have to be abolished. The Church, allied to the State and the Army, can never achieve 'a recall to Christ', 'for the false pride of patriotism and the humility of Christianity can never be r econciled'.[30]

Like so many prophets of doom in the 1930s Crozier's impassioned harangue was inspired chiefly by the rapid development of air power and the horrifying predictions of what aerial bombing would do to densely-packed cities. In Crozier's view, there will be no immunity for the most helpless and the most innocent. The airman's target is no longer the machines of his enemy but the women and children in his cities. All will be victims of the diabolical invention and perversion of their fellow-men in times of 'just wars' which in practice means all wars.

The only solution, he suggested, was for the ordinary people to take defence out of the hands of the professional militarists and to associate themselves with a universal plan of peace construction. He envisaged the gradual disarmament and eventual abolition of Britain's armed forces, which would set an example to the rest of the world.[31]

Though Crozier was clearly voicing the fears of millions of ordinary people as regards the very real threat of aerial bombing of cities – underlined by Stanley Baldwin's grim prediction that 'the bomber will always get through' – his discussion was completely lacking in specific details and, at the time of writing, considerably exaggerated what any bomber could then achieve against distant, defended targets. Where he strayed beyond the general public's fears was in his belief that aerial bombing would lead to a popular revolution in England against the rulers who had failed to defend them. There would be a 'stringing up to the lamp posts [of] those responsible for the visitation of horrors and massacre'.[32] This was a notable failure to foresee the British people's stoical willingness to endure the Luftwaffe's assault in 1940 and 1941. But, ironically, it also underestimated the German public's stubborn resistance, under much more sustained bombing, and its failure to rebel against its tyrannical Nazi rulers, as the British Government had hoped it would.

There is clearly no point in subjecting Crozier's polemic to a detailed critique. Polemicists rely on rhetorical, one-sided arguments to make converts to popular movements and seldom mention exceptions or qualifications which would weaken their case, or provide details which could be challenged. Nevertheless, four brief criticisms are offered to suggest Crozier was neither sophisticated nor well informed.

First, he makes sweeping assumptions about the universal desire for peace with its corollary: the willingness to subordinate national interests – with all their grievances, bitter memories and aspirations – to an international ideal. The British people did indeed wish for 'peace' in the 1930s but had to be prepared to defend themselves against likely aggressors. As Clausewitz wryly remarked, 'the aggressor is always peace-loving. He would like to occupy your country.'

Second, Crozier displays a cavalier disregard for the pro-war policies of Hitler and Mussolini (the latter by the time he was writing had occupied Abyssinia), who received sympathetic mentions as does also Stalin and Soviet Communism. Like so many anti-war publicists in that decade, including Capt. B. H. Liddell Hart, he found it impossible to accept that leaders of some of the major powers actually wanted war, and could command an impressive amount of popular support.

Third, there was a certain irony to his gibes against the British governments in the 1930s since they were profoundly anti-war and very reluctant to rearm. Governments by their very nature, however, have to take notice of military threats, such as aerial bombing, and do the best they can to counter and defeat them. Even Siegfried Sassoon acknowledged this reality when he abandoned the Peace Pledge Union about the time Crozier was publishing his book.

Lastly, as an ex-soldier whose only real claim to expertise lay in his personal experience, Crozier gives no evidence of being *au fait* with military developments. While he could not be expected to know about the secret experiments with radar before 1937, he might have been aware that Britain was developing impressive modern fighters in the Hurricane and Spitfire. It was no means self-evident that 'the bomber would always get through' or would do substantial damage to camouflaged, defended targets. He also endorsed Liddell Hart's argument that the Luftwaffe would completely prevent the British Expeditionary Force from sailing to France in the event of war. But in September 1939 this proved to be quite mistaken.

These criticisms could easily be expanded but the exercise would be pointless. Suffice it to conclude that Crozier's book would have stood a better chance of convincing educated readers had he displayed a little more accurate evidence to underpin his warnings about an imminent Armageddon.

Frank Crozier excelled as a zealous battalion and brigade commander who was ruthless in his determination to convert raw, ill-disciplined soldiers into killing machines who would seize and hold trenches and would never retreat without orders. Although he stressed the role that fear of being executed played in his soldiers' tactical achievement, it seems clear that he successfully inculcated positive factors such as patriotism, *esprit de corps* and belief in victory. He was unpopular with some of his fellow officers in the Ulster Division, due in part to his advocacy of trench raiding. One officer recalled that he was particularly keen on sending out such patrols 'all to no purpose except to show off. He had the reputation of being a callous and overbearing martinet.'[33] After the battle of Cambrai his former Divisional Commander, Sir Oliver Nugent, told him in a rare moment of candour: 'I am sorry for you Crozier, you are in the wrong shop; you have cut off too many heads to be popular!' Crozier probably took this as a compliment because he repeatedly refers to various officers he had summarily sacked throughout his time as a battalion and brigade commander. On the other hand it seems clear that he had won the devotion of the staff and battalion commanders of his Welch Brigade, and at least some of their successors, notably lieutenant-colonels Brown and Metcalfe in the reconstituted brigade in 1918. A curious photograph published in *Impressions* (page 212) shows Crozier seated and surrounded by his reverential headquarters staff after the Armistice in an almost Napoleonic tableau. Philip Orr, author of a book on the men of the Ulster Division, describes Crozier as 'infamous' and mentions that he flirted with Irish nationalism and embraced fascism of the Mussolini brand for a while before his final phase of crusading pacifism. Orr concludes severely that he 'scaled the heights of egotism with his ill-written and eccentric books of personal reminiscences and pontifications, and he gave English literary history one of its most tasteless book titles – *The Men I Killed*'.[34]

It is true that Crozier is not an easy man to like because of his anecdotal, undisciplined writing; his militarist attitudes; and his unprepossessing appearance. Quite apart from its title, *The Men I Killed* is an irritating book and my own marginal notes on it include exclamations such as 'dotty' and even 'raving'. However, while it seems plausible that 'no gentleman is a hero to his valet', it is worth noting that Crozier ('The Master') retained the devotion and hero-worship of his batman, David Starrett. Crozier took on the naive Belfast lad, aged only 16 on the outbreak of war, treated his numerous blunders and indiscretions with amused tolerance and regarded him almost as a son. Starrett knew that he was a martinet, feared by some of his subordinates more than the enemy, but insisted that this was a professional persona which did not properly reflect his private character. Starrett evidently remained in touch with Crozier after the war and, at his death, became his literary executor.[35]

Judging by his memoirs it seems clear that Crozier was deeply affected by his rejection by the Army in 1896 and his failure to gain admission to the Staff College a decade later. Between 1900 and 1909 his turbulent life as a military adventurer in the Boer War and West Africa, handicapped by poor health and shortage of money, involved him in numerous 'scrapes' which culminated in bankruptcy and dismissal from the Army. His wayward, undisciplined behaviour continued in Canada until he gave up alcohol completely and became a campaigner for total abstinence. Even so, after he returned to Britain and resumed a form of military service with the Ulster Volunteer Force, his military prospects still seemed bleak. The advent of war in 1914, aided by the War Office's failure to check his previous record, gave him his second opportunity to prove himself as an officer and he seized it impressively. After 1919, however, he was not promoted Major-General and there seemed to be no future for him in the rapidly shrinking regular Army. Consequently, he embarked on further irregular soldiering in Lithuania and Ireland, the former venture ending in farce and the latter in tragedy and resignation in controversial circumstances which made it impossible for him to rejoin the Service. Astonishingly, in 1921 he was still aged only 42 but in the

16 years remaining to him he did not find a satisfying alternative career. He devoted his considerable energy to autobiographical writing and later, in the 1930s, to whole-hearted involvement in the Peace Movement. Crozier had an extremely colourful life to write about and two of his memoirs, *Impressions and Recollections* and *A Brass Hat in No Man's Land*, remain well worth reading for their graphic and eccentric portrayal of soldiering in the period 1900–21. Most importantly, for the student of the First World War, Crozier provides unique insights into the organizing, training, inspiring and commanding of troops at the battalion and brigade levels. He ruthlessly exposes the fundamental inhumanity of combat and the harsh measures which he believed to be essential for the maintenance of discipline and morale in the unwavering pursuit of victory.

9

The war in the air: Cecil Lewis and Billy Bishop

As a completely new and revolutionary form of warfare, aerial combat had tremendous appeal for servicemen and civilians alike in the First World War and still retains much of its magic for us today, despite – or perhaps because of – later manifestations of air power. War in the skies contrasted starkly with the virtually static trench lines on the ground and, despite being ultra-modern and mechanical, nevertheless allowed considerable scope for personal skills and courage. Furthermore, although the Royal Flying Corps (and from 1 April 1918 the Royal Air Force) increased prodigiously from only 41 aircraft in August 1914 to 1,799 in November 1918 on the Western Front alone, organized in 99 squadrons, the key unit remained the squadron with 12 front-line aircraft, usually commanded by a major.[1]

Soldiers condemned to the 'long disgusting drudgery of trench warfare' often expressed envy of the free adventurous spirits flying above them, and with good reason. As Cecil Lewis recalled, 'Under the most arduous conditions we were never under fire for more than six hours a day. When we returned to the aerodrome our war was over. We had a bed, a bath, a mess with good food, and peace until the next patrol.' Airmen were relatively well paid and enjoyed ample leisure with good transport, which enabled them to visit neighbouring towns and squadrons. Most of the pilots and observers were very young, so the ethos of the RFC was set by devil-may-care fast drivers and risk-takers. They felt they were 'the last word in warfare [and] the advance guard of wars to come' – as indeed they were.[2]

War in the air was certainly exciting but its romantic side can easily be exaggerated, as it was by many civilians at a safe distance. In addition to fatalities in combat those in accidents were extremely common. During the great battles, such as the Somme, Arras and Third Ypres, a pilot's life expectancy was reckoned at between three and six weeks. Even when on the ground the pilot's life was full of uncertainty and stress, for example in coping with the almost daily disappearance of colleagues from the mess table, so that it was very hard to remain fit for combat for more than six months without substantial leave.

It is also easy to exaggerate the analogy with the chivalrous jousting of medieval knights. True, in the first year or two of the war there were more opportunities for duels between just two aircraft before fast and very confused 'dogfights' involving many machines became the norm. A few acts of chivalrous restraint were recorded, with astonishment, by the beneficiaries, as when the French ace George Guynemer apparently showed mercy towards his German opponent Ernst Udet; and Ira Jones also believed he had been allowed to fly away after his Lewis gun had been ripped off in combat. But in general a ruthless combat ethic prevailed: never give the slightest chance to any enemy in the sky at any time. It was a simple matter of kill or be killed. Although pilots did admire the technical skill and courage of their opponents, and would exchange civilized enquiries about the fates of missing comrades such as Manfred von Richthofen or Albert Ball, the paramount duty was to kill one's opponents and so weaken the enemy's air force. Consequently, however romantic and heroic the most famous air aces might appear to outsiders, most of them were ruthless and ambitious killers.[3]

This chapter focuses on just two classic accounts of war in the air from the many that might have been chosen; namely W. A. Bishop's *Winged Warfare* (1918) and Cecil Lewis' *Sagittarius Rising* (1936). Their backgrounds, flying exploits and subsequent careers were very different. 'Billy' Bishop was a Canadian, born in 1894 at Owen Sound in Ontario, who arrived in England as a cavalry officer but soon transferred to the RFC, became a fighter ace – despite notoriously poor flying skills – was rapidly promoted and much decorated – and went on to have an adventurous career in aviation, business and social life in high society. Cecil Lewis, the only son of a Congregational minister, was born in March 1898 and was already 'air mad' about aircraft types and every aspect of aviation before 1914. He contrived to enter the RFC straight from school when barely 17 (and already 6 ft 4 in. tall), and became an excellent pilot, though his distinction would lie more in scouting, liaising between infantry and artillery, and navigational feats than in his total of 'kills'. The rest of his very long life (he died in 1997) was so varied, fascinating and bizarre that it really merits the cliché 'stranger than fiction', as will be shown later. The key difference, however, lies in the dates and circumstances of the publication of their books. Bishop's *Winged Warfare* was published in 1918, after a period of leave and while he still had another tour of duty in France as a squadron leader ahead of him. The memoir was republished by Penguin Books in 1938 in its series on 'Travel and Adventure'. This was appropriate because it is written in a 'Boy's Own Adventure' style packed with exciting accounts of the author's combat experience, narrated in remarkable detail as though drawn directly from his log books.

Billy Bishop was a fast-living unintellectual daredevil who was slow to mature. For obvious reasons his book is much stronger on the joys (even the ecstasy) of flying, risking one's life and downing 'Huns' as though in sport, than in introspection or reflections about comrades or the war in general. By contrast, Lewis' elegantly written memoirs benefit greatly from the delay in writing and publication because by the mid-1930s he had already experienced a remarkable career. After a brief spell as a manager of civil aviation with Vickers he visited

Peking in 1920–1 to train the nascent Chinese air force but this proved frustrating, except for his marriage to the daughter of a White Russian general in exile. In 1922 he was the junior member of the quartet who founded the BBC, but four years later he abandoned a promising career there because, although he got on well with the overbearing John Reith, he felt the need for greater independence. This he used initially to produce plays, especially those of George Bernard Shaw, who influenced him greatly, and he went on to become a prolific director and writer of plays for radio, film and television. In the early 1930s he acquired a neglected plot of land on Lake Maggiore and, with local help, built an idyllic retreat there.[4]

It was at Lake Maggiore, when faced with the apparent collapse of his career, that Lewis completed his memoirs of flying in the First World War and in China, entitled *Sagittarius Rising*. His marriage had broken up, his wife had returned to China, and his two children were being taken care of abroad. He was never lacking in female company but 'The young women who at that time flocked to my bed did not console me'. His career as a film producer had come to a sudden end, he was without any means of support, and he felt like a 'mercurial antelope' (G. B. Shaw's description) who has lost its jump.[5]

His book was an immediate success in both Britain and America. Shaw gave it a rave review in the *New Statesman* and his fortunes at once brightened. The BBC, which had just opened its television service, took him on as Director of Outside Broadcasts, but he never settled at the cavernous Alexandra Palace and was soon tempted to Hollywood on a well-paid but ill-fated venture to collaborate on a script on the history of aviation.

Thus Lewis brought to his war memoirs a much more mature outlook than the naive young pilot of 1918. He had had valuable experiences outside the world of the Royal Air Force, and in particular had developed the skills of a professional writer. Consequently, *Sagittarius Rising* has considerable merits as a work of literature. It is also distinguished by reflective passages on the author's reactions to the follies and futility of the war in which he had fought, and his anxieties about the terrifying role which air power was likely to play in the next great conflict already looming.

Cecil Lewis entered the RFC as a schoolboy straight from Oundle, where he had enjoyed the practical and scientific subjects but loathed the beatings. He arrived in France in March 1916, aged just 18 and with only 13 hours of solo flying to his credit. Fortunately, as a very promising pilot, he was posted to the great air depot at St Omer to train on a notoriously difficult aircraft, the French Morane Parasol, a two-seater monoplane. It had a powerful and reliable engine but no tailplane, hence the elevator was extremely sensitive and the machine had to be firmly controlled every second it was in the air. In less skilled hands the Parasol was certainly a death-trap, but Lewis flew 'her' throughout the Somme battle, and in all for over 300 hours, winning his MC and mentions in despatches, without ever having a crash and with only one case of engine failure. She was ideal for ground observation because both pilot and observer had an uninterrupted view below. Lewis grew to love this aircraft more than any other and found all the RFC's other planes child's play after the Morane.[6]

When posted to the front in 3 Squadron Lewis began the simple, but terribly dangerous life of a pilot in Spring 1916: no parachute, no oxygen, no ground control, no crash or fire wagons. His role was to pioneer a new form of liaison with the ground forces, called 'Contact Patrol'. The procedure might sound almost comical were it not so hazardous. It involved continually circling and patrolling up and down the front line at a very low altitude (maximum height 500 ft (150 m)), which put the aircraft right in the path of the smaller field guns and machine-guns. Many planes were also hit by British shells. The observer could signal down to the infantry by sounding a loud klaxon horn or by dropping messages in small weighted bags. The ground forces could signal back by opening a spring-operated black and white blind, which could send messages in Morse, or by lighting small red flares which would in theory pinpoint the advancing battalions' precise positions.[7]

In the days preceding the opening of the battle of the Somme, Lewis' task was to photograph the enemy trenches and plot the effects of the British bombardment. Low cloud cover and heavy rain made this a terrifying experience. At one point he felt certain that thousands of British guns were deliberately firing at him: 'the malevolent fury of the whole bombardment was concentrated on us!' He was gripped by a nightmare terror as the machine lurched and rolled, but somehow he brought it through intact. Meanwhile his observer, Sergeant Hall (who was awarded the DCM for his work that week), had to operate his camera, change the plates and make the fresh exposures. The mission lasted for an hour.[8]

When the great offensive began early on 1 July, Lewis enjoyed a perfect bird's-eye view as he flew down the German front line from Thiepval to La Boisselle, where he witnessed the tremendous explosions of the two British mines. Unfortunately, despite his heroic efforts, the attempt to liaise directly with the advancing infantry was a complete failure. Not a single ground sheet for signalling was displayed at battalion or brigade headquarters, and only two flares were lit in the whole area of the two-corps front. In his afternoon flight he saw and reported many enemy batteries but there was no British response. It was a complete wash-out and he was deeply disappointed not to have been able to assist the wretched infantry. But, as he soon realized, at many points the offensive had failed utterly and there was no progress to report. From the second day he changed his methods by flying even lower, in order to see the men in the trenches and accurately report their positions. Thus he observed British infantry advancing beyond Fricourt and the communication trenches between Mametz and Montauban full of troops. Their positions were noted on scraps of paper, put into the message bag and dropped in low swoops on the ground sheet laid out near brigade headquarters.[9]

Flights on subsequent days revealed that there had been quite promising advances to the east of La Boisselle and Fricourt, but Lewis rightly concluded that the setbacks on the first day had been decisive. For a sensitive man, who hated killing animals, it is interesting that Lewis mentions that he and his observer shot up two German horse-drawn limbers on the road between Bapaume and Pozières. The leading horse crumpled up 'and the others, with their tremendous momentum, overran him, and the whole lot piled up in the ditch a frenzied tangle of kicking horses, wagons and men'. They returned to base elated at their contribution to winning the war.[10]

The Canadian fighter ace W. A. (Billy) Bishop had been sent to study at the Royal Military College, Kingston in 1911 to give him some discipline after an unruly boyhood, but his wild, unscholarly ways persisted. He hated RMC and was fortunate not to be expelled for cheating in an exam. He had not decided to follow a military career until August 1914 when, like so many other young men, he became impatient to get to Europe in time to experience combat. He sailed to England, as a subaltern, with a cavalry detachment in the Second Canadian Division – a memorable voyage of 15 days with 700 sea-sick horses in an old cattle boat. In July 1915 the muddy, slimy conditions in his dreary training camp at Shornecliff persuaded him that the only way to go to war was in the air. By a characteristically bold approach to Lord Hugh Cecil, he secured an immediate transfer to the RFC, but was obliged to spend his first four months in France as an observer. He did not fire a single shot from his machine-gun in this period and longed to become a pilot, but only after a crash landing and a long recuperation in 1916 was his ambition fulfilled. He returned to France in March 1917, to join the same elite 60th squadron as Captain Albert Ball (who was killed a few weeks later), and to fly the elegant single-seater Nieuport Scout, whose guns could by now fire between the propeller blades.[11]

In view of his outstanding record of 'kills', surpassed on the Allied side only by Edward Mannock and the French ace René Fonck, it is surprising to learn that Bishop was not a particularly gifted pilot; indeed, 'Bishop landings' became an unflattering byword in his squadron. But he quickly developed sufficient skills to survive innumerable aerial combats as well as low-level attacks on ground targets. He was 'a cold and gifted hunter' whose outstanding attributes were exceptionally good vision and remarkable accuracy of fire – a gift which he sedulously maintained by practice in his leisure time. As to his character, a colleague remarked 'There was something about him that left one feeling that he preferred to live as he fought, in a rather hard, brittle world of his own.' But he enjoyed a riotous social life off-duty, getting into endless scrapes, and also showed a gift for friendship not only with fellow-airmen but also, later, in high society.[12]

Bishop's hyper-aggressive attitude is revealed in his account of an attack on an enemy balloon – a notoriously difficult and dangerous undertaking – in his early days as a fighter pilot. The balloon was rapidly pulled down to the ground but, disobeying an order not to go under 1,000 ft (300 m) after the 'sausages', he continued to dive until only 50 ft (15 m) above the bag. Failing to set it alight, he turned his machine-gun on the balloon crew and also fired on an anti-aircraft gun. He escaped by flying over the enemy guns and trenches at below tree-top level. For this daredevil exploit he received a congratulatory wire from the General commanding the Flying Corps, Hugh Trenchard.[13]

Before discussing Bishop's remarkable combat accounts in more detail, Cecil Lewis' experiences after the opening of the Somme campaign must be briefly described. In September 1916 Lewis, with a new observer keen to win the MC, had a very active role, involving photography, trench reconnaissance and artillery observation in support of the operations around Ginchy and Flers, including the first employment of tanks. On his twice-daily patrols he resolved to fly lower (below 1,000 ft (300m)) in a determination to 'deliver the goods'. In contrast to his negative experience in the opening phase of the battle, the infantry were now regularly lighting their flares so that he could promptly report the precise positions of the leading units to headquarters. On the debit side enemy machine-gunners were now more active, to the extent that 20 or 30 bullet holes in the aircraft was the average for each mission. Lewis was incredibly lucky to escape serious wounding; on several occasions bullets came up through the floor between his feet, one knocking the control stick out of his hand, causing a near-fatal dive, while another penetrated the oil tank but miraculously missed setting the engine on fire. He was cheered to observe tanks 'waltzing' through Flers and flew low enough to see a white terrier following one of them. But his log book bleakly recorded the repeated failure to break through the German third line of defences.

After this tour of duty Lewis was obliged to return home on sick leave due to severe eye problems, caused by leaning out of the cockpit without goggles to make sure of identifying the uniforms of the men in the trenches. Secretly, he hoped for a longer rest because he was 'utterly tired of it all'. On his return to duty he graphically recounts the laconic answers to his questions about missing friends, including his former observer Pip: 'Done in last night. Direct hit, one of our own shells. Battery rang up to apologise.' He is formally congratulated on the award of his Military Cross, but reflects gloomily: 'five ghosts in the room, five friends. Congrats!'[14]

In the spring of 1917 Cecil Lewis, still not quite 19, was posted to No. 56 Squadron at London Colney, which was equipped with the new SE5, the last word in fighting scouts, produced by the Royal Aircraft Factory. He took part in several Offensive Patrols in France in April and May, quickly discovering that the

SE5 was still not equal to the enemy fighters. Scrapping at high altitudes, 15,000 to 18,000 ft (4,500–5,500 m), the Huns' aircraft had a marked superiority in performance. Once down to the enemy's level it was very difficult to climb above him again. Since the scout's guns were fixed, firing forward, it was necessary for the pilot to aim the whole machine at the target. If the enemy was above him, he would be forced to pull his machine up on its tail to get him in the sights. By now dogfights between many planes on both sides were much more common than duels. A pilot would aim to go down on the tail of a Hun, hoping to get him with the first burst, but he would be wise to zoom away rapidly because another Hun was almost certain to be on *his* tail. Such flights, Lewis explains, were really a series of rushes, aiming to catch an enemy at a disadvantage, or separated from his colleagues. Apart from the essential flying and shooting skills, Lewis believed that the crucial quality in air combat was absolute cold-bloodedness – 'a set steely courage, drained of all emotion, fined down to a tense and deadly effort of will'.[15]

On 7 May 1917 Lewis took part in an evening patrol to deal with Richthofen and his 'circus' of Red Albatrosses. After the ensuing dogfight only Lewis' plane and four other scouts of the 11 who had set out returned to base. Four of the missing pilots were soon accounted for – two wounded and two forced down by engine failure – but Albert Ball was never seen again. Lewis flew Ball's Nieuport back to the depot. Statistically, Lewis' chances of survival were slim, but in June he was fortuitously 'rescued' by the outcome of the first Gotha bombing raid on London. A crack squadron was immediately requested by the Air Ministry for the defence of London and No. 56 Squadron was selected. Though these duties were far from risk-free – night flying without lights was extremely dangerous and there were frequent crashes, some resulting from over-confident stunts – nevertheless Lewis could now be fairly confident that he would survive the war.[16]

In a frenetic period of aggressive flying between March and August 1917 Billy Bishop accounted for the majority of his 'kills'. Bishop made no secret of his ambition to shoot down as many victims as possible, and expresses disgust at the numerous occasions when he had patiently stalked his opponent and pounced, but failed to obtain the kill, often because his guns jammed or he ran out of ammunition.

> I began to feel that my list of victims was not climbing as steadily as I would have liked. Captain Ball was back from a winter rest in England and was adding constantly to his already big score. I felt I had to keep going if I was to be second to him. So I was over the enemy lines from six to seven hours every day, praying for some easy victims to appear. I had had some pretty hard fighting. Now I wanted to shoot a 'rabbit' or two.[17]

On 30 April, which he describes as a red-letter day for 'very pleasant fighting', he had nine separate scraps in less than two hours in the morning, and went up again before tea with his squadron leader to take on four scarlet enemy scouts of Richthofen's circus. He was always willing to take on odds of three or four to one and would fly as far as 15 miles inside the German lines in search of unwary prey. Shooting down two enemy planes in flames put him in good humour. 'It is so certain and such a satisfactory way of destroying Huns.' Another Hun 'crashed in the most satisfactory manner. I turned and flew south, feeling very much better.' He expresses bitterness and a desire for vengeance against enemy two-seaters which, he believes, tried to lead him into an ambush against great odds. Faced with such an aggressive opponent as Bishop, it is not surprising that the enemy, especially two-seater spotter planes, frequently tried to escape. Bishop found it 'very aggravating to chase machines that will not fight'. He admitted getting into a tremendous temper when frustrated in this way and was apt to run unnecessary risks in his next encounter: anything to relieve his feelings. A few pages later in his memoirs he says he has decided to be more cautious and take no unnecessary risks. Whether he heeded his own watchword of greater caution may be doubted. He so loved the chase and fighting that he was reluctant to go on leave. For him war was just a wonderful game.

> To bring down a machine did not seem to me to be killing a man; it was more as if I was just destroying a mechanical target, with no human being in it. Once or twice the idea that a live man had been piloting the machine would occur and recur to me. My sleep would be spoiled perhaps for a night. I did not relish the idea even of killing Germans, yet, when in combat in the air, it seemed more like any other kind of sport, and to shoot down a machine was very much the same as if one were shooting down clay pigeons.[18]

Bishop admits that on returning from leave after his initial three months tour of active duty he was ambitious to bring down as many enemy machines as possible, and to this end he planned many little expeditions on his own. Consequently, on 2 June 1917, a day when off duty, he attacked an enemy aerodrome, hoping to shoot down the enemy planes as they attempted to take off into the wind. He found an enemy base at Estourmel with some aircraft in the open and swooped to 50 ft (15 m) to machine-gun the ground crews, laughing to himself as he watched the fun. He managed to destroy three planes before making a lucky low-level escape, his plane riddled with bullets. He suffered an acute spell of dizziness and nausea but quickly recovered, much gratified at the congratulations of his colleagues, and the higher authorities, at the success of his hare-brained stunt.[19]

 As the date of his second, and possibly final, leave approached he became desperate to put in as much flying time as possible and counted his growing list of victories – 45-46-47 and another on the very evening of his departure – a lucky hit from directly behind and at long range which must have killed the pilot. As commander of 85 Squadron in France in May and June 1918, Bishop raised his final tally of victims to 72, the last 25 in only 12 days, including five in about

15 minutes on what he knew would probably be his final hours of active service. For this remarkable performance he was awarded the newly-created decoration, the Distinguished Flying Cross.

Bishop had been promoted first to captain and then to major in 1917, and in 1918 he would be further elevated to lieutenant-colonel. In the final pages of *Winged Warfare* he suggests that his attendance at an investiture at Buckingham Palace caused him more anxiety than any episode at the front. The King presented him with his decorations: the VC, DSO and MC. He would later win a bar to his DSO and be awarded the DFC.[20]

These personal accounts of air warfare raise several interesting questions. Did these fliers hate the enemy and did they recognize a special kind of chivalry in air combat? How did they experience stress and what steps did they take to offset it? Did their experiences as very young men permanently affect their lives and, in particular, their attitudes to war in general?

As Denis Winter has pointed out, in contrast to the Second World War there was no systematic propaganda effort to dehumanize the opposition or turn the enemy into a sinister threat with whom there could be no civilized contacts. Furthermore, the generally static nature of the war, added to the novelty and special hazards of air warfare, permitted frequent communications between the antagonists in the comradely spirit of fellow aviators. Winter cites several touching enquiries about missing airmen, some famous like Albert Ball but others undistinguished like Fritz Frech, whose friends grieved for him. They provided details of his crash and added: 'His respectable and unlucky parents beg you to give any news of his fate. Is he dead? At what place found he his last rest?' (and the parents' address was given for a reply). Equally moving were the enemy tributes to gallant opponents. For example, a German pilot wrote regretting the deaths of two British officers who had 'bravely defended till the pilot received a shot in the head'. Another German letter to a captured pilot's parents assured them that he was being well-treated: 'He fought me very bravely ... and I am proud to have combated with such a sport and a gentleman.' Winter even cites the case of a German aristocrat ('the Black Knight') who, finding his captive opponent in plimsolls and flannels, took him to his local tennis court to play the deciding set.[21]

The same author also provides an excellent account of the generally shared revulsion and pity when witnessing opponents' deaths close-up. Most fatalities in the air war were horrific. Men in their final moments were seen falling out of their doomed planes or, worst of all, going down in flames. Many pilots were 'horrified and sickened' by such 'flamers'. Even Albert Ball, in one of his last letters, wrote that he was getting tired of always living to kill and was beginning to feel like a murderer. The German ace Ernst Udet confessed that he had to repress the thought that somewhere a mother wept for every man shot down. Cecil Lewis, writing in the mid-1930s, felt the need to justify his invariable reference to the enemy as 'Huns' because nothing derogatory was intended. They usually treated our captured airmen with courtesy and gallantry as he thought we did in return. They were simply 'the enemy'; their machines had black crosses, and it was our job to bring them down.[22]

As we have already noted, Billy Bishop's attitude to the enemy was more ambivalent. He was an enthusiastic hunter and killer of 'Huns', both in the air and on the ground, who regarded his activities as sport with little concern or empathy shown for his victims. Thus early in *Winged Warfare* he writes of the 'great fun' of flying very low along the German trenches and giving them a burst of machine-gun bullets: 'we love to see the Kaiser's proud Prussians running for cover like so many rats.' Later he recounts flying so low over the enemy trenches that he could make out every detail of their frightened faces. 'With hate in my heart I fired every bullet I could into the group as I swept over it.' He admitted that he found it difficult to realize that men were dying and being maimed beneath him. As British troops advanced to occupy enemy trenches, 'I felt that I had seen something of that dogged determination that has carried British arms so far.' Regarding his first 'flamer' he recalled that without wishing to make himself appear as a bloodthirsty person 'I must say that to see an enemy going down in flames is a source of great satisfaction.' Of another 'flamer', whose doomed crew he had just seen close-up, he says he 'reflected briefly on their fate, but it was fair hunting, and I flew away with great contentment in my heart'. He admitted to a particular hatred of Hun two-seaters because 'they always seemed so placid and contented in themselves'. So outraged was he when a two-seater appeared to have escaped him by landing that he dived to within a few feet of it and pumped a stream of bullets into the machine. Neither the pilot nor the observer emerged from the wreck. Towards the end of his first combatant tour in France in 1917 Bishop reflected that, while killing was against his nature, he did not mind it for two reasons: the more important was that every Hun shot down was a contribution to the war effort; and the lesser was revenge for all his lost friends. Furthermore he did not altogether feel the human side of it; it was not like killing a man so much as just bringing down a bird in sport. Towards the end of his time in France he admits he was losing the thrill of anticipation before a fight, but as soon as he fired his machine-gun the old exultation returned and remained with him in all his combats.[23]

Cecil Lewis clung to the notion that chivalry had persisted in the air war in sharp contrast to the senseless, brutal, ignoble murder of war in the trenches. He even likened air combat to the 'lists of the Middle Ages, the only sphere in modern warfare where a man saw his adversary and faced him in mortal combat'. It was a fair battle of skill, courage and wits, and if the enemy went down 'a falling rocket of smoke and flame, what a glorious heroic death!' Sometimes it even seemed a pity to him that he had survived to die peacefully in bed – an event still 60 years ahead at the time of writing. This must appear a somewhat idealized portrayal of aerial combat in view of the chaotic and merciless dogfights which characterized the later stages of the war. But he is surely right to contrast the 'majesty of the heavens' in these early days of flying, which gave them an inspiration unknown to 'sturdier men who fought on earth'. 'Nobility surrounded us. We moved like spirits in an airy loom, where wind and cloud and light wove, day and night long, the endless fabric of the changing sky.' Lewis' literary and poetic view was clearly genuine and, with the romantic expressions of similar writers, has profoundly influenced our views of the air in the First World War. But Lewis would surely acknowledge the gulf between the thrill and the ecstasy of flying *per se*, and the deadly business of aerial combat; indeed he fully described the thorough, systematic and utterly unromantic routines and tactics of dedicated killers such as Ball, McCudden and Guynemer.[24]

Cecil Lewis surely spoke for the vast majority of airmen when he wrote that they were vastly better off than the poor, bloody infantry: they were never filthy, verminous or 'exposed to the long disgusting drudgery of trench warfare'. But, quite apart from combat, flying itself exerted new and terrible physical and mental pressures which quickly took their toll on even the bravest and fittest pilots.

The camaraderie, high jinks and forced gaiety in the officers' messes barely concealed the underlying anxieties. There were the unavoidable uncertainties of the flying routine; usually two hours in the morning and two more in the afternoon, but with the constant prospect of sudden 'scrambling' to meet emergencies. Pilots might appear outwardly cheerful and confident, but many suffered from nervous tics and insomnia. Lewis' description of the five empty places at the mess table on return from sick leave captures the daily tragedy of lost comrades. Even without enemy interference most pilots, including Lewis and Bishop, were fearful of getting lost, particularly when flying behind enemy lines. Also, though both made light of the dangers posed by anti-aircraft artillery in their breezy narratives, they privately admitted that this was their worst fear. Bishop's son vehemently denied that his father was fearless; not only enemy action but even high altitude terrified him.[25] Lewis captures the sheer challenge of 'sticking it out'.[26]

Flying itself was extremely tiring: most of the aircraft demanded considerable physical strength as well as unwavering concentration from their pilots; the engines were very noisy and vibrated alarmingly; freezing cold caused numbness and the risk of frostbite; and at high altitudes there was an acute problem of oxygen deficiency. Having survived all the hazards of flying and enemy action, mental and physical exhaustion frequently led to crash landings, of which about 70 per cent wrote off the aeroplane and 50 per cent injured the pilot. Every flyer was acutely aware of the horrific forms which death might take and the high odds against his survival. In 1916 the average life expectancy for pilots on the Western Front was calculated at three weeks, but early in 1917 it fell to two weeks. French pilots tended to be more cautious and professional, but even so René Fonck noticed early in 1918 that at 24 he was the oldest pilot in his squadron. Estimates of how long pilots could be expected to endure in combat conditions varied slightly, but a year was the absolute maximum. Billy Bishop precisely fulfilled the standard requirement of a six months tour with a fortnight's leave in the middle.[27]

Lewis, in writing his memoirs, frankly acknowledged the effects of fear, anxiety and nervous strain and came to understand, in retrospect, why so many pilots cracked up. Nobody could stand the strain indefinitely but you could not openly admit you were afraid. Day after day you had to conquer your fears but the challenge did not go away. Lewis thought it was not like bodily fatigue, from which you could recover completely, 'but a sort of damage to the essential tissue of your being'. Billy Bishop, writing while the war was still in progress, and with a different temperament to Lewis, did not indulge in introspection or admit to fears, but even he was in a very nervous condition when he arrived in England on leave. At first he could not keep still but after a week's enjoyment he became quieter and more relaxed. He appreciated that this short rest had quieted his nerves and left him in a much better state of health, so that he actually looked forward to rejoining his squadron. After the war he was troubled by a persistent nightmare of the time he had crashed in flames and was left hanging upside down in the burning machine. His blond hair had turned completely grey by the time he was 30.[28]

Given the daily risks they faced and the possibility that any day might be their last, it is understandable that many of the officers indulged in an extravagant, devil-may-care round of pleasure when off duty. Also, compared with junior Army officers, they enjoyed far more freedom: there were fewer other ranks to command and these few mostly mechanics and riggers devoted to 'their' pilot and his aircraft; no senior NCOs; and fewer senior officers above the rank of major, and these often not much older than the flight crews. Consequently there were frequent wild parties, heavy drinking and forays in search of sexual conquests. Billy Bishop indulged in gargantuan binges in France and on leave in England. Though already engaged (and to be married in October 1917), he admitted to his fiancée that he had had a French mistress in Amiens. He also found relaxation in capturing pigs or piglets (no easy feat) and confining them in the quarters of absent colleagues. In a bizarre elaboration of these capers, pigs – and also ducks – were painted in red, white and blue. By way of variation, one large sow was painted in German colours with a large black cross on each side and inscribed 'Baron von Richthoven'. Among numerous pets, dogs were their special favourites, and every stray they encountered was brought back to the mess and cared for. Other sports and pastimes included ratting, shooting at pigeons on the wing, tennis and riding. In contrast to these social group activities, Lewis described Albert Ball as a quiet, little man with simple pleasures. His one relaxation was the violin, and 'his favourite after-dinner amusement was to light a red magnesium flare outside his hut and walk round it in his pyjamas fiddling!'[29]

Cecil Lewis loved flying and carried out his duties in the First World War courageously, but it seems likely that he had come to loathe war itself – and the human imperfections which caused it – long before he wrote his memoirs in the mid-1930s. In particular his service in the latter part of the war in the (largely ineffectual) defence of London had impressed on him the terrible fate likely to befall urban populations in the next conflict. His most disturbing memory of the war was the sight of gas, 'a long creeping wraith of yellow mist', seeping into German trenches near Thiepval in 1916, and his understanding of how it would affect the soldiers trapped below. He later saw this as a symbol of the enlightened twentieth century: science being exploited by a world without standards or scruples, spiritually bankrupt. He believed that future horrific conflicts, including the use of poison gas against civilians, could be averted, but drastic new thinking was necessary and it would probably take two or three more world wars to secure such changes. The eventual solution must be the protection by an 'International Guard', just as citizens now expect protection from a policeman. In an impassioned outburst, better informed but only a little less shrill than Crozier's, he deplored the failure to obtain an international agreement to control air power, and concluded gloomily with what must still seem a Utopian solution:

> If we cannot collectively rise above our narrow nationalism, the vast credits of wealth, wisdom and art produced by Western civilization will be wiped out. If we really want peace and security, we must pool our resources, disarm, and set up an international air police force, federally controlled. That force must be as incorruptible, free from bias and self-interest, and devoted to law and order as our civil police are today. There is no other way.[30]

When the war ended in November 1918 Lewis was aged only 20 and Bishop 24. They had survived physically unscathed and with a normal lifetime's worth of challenges, danger and achievement behind them. Lewis was a brilliant pilot and Bishop a uniquely decorated Canadian hero with a remarkable range of high-level social and political connections, including Churchill and Beaverbrook. The latter's subsequent career, to his comparatively early death in 1956, was a roller-coaster of triumphs and near disasters.

Bishop left the RAF in 1919 and, as his son admits, he found it difficult to adjust to civil life and stay on an even keel. Though now happily married, he was still rather immature and unsophisticated, yet accustomed to an extravagant life-style which he would never abandon. He set up one of Canada's first chartered airlines with another fighter ace, William Barker, but this venture failed, in part because Bishop had nearly killed himself in yet another crash landing. He then experienced a 'high' for the remainder of the 1920s, as a well-paid sales representative in London for two metal companies. As a lucrative sideline he bought and traded polo ponies. He and his family lived in a fine house in Regent's Park and his numerous social activities included playing in a polo team with Winston Churchill. He spent his holidays at Cannes and Le Touquet; he owned a chauffeur-driven Rolls-Royce; and his friends included Scott Fitzgerald, Hemingway and the Prince of Wales. In November 1929 he was immediately bankrupted by the Wall Street Crash, but a Canadian friend came to the rescue by securing for him a vice-presidency in an oil company, a lucrative position which he only relinquished, due to failing health, in 1952. Meanwhile he was successively promoted Group Captain (1931), Air Vice-Marshal (1936) and Air Marshal in the Royal Canadian Air Force, but until the advent of war in 1939, these appointments were honorary and unpaid. When Canada entered the war Bishop returned to full-time service as Director, RCAF, with wide responsibilities in recruitment, liaison in air matters with the USA, and promoting Canadian and Allied air power generally. He wore himself out in this work and his health deteriorated rapidly after he collapsed in public while making a speech to air cadets in November 1942. He returned to duty the following year, working harder than ever, but by 1944, though still only 50, he looked 20 years older. Though outwardly cheerful he was 'close to total exhaustion in body and soul' by the end of the war.

After the war he lived in semi-retirement in Montreal. As his son testified, 'he no longer had his old energy and enthusiasm. The great challenges which had inspired him in two world wars no longer existed.' He went through the motions in public, but his career was effectively over. He spent his last winter in Palm Beach, Florida, and died there, in his sleep, on 10 September 1956.[31]

Cecil Lewis had such an array of talents that he could have risen to the very top in several careers including aviation, radio and television, producer and playwright, novelist, travel writer, perhaps even boatbuilder. But, by his own admission, he had a knack of being in at the start of promising ventures (civil aviation, the BBC, television, Hollywood) but never staying long enough to reap his own personal reward from them. In a few cases, such as his brief stint in Hollywood, the venture had failed, but more often his urge for travel, new experiences and, above all, independence, caused him to move on precipitately, often when there was no alternative employment in view. His private life was similarly complicated; clearly a charmer and very attractive to women, he was married three times and admitted to 'a prodigious appetite for seduction'.[32]

Cecil Lewis returned to the RAF in 1939, served throughout the war and achieved the rank of Wing-Commander. After a relatively dull period as a flying instructor in Britain he had an adventurous though largely non-combatant role as the organizer and controller of advanced air staging bases in Egypt, Italy and Greece. At the end of the war he was still only 47 and halfway through his life. His later career, though full of colourful incidents and a good deal of successful writing, was decisively influenced by his profound commitment to the spiritual movement associated with the exiled Russian guru George Gurdjieff and his disciple P. D. Ouspensky. In the later 1940s he helped to set up and run an idealistic, inexperienced farming community in South Africa which failed disastrously, receiving its death-blow when it was discovered that the Master was not dead after all, but very much alive and holding court among his devotees in Paris. Lewis embarked on an endless, indeterminate mental journey to discover his 'true self'.[33]

By the time Lewis published his fascinating memoirs *Never Look Back* in 1976 he had already embarked on another remarkable adventure by sailing a yacht to Corfu, with his new wife, and settling there. As he frankly admitted, he had always mistrusted success, whether in wealth, power or position. Consequently his life had fluctuated wildly and he had never been influenced by ideas of saving, safety or security. He died on 27 January 1997, a few weeks short of his 99th birthday.[34]

10

Having a 'good war': Anthony Eden and Harold Macmillan

Anthony Eden and Harold Macmillan were close contemporaries, the former born in 1897 and the latter three years earlier. Their schooldays at Eton did not quite overlap because poor health caused Macmillan to leave early – in 1909, two years before Eden arrived. Macmillan went up to Oxford before the war and Eden after it. Both served gallantly as infantry officers on the Western Front, and in terms of later Conservative party credentials, had particularly 'good wars'; Eden especially achieving responsible positions and winning the Military Cross while still astonishingly young; likewise Macmillan had also done well as a Grenadier Guards subaltern until very badly wounded in September 1916. Both published their recollections of the First World War late in life: Eden an elegant little volume evoking, as its title proclaimed, *Another World, 1897–1917* (1976), and Macmillan a chapter in his first volume of memoirs, *Winds of Change, 1914–1939* (1966). Their family backgrounds differed, Eden's deriving from the landed aristocracy, Macmillan's from fairly recently acquired wealth in 'trade' (the distinguished publishing house). Both served in elite regiments and were permanently influenced by their wartime experiences, notably in meeting and making friends with a great variety of people they would not have encountered at Eton or Oxford. After the war both were politically ambitious: Eden's route to Cabinet rank was much quicker and more spectacular, but Macmillan proved to have more staying power and was more successful when he at last reached the top of the 'greasy pole'. In 1918, and indeed for a long time afterwards, it would have been impossible to foresee that they would become successive Conservative Prime Ministers, Eden in 1955–7 and Macmillan 1957–63.

Anthony Eden enjoyed a privileged and comfortable if not particularly happy childhood at the family's early Victorian mansion Windlestone on an estate of about 8,000 acres (3,200 ha) in County Durham. As the third son in a family of five children, Anthony knew he was most unlikely to inherit the estate and was uncertain about his career. His father, Sir William Eden, was an artist, a collector of modern pictures and otherwise absorbed in country pursuits and travel. He gave Anthony little time and no encouragement. His beautiful but very difficult mother, Sylvia Grey, was born in India, the daughter of Sir William Grey, Governor of Bengal, and she was also related to Sir Edward Grey, the Foreign Secretary between 1905 and 1916. Eden conveys the impression that his parents were dutiful but distant towards their children. Lady Grey, a tireless worker for good causes in the county, perhaps 'preferred the singular relationship which existed between donor and recipient to the more complicated one between mother and child'. Her huge, unpayable debts and selfish behaviour would throw the family into bitter quarrels after the death of her husband and eldest son.[1]

Although a member of the OTC at Eton, Eden admits that he took little interest in international or military affairs before the outbreak of war in 1914, but thereafter became increasingly restless, fearing that the conflict would be over before he could see action. By the time he left Eton in the summer of 1915 tragedy had already struck the family twice: his eldest brother Timothy had been studying in Germany in August 1914 and was interned until 1916, while his elder brother Jack had been killed in action as a cavalry officer in France in October 1914. In 1916 his younger brother Nicholas would go down with his ship *Indefatigable* at Jutland aged only 16.

By his own admission naive and inexperienced in all practical matters, and too short-sighted to be acceptable at Sandhurst, Eden was fortunate in the way he entered the Army. A close family friend, Lord Feversham, was authorized to raise and command a battalion of Yeomen Rifles in Northern Command in which all the yeoman volunteers would serve together as one unit. The battalion would form the 21st Battalion of the King's Royal Rifle Corps (60th Rifles). Though only just 18 and lacking military experience, Eden was instructed to raise a platoon which he would then, subject to some basic and perfunctory tests, command as a second lieutenant. Suppressing the criticism and impatience he displayed in letters home, he charmingly describes how the platoon was recruited from local tenant farmers, horsemen and other sturdy Durham countrymen who all learnt the soldier's trade together from scratch before going on to field exercises on 'Charlie' Feversham's Yorkshire estate. Nearly all were very young, like Eden himself, and keen to see action. A sense of comradeship was created which 'took the bite out of the most cheerless duties and endured among the survivors to the time of writing'. He described this bond as 'the finest form of friendship' and cites amicable meetings with former private soldiers and NCOs long after the war. From long conversations with company sergeants in England and France, Eden gained hope that the great social mixing of volunteers in the Army would lead to a more united nation after the war. Though disappointed in this ideal he claims that he retained 'a sense of the irrelevances and unreality of class distinctions'.[2]

In April 1916 the battalion was deemed fit for active service and, as part of 41st Division, took up residence in Ploegsteert Wood a few miles south of the Ypres Salient. Later to acquire grim associations, the Wood in the spring and summer of 1916 was relatively quiet and unscarred by shell-fire; indeed nightingales and other songbirds could be heard even while the guns were firing. Since this section of the front had been held by the renowned Ninth (Scottish) Division, the unfledged Yeomen were fortunate in their introduction to trench warfare. These countrymen were not perplexed by frequent night patrols in No Man's Land which, for Eden, became 'a war within a war', but he admits to suffering anguish over early fatalities among his riflemen, whom he had grown to respect and admire. He later reflected that it was these chance deaths of individuals in the trenches which left a sharper imprint than the wholesale slaughter of a battle. As by several years the company's youngest subaltern, Eden was dubbed 'the Boy' until heavy casualties on the Somme left only a memory of most of the officers who had used it.[3]

While still at 'Plugstreet' Eden proved his mettle in leading a small raiding party across No Man's Land in the dark with the aim of capturing a prisoner in order to identify the unit opposite them. Careful plans were laid and the wire-cutting was nearly complete when they were detected and 'all hell broke loose'. Luckily they were so close to the German trench that the rifle and machine-gun fire passed over them, but before they could crawl back to their own lines their much-respected sergeant (Harrop) was badly wounded and seemed likely to bleed to death. Eden showed coolness in staunching the flow of blood and deciding that the stretcher bearers should return over-ground in view of the enemy. Harrop endured two years in hospital and 33 operations but eventually recovered. A memento from the sergeant's native Sheffield remained for ever on Eden's writing table. Eden was recommended for a decoration but did not receive the Military Cross until later the following year.[4]

Early in September 1916 the 41st Division, including the Yeoman Rifles, moved to the Somme theatre near Albert, where Eden observed the horizontal statue of the Virgin on the Basilica and was thrilled at last to encounter the sights and sounds of war. The battalion was ordered to take part in the offensive north of Delville Wood and east of Flers on 15 September which at once became memorable for the first use of tanks, one in particular becoming famous for its 'walk' through the straggling village of Flers.

Eden was furious to be named as one of the two officers kept in reserve but this probably saved his life. Despite numerous casualties the battalion made good progress against units of a Bavarian division and by afternoon was ahead of the brigades on either side but facing formidable German defences on the Gird ridge east of Flers. The brigade received an ill-informed order to attack and capture the next objective, which its commander deemed to be impossible without reinforcements and a bombardment. But knowing that the advance towards Lesboeufs on the right had been held up, the brigadier decided that the order must be obeyed. Predictably, the attack failed, and all the senior officers were killed or wounded, including Lord Feversham, whose body Eden found and buried a month later. It fell to the surviving subalterns and NCOs to rally the men and dig in for the night without losing much ground. After the melancholy roll-call on 16 September the new battalion commander, a regular soldier, Major the Hon. Gerald Foljambe, called Eden over and said quietly 'You'll be adjutant' – a remarkable promotion for a comparatively inexperienced subaltern aged just over 19.[5]

When the remnants of the brigade were inspected on the morrow of the battle Eden experienced an 'aching sadness' at the gaps in the ranks, and it was only a slight consolation that his former platoon was singled out as the best on parade. As adjutant it was his duty to compile the battalion casualty figures for 15 September which were as follows: killed 4 officers and 54 other ranks; wounded 10 officers and 256 other ranks; missing 70 other ranks. Since no ground had been conceded it was a grim presumption that almost all the missing would be dead, not prisoners of war.

Early in October the battalion, still under strength, was ordered to take part in another attack over the same ground, now in an appalling state after persistent rain. Eden describes how an inexperienced draft of replacements, straight from England and not even from the reserve battalion, were loaded up with the unit's rations and started on the weary trek up the line. This involved a five-mile slog (8 km), first on a crowded road and then up the single communication trench (Turk Lane), already jammed with casualties coming down. The draft at last arrived, exhausted, and in low spirits, on the morning of 7 October, only to be thrown into battle the same afternoon.[6]

Foljambe and Eden sheltered on the forward slope of a ridge ahead of the start line to escape the enemy bombardment which began with tremendous force at 2.00 p.m. They then witnessed the strange sight of their battalion advancing down the slope towards them but taking heavy casualties. Nothing went according to plan. It had been a mistake to attack in the afternoon, there was no element of surprise, and enemy machine-guns took a deadly toll along the whole front of the line. Worse still, shells from their own heavy artillery began to fall among them. In trying to locate B Company Eden stumbled across dead and wounded fusiliers and riflemen everywhere and met a very young-looking NCO who reported 'Lance Corporal X in charge of B Company, sir'. All the officers and senior NCOs had been killed or wounded and he had only been able to collect six riflemen whom he had put to digging a support trench. Most of the casualties had resulted from trying to take on securely entrenched German machine-gunners who had not been knocked out by the British barrage. Foljambe and Eden remained in the front line through the night, rallying the mixed troops available to meet an expected dawn counter-attack. Their greatest anxiety was for the rescue of the wounded since it would take four men about eight hours to carry each casualty to the nearest point at which they could be met by an ambulance.

The remnants of the battalion were pulled back to support trenches with its headquarters at a very exposed spot known as Factory Corner. On 9 October

Eden received the astonishing news that a new draft was on the way to reinforce them, crossing several miles of battle-torn landscape and under intense shell-fire to get to the line. Their morale was understandably low. Eden feared they might be thrown straight into combat since higher command would assume the battalion was now up to strength. Foljambe protested vigorously and the attack did not take place. Foljambe received a DSO for this battle and Eden was recommended for an award.[7]

The Yeomen Rifles, as a battalion of friends who had trained and come out together, virtually ceased to exist after the two disastrous Somme attacks in September and October. After the latter battle they were reduced to only six officers and 170 other ranks, with many of the latter from the recently arrived drafts which had been drawn from the battalion's reserves.

Eden was very critical of the placing of brigade headquarters much too far behind the lines. The wires were repeatedly cut and runners frequently failed to get through; consequently there were not merely poor communications between brigade and the front line, but also between front-line battalions on either flank. During the ten days of the approach march and the battle Eden never saw an officer from brigade headquarters, and certainly no officer came up from the divisional staff. The troops were acutely aware of this failure and allegedly made sarcastic comments about a general who later claimed to have been 'with them on the Somme'.[8]

After several days of being shunted about in cattle trucks and apparently aimless marching, the Yeoman Rifles, now reconstituted with a new draft, found themselves just south of St Eloi on the edge of the Ypres Salient, the scene of bitter fighting in 1914 and 1915. They followed a dreary routine for several weeks in one of the harshest winters in Flanders' history; namely six days in the line, followed by six in 'rest' in a camp at La Clytte which Eden described as 'an unfriendly place, deep in mud and with a scarcity of duckboards'. Here the enemy commanded the higher ground so could drain his defences into the British lines, making it impossible to dig trenches. The chief enemies, however, were cold, mud and rats. In six months of monotonous routines there was only one emergency summons to the front and even this proved to be a false alarm. When the battalion was in the line Eden's most exacting task was the nightly visit of inspection to companies at the front, made hazardous by the strict ban on using torches. The periods in support in Ridge Wood were tolerable but heating the cramped dug-outs was difficult. He had to organize and supervise endless working parties up to the line.

On the positive side, as quickly became apparent in the spring of 1917, the battalion was now in X Corps area commanded by General T. L. N. Morland, a 60th Rifles officer, who was both respected and liked. More important still the battalion was now in the sector of Second Army, commanded by the portly and most unmilitary-looking General Sir Herbert Plumer. Like thousands of other young officers, Eden quickly learnt that in Plumer's case appearances were deceptive: to hear him speak and watch his methods soon revealed a keen, well-informed and diligent commander 'who was master of every detail of his job'. He seemed to take a special, almost avuncular interest in the riflemen because he had been a friend of Lord Feversham before 1914 when holding Northern Command and was familiar with the men's home towns and villages. Plumer not merely noted deficiencies but quickly had them put right. The Yeoman Rifles experienced to the full the thoroughness in planning and training, under the direct supervision of Plumer and his extremely able Chief of Staff 'Tim' Harington, which made the set-piece attack and capture of the Messines Ridge on 7 June 1917 such a rare and spectacular success.[9]

Eden's battalion was plunged into an intensive system of training such as it had never known before. Plumer and Harington both inspected the work and, most unusually, even riflemen were encouraged to ask questions. Eden himself asked Harington about a middle-distance objective and received a reassuring reply. Since they were to attack from the heavily mined area of the St Eloi craters where the lines were scarcely 50 yards (45 m) apart, and then capture successive lines, it was essential to practise the attack over similar terrain.

> Over and over again we exercised across this ground to a meticulously accurate timetable. Flags represented the creeping barrage and over and over again we practised advancing in close time with it, until our rate of progress became almost automatic. This we did first by companies, then by battalions and finally as a brigade.[10]

As Eden appreciated, these exercises, with the additional aid of an elaborate small-scale model of the battlefield, also gave a valuable boost to morale.

Although the thoroughness of Second Army staff's planning gave the battalion a real hope of success, the horrendous experience on the Somme in October 1916 still cast its shadow. Eden admits that he prayed that if he were to be hit he should be lightly wounded or killed; he could not face the prospect of mutilation. This was the only occasion that he wrote a last letter to his mother and sister, and afterwards he felt rather ashamed that he had done so.

By 2.00 a.m. on 7 June the whole battalion was tightly packed into the front trenches so that all the troops could be clear of their positions within seconds of zero hour to avoid the inevitable enemy barrage. At 3.00 a.m. the St Eloi mine exploded just to the left of the battalion, where Eden and the headquarters were stationed, and the infantry advanced close behind the creeping barrage. The attack, which lasted five hours, succeeded beyond their wildest dreams. The pre-battle planning and staff work on the day were far superior to anything they had experienced before.

During the five hours which our advance was planned to last, we were scheduled to attack a series of lines, red, blue and black on our maps. The rate of our advance and the length of the pause at each captured objective was perfectly timed to give us just long enough to regroup before the barrage moved on again and the enemy no sufficient opportunity to rally and fight back.[11]

By 8.00 a.m. the battalion had captured its final objective and could view the impressive westward panorama from the crest of the Messines ridge, while to the east the enemy was pulling out his guns and infantry. They dug in to await a counter-attack but none followed. The battalion's casualties were light: a total of seven killed and 64 wounded. Only a week later, however, any lingering euphoria was sharply dissipated. In an attack to the left of their previous position at Ravine Wood the battalion suffered more than 200 casualties from shell-fire alone. It was Eden's 20th birthday.

In the following weeks of attrition, still in the captured area near Messines, the battalion was again torn apart by the steady loss of men and exhaustion of the survivors. Though Eden is very sparing with scenes of massacre, preferring to highlight the fate of individuals, he recounts one incident which 'broke through to another layer of horror'. Battalion headquarters occupied a concrete German pill-box which had proved impervious to British shelling but had an exposed entrance on the eastern, or former German side. After six days in this dangerous place, the staff were about to depart when a German 5.9 shell penetrated the aperture and burst in the doorway of their larger room, which was packed with their own men and the headquarters of the relieving battalion. There was an over-whelming stench of cordite and indescribable carnage. It took several hours to disentangle the bodies and evacuate the wounded to the first-aid post. Eden lost companions with whom he had worked daily as adjutant; he and the survivors felt sad and bereft as if they had lost a limb. On this occasion, he confessed, even the strength of wartime comradeship could not compensate for the loss.[12]

Soon after this incident Eden was transferred to Second Army headquarters as a junior staff officer or GSO3. He had been adjutant for a year and was the only combatant officer to have served continuously with the battalion since it landed in France. In the autumn, when Plumer and Harington left to take command of British troops in Italy, the latter recommended that Eden be promoted brigade major. This remarkable testimony to his outstanding war record he duly achieved early in 1918 with 198th Infantry Brigade, under a brigadier who had been an officer in his own regiment. Eden became the youngest brigade-major in the Army. This was an exacting, strenuous appointment, but one that was much sought after and carried considerable prestige. Eden noted that the brigade and its staff offered scope for individual efforts to be rewarding, while there was sufficiently close contact with the three battalions involved to have a human interest. He chose to end his memoirs at this point because he had particularly wished to commemorate the 'close personal character of comradeship' with the Yeomen Rifles. 'The more beastly and dangerous the conditions, the more this association seemed to count.' He was demobilized in June 1919 in a camp on the raw Wiltshire downs.

> I had entered the holocaust still childish and I emerged tempered by my experience, but with my illusions intact, neither shattered nor cynical, to face a changed world.[13]

Eden was only 21 when the war ended, with an outstanding military career behind him but an uncertain future. He had no money of his own; there was bitter family discord in which his mother sided with Tim against him; and he saw no future in the Army.[14] On the positive side he was handsome, charming, a good speaker and with a quick intelligence that enabled him to master detail easily. After demobilization he went up to Christ Church, Oxford, and in 1922 graduated with a first in oriental languages. In 1923 he entered Parliament as MP for Warwick and Leamington and within two years had become Parliamentary Private Secretary to the Foreign Minister, Sir Austen Chamberlain. In 1935 he himself became Foreign Secretary at the very early age of 38, but it would be another 20 years before he would fulfil his burning ambition when he at last succeeded Winston Churchill as prime minister.

Eden's war record, academic and political expertise in foreign affairs and attractive appearance together ensured a rapid rise in the Conservative Party but, inevitably, he encountered doubters and critics from the start. He was said to lack staying power. He was irritable, impatient, quick to take offence at perceived slights and did not conceal his ambitions or his scorn for some senior party men who had not served in the war. Even a younger admirer thought him 'nervous and excitable' and, in Simon Ball's summary, 'There was a brittle quality to Eden, an inconsistency of temperament and policy that would always dog him.'[15]

These limitations in the harsh world of party politics, however, should not undermine for us his admirable performance as a very young officer on the Western Front and his remarkable swansong in the form of a literary tribute paid to his comrades and enduring friendships with survivors of the Yeomen Rifles.

MACMILLAN

When Harold Macmillan published the first volume of his memoirs, *Winds of Change, 1914–1939*, in 1966 he had already been in retirement for three years and was beginning to affect the persona of a world-weary Edwardian 'old fogey', an antediluvian survivor of the 'Lost Generation'. Nevertheless the all-too-short section he allotted to his youth and wartime military service has the essential ring of truth. This becomes clear in comparing his own recollections with the account of his official biographer, Alistair Horne.[16]

Harold's grandfather, the son of a poor Scottish crofter, had established the successful publishing company of Macmillan in 1843 and it remained a prospering family business. His father, Maurice, was shy and reclusive whereas his mother Helen (always known as Nellie), the daughter of an American surgeon from the Mid-West, was the driving, dominating force in the family, determined to push her children to the very limits of their potential – and beyond. It was Nellie who had purchased Birch Grove, the country home in Sussex, and whose ambition secured a place for Harold at Eton and then Balliol, following his more academically brilliant elder brother Daniel. Later she would get him transferred from the prestigious Rifle Corps to the ultra-smart Grenadier Guards and, after the war, help to launch his political career, even playing a part in securing his marriage to a daughter of the Duke of Devonshire.

Consequently Harold's childhood, though superficially comfortable and privileged, was in reality austere and joyless; indeed like so many upper-class children of that era his only really affectionate relationship was with his nanny, Mrs Last. Born on 19 February 1894, Harold in his memoirs would express profound gratitude to his mother for her ceaseless support and encouragement, reassuring him after every setback, 'You will win in the end', but he admitted that she was rigid in her views and somewhat puritanical. She was 'a formidable character, not easily deterred from anything on which she had set her mind', and expected those around her to meet her own high standards. She exerted an inhibiting effect on all her three sons, and had an adverse influence on Harold's relations with women.[17]

Harold entered Eton as a Colleger (he had won the Third Scholarship in 1906) but, being shy, repressed and highly-strung, was never very happy there. Clearly ill-health was the main reason for his leaving early in 1909 – he had heart trouble and suffered from bouts of depression ('the Black Dog') – and if there were any other causes they have not come to light. Among his private tutors after Eton one was outstanding in intellect, moral seriousness and influence; namely Ronald Knox, who was already displaying tendencies which would eventually draw him into Roman Catholicism. Knox's emotional and intellectual effects on his young pupil were tremendous and might well have caused Harold to follow his own religious path had he not been summarily dismissed by Nellie, who was an unbending Protestant.[18]

Knox's influence was still quite strong, but no longer dominant, at Oxford where Harold was an Exhibitioner at Balliol between 1912 and 1914. Harold found Oxford wonderfully liberating and enjoyable: he threw himself into his studies, reading parties and college activities, and made rapid progress at the

Union, where he would almost certainly have been elected President but for the outbreak of war. In his own modest phrase he 'scraped a first' in Honour Moderations but never returned to complete his degree. In contrast to Eton, he retained a lasting affection for Oxford.

In the autumn of 1914 Harold was commissioned into a New Army battalion of the King's Royal Rifle Corps. Although the regiment was famous, Harold's battalion, stationed at Southend-on-Sea, had little equipment, no rifles and was in a low state of readiness for operations. Fearing that the war would be over before he could get to France, Harold, through his mother's contacts, gained a transfer to the 4th Battalion Grenadier Guards, which was just being established. He was alarmed, but also impressed, by the exacting drill, dress and etiquette standards at Chelsea barracks, but then enjoyed an idyllic period of field training in and near Marlow, Bucks. Their host was the 'greatest living Grenadier', General Sir George Higginson, on whose riverside estate they were entertained. Field exercises took place nearby at Bovingdon Green where some 20 acres (8 ha) of trenches, perhaps a mystery to later generations, can still be seen.[19] The battalion embarked for France in August 1915, just in time to take part, in the newly-formed Guards Division, in the disastrous battle of Loos.

Macmillan and his battalion had an unsettling, depressing experience even before the battle began. Owing to crowded roads the troops were obliged to wait for six hours in the mud in pouring rain and were not allowed to break off for refreshment or rest. After at last reaching billets with plenty of straw they enjoyed only three hours' sleep before being woken at 4.30 a.m., to suffer further delays to allow a cavalry corps to pass. After a long approach march through a devastated area, passing the bodies of the dead and wounded from the previous day's attacks, the battalion reached the vicinity of Loos on the morning of 27 September. These chaotic scenes, in which some units had lost all discipline, gave Harold nightmares for many years. His battalion was ordered to attack Hill 70 to the east of the town. Already being heavily shelled and enfiladed by an enemy machine-gun on its right, the battalion entered a captured communication trench but was then ordered by the brigadier, who dashed up on horseback, to follow him in a completely different direction. This counter-order caused utter confusion; the battalion split up and the main body attacked Hill 70, overshot the objective, and suffered horrendous casualties from the enemy's second line. Macmillan's section, having no orders whatever, attached itself to other Guards units of the 2nd Brigade and attacked a strongpoint to the north (Puits 14). This too met with disaster and the survivors were ordered to crawl away from the enemy line. Unfortunately, Macmillan's company commander, Captain J. A. Morrison, was too fat to do this so the pair walked above ground, Harold suffering a glancing superficial wound to the head, but some hours later a more damaging and painful wound to his right hand. As the small group of bewildered survivors tried to dig in, Macmillan was sent to the casualty clearing station and, within a few days, was dispatched to Rouen. He never fully recovered from the wound to his hand, which also affected his arm.

At the time, as he honestly admits, he had only the dimmest idea of what was happening: he only recalled that they had advanced to attack in the conventional open-order formation, under intense fire from shells and bullets. 'There is a kind of daze that makes one impervious to emotion.' Since it was his first experience of battle he did not assume it was any worse than usual. He had memorably experienced 'the fog of war' in a disastrously mismanaged battle. He had behaved with more *sangfroid* and courage than his own modest account suggests; indeed his bravery under this baptism of fire became legendary in the battalion. It was a real mark of courage to be 'nearly as brave as Mr Macmillan'. His biographer makes a strong case that he should have been decorated but two considerations probably ruled it out: the confused attack in which he had taken part had failed; and there were no senior battalion officers present to recommend him because all had been killed or wounded.[20]

When Macmillan was fit enough to return to France in April 1916 he was posted to the Second Battalion in the Ypres salient. His new commanding officer was the eccentric Colonel Crawley de Crespigny, an inspired leader who often disregarded orders, especially those regarding uniform, and was reputed never to read a book. In sharp contrast Macmillan was extremely scholarly and bookish: he had taken an impressive mini-library to France and in any lulls in routine was to be found reading Samuel Richardson's *Pamela,* some of Scott's Waverley novels, and Boswell's *Life of Johnson.* The Colonel, however, treated him jovially as a strange animal who read books and was keen to discuss politics and philosophy, subjects not generally encouraged in the Mess. Macmillan experienced the squalor, discomforts and daily hazards of routine duties in the salient: 'The mud, the duck-boards, the darkness, the shell-holes', the sniping and the shelling. The most tedious aspect he found to be the process of relieving units in the front line.

He made his name in his new battalion on 19 July when leading a small patrol. He was doubtful about the value of such forays into the enemy trenches particularly, as in this case, his men failed to capture a prisoner. They encountered a German party digging a trench and came under fire. In the hasty retreat Macmillan suffered a glancing blow to the head from a grenade burst and was badly concussed. Though doubtful that he had achieved anything, he was commended by the brigadier. This injury gave him a perfect ticket to 'Blighty', but he managed to persuade first the medical officer and then his colonel not to send him home.[21]

In trying to describe his experiences in letters to his mother the aspect of the modern battlefield that struck him as most extraordinary was the desolation and emptiness of it all. 'One can look for miles and see no human being. But in those miles of country lurk (like moles or rats, it seems) thousands, even hundreds of thousands of men, planning against each other perpetually some new device of death.' What was needed in this new and very unglamorous form of warfare, he told her, was 'indomitable and patient determination'. 'If anyone at home thinks or talks of peace, you can truthfully say that the army is weary enough of war but prepared to fight for another 50 years if necessary, until the final object is attained.' Although he did not quote this letter further in his memoirs, he went on to say that he viewed the war as a crusade and every British soldier killed in it as a martyr. He believed that the men shared his conviction that the cause was just and so certain to triumph in the end. His mother, worried sick by his second head wound, offered to send him a steel waistcoat which he politely declined. Her son, though far from fearless, had a deep conviction that he would not be killed.[22]

At the end of July the 4th Battalion Grenadier Guards was transferred to the Somme battle area and, a few weeks later, moved up to the front towards Ginchy in preparation for the second great offensive push, incorporating tanks for the first time, and due to be launched on 15 September. Before that, on the night of 12–13 September, Macmillan led two platoons in support of a preliminary action to clear enemy machine-guns from an orchard to the north of the village. This succeeded but the Germans continued to shell the position, causing several casualties. The group dug in to await a counter-attack until relieved in the evening of the 14th when they bivouacked just behind Ginchy. Soon after dawn Colonel de Crespigny, smart but irregularly dressed as usual, led the battalion back towards Ginchy as part of the larger-scale offensive intended, on this sector, to capture the strongly-fortified village of Lesboeufs a few miles to the north-east.

Very quickly the whole of the attacking brigades in the Guards Division were thrown into confusion.[23] A heavy barrage fell near Macmillan's battalion as it approached the start line and, very disturbingly, it came under enemy rifle fire and machine-gun fire from the flanks and rear. The supporting divisions on either side failed to advance, with the result that the Guards were completely isolated. The three neatly marked, coloured lines denoting successive objectives on the map soon lost all meaning in the featureless, cratered terrain, the leading battalions mistakenly believing that they had captured the enemy's front line and were advancing on the second. As if this confusion was not enough, the Grenadiers were faced with another problem. The two Coldstream battalions ahead of them had veered a long way to the left and were out of contact; consequently the Grenadiers found no one to support, and when they reached the front line it was still in German hands. Since the Royal Artillery's creeping barrage had now moved on they were completely exposed.

Early in the advance a shell fragment had struck Macmillan just below his right kneecap, but he felt little pain at first and stayed with his men until the front line of enemy trenches had been occupied. Then, in leading a party of troops to silence a machine-gun on their left flank he was shot at close range while half crawling and half crouching. Machine-gun bullets penetrated his left thigh and some, as he discovered later, stuck in his pelvis. Knocked over, but not in great pain at first, he rolled down into a deep shell-hole and dosed himself with morphine.[24]

His position was particularly desperate since he lay between the trench line already captured and the next objective. In the event, due to the utter confusion and heavy casualties already suffered by the Coldstream and the Grenadiers, no further advance was attempted; but he lay close to where the German barrage was falling. Moreover, on several occasions enemy soldiers, counter-attacking, ran round the lip of his shell-hole. He lay 'doggo' and feigned death. What is truly astonishing is that he happened to have a copy of Aeschylus' *Prometheus* in Greek in his pocket – a play he knew well and one that seemed 'not inappropriate to my position' – so he read it 'intermittently'. He lay out all day, for more than 12 hours, without water and fearing that he might have been wounded in a vital place. At last, after dark he was found by a company search party and carried back to the captured trench.

His ordeal had been terrible but even worse was to come. He and another wounded officer were carried by guardsmen into Ginchy but no advance dressing station was found there and so intense was the shelling that the two officers decided to release the stretcher bearers and somehow make their own way back. In the darkness and confusion they became separated and at that terrible moment Macmillan admits that fear, even panic, seized him. He was no longer part of a team with leadership responsibilities but alone, unable to walk and very frightened. Somehow he managed to crawl or scramble through Ginchy and fall into a ditch on the southern side, where he was eventually picked up by the transport of another battalion. He was taken half-conscious to a dressing station but remembered nothing more until, some days later, he reached a French military hospital at Abbeville. He managed to get a message through to his mother to say he was all right. He links with this experience a strange and moving incident which occurred 27 years later. In 1943, when he was Minister-Resident in North Africa, he was involved in a plane crash near Algiers in which he was badly burned and shocked. Once again taken to a French hospital, which must have been associated in his confused mind with Abbeville, he insisted that a similar reassuring message be sent to his mother – who had been dead for seven years. 'For a day or two, I was persuaded that I was a wounded officer from a battle nearly thirty years before.'[25]

When Macmillan arrived back in London in late September 1916 he was dangerously ill. Because no tube had been inserted in his stomach the wound had healed superficially, but a deep abscess had formed. Realizing that he might not survive a long ambulance journey to a military hospital, he insisted that he be taken to his mother's home in Cadogan Place. She at once took charge, telephoned a first-class surgeon, Sir William Bennett, and took her son to a hospital in Belgrave Square run by two titled ladies of American birth, where he was promptly operated on. His mother's intervention had undoubtedly saved his life but recovery was very slow. He was still in hospital when the war ended and, after release, had to return frequently to have the wound reopened for the extraction of bits of metal or bone. The tube was removed early in 1919 but another year passed before the wound finally healed. For the remainder of his life he would have a daily reminder of his war service due to pains in his head, pelvis and leg.[26]

Macmillan was still very critical of the British High Command and its staffs when writing his memoirs in the 1960s. He shared a widespread view that senior commanders and staffs did not visit the front line and were ignorant of conditions there; how otherwise could they have permitted the continuation of the Passchendaele campaign? A little unfairly (though making an exception for Plumer's Second Army), he summarized the contrast as follows: 'the Second World War was fought by great generals from their caravans. The First World War was conducted by men of lesser ability from their châteaux.' But he allowed that, on various levels, lessons had been learnt from the experience of 1914–18.[27]

Coming from a completely unmilitary background, Macmillan was at first unsettled by unfamiliar routines and traditions, but in retrospect he became tremendously proud of his service in the Grenadier Guards. He took genuine pleasure in the high standards of discipline, including the smartness and beauty of drill. The Guards' standard of excellence, he considered, provided a good working rule for civilian life.

Among the particular lessons he learnt was that many officers had wider interests and talents than were immediately apparent; indeed he became somewhat ashamed at the narrowness and intolerance of the intellectual classes to which he belonged. Next he learnt the meaning of courage and the unique quality of comradeship and sense of triumph fostered by shared dangers and achievements. He went even further, admitting to a certain contempt for gentlemen, in either of the world wars, 'who voluntarily missed their chance or chose to avoid danger by seeking positions of security'. Most importantly, he believed that military service with officers and soldiers from very different backgrounds to his own had given him the ability to get on with all sorts of people.

> By the daily life, working in close contact with the men in one's platoon or company, we learnt for the first time how to understand, talk with, and feel at home with a whole class of men with whom we could not have come into contact in any other way. Thus we learnt to admire their steadfastness, enjoy their humour, and be touched by their sentiment.[28]

Like virtually all the individuals discussed in this book, Macmillan was haunted by his war experience: 'We almost began to feel a sense of guilt for not having shared the fate of our friends and comrades. We certainly felt an obligation to make some decent use of the life that had been spared to us.'[29] He could not face returning to Oxford, which now seemed 'a city of ghosts', and soon threw himself wholeheartedly into 'the game of politics'.

He was elected to Parliament at his second attempt in 1924 and was seen as one of the Party's most promising young men. In the inter-war decades, however, his progress towards office was much slower than Eden's. He sensibly – for the longer term – chose to specialize in economic and social issues (such as pensions), but these subjects lacked the glamour of foreign affairs.

In 1929 his political career and private life were thrown into turmoil: he lost his parliamentary seat in the Tory party's disastrous election; and his wife Dorothy's affair with Bob Boothby was flaunted in public. He was devastated by this double betrayal by his wife and close friend, and everyone knew it. Curiously, his wife never entirely abandoned the family home during the protracted affair, while for his part Harold was desperate to preserve the marriage. Demoralized by his public humiliation, he suffered a nervous breakdown and, helped by his mother, sought refuge abroad, spending several months in a sanatorium near Munich. His career seemed to be in ruins.[30]

Although he regained his Stockton seat in 1931 his political reputation remained in the doldrums. He seemed to lack vigour; his speeches on economic matters were held to be tedious; and enemies derided him as an advocate of 'naked socialism'. Even a sympathetic MP thought he was becoming a monomaniac about himself and his policy and 'a colossal bore'. He openly criticized Baldwin and resigned the Party whip, only to slink back once the latter had resigned. On the positive side he opposed appeasement and supported rearmament, associating himself with Eden after the latter resigned as Foreign Secretary in 1938. In May 1940 his opportunity came at last when Churchill appointed him parliamentary secretary to the Ministry of Supply. As a committed Churchill supporter whose abilities could now at last be demonstrated, Macmillan's reputation rose so rapidly during the Second Word War that by 1945 he was one of the outstanding members of the Conservative Party.[31]

Eden and Macmillan both had an advantageous start to their careers in that they were educated at Eton and Oxford, and both served in elite regiments, the Rifle Corps and Grenadier Guards respectively. The war gave them experience of hardship and suffering at a very early, formative stage of their lives; but also offered them an opportunity for responsibility and leadership, and comradeship with a wide variety of men which they would not otherwise have found in their scholarly, bookish backgrounds.

After the war, however, successful careers in politics were far from guaranteed.

Eden had recently experienced terrible family quarrels over the Eden estate and finances, and had effectively lost his home; he had no private income; he had still to take his degree; and his health was suspect. Macmillan had secure employment in the family publishing business but continued to suffer from his war wounds and struggled to make his mark in politics right through the inter-war decades. Both had had 'good wars', Eden outstandingly so, but this did not seem to count for much in an era when the political leaders – Ramsay MacDonald, Baldwin, Austen and Neville Chamberlain, Halifax, Simon and Hoare – had not served at all. Only with the failure of appeasement, the advent of war and the demotion of Neville Chamberlain did the 'warriors' of 1914–18 (including Duff Cooper) find favour in the coalition led by Winston Churchill, who had himself briefly commanded a battalion on the Western Front. Henceforth, and for many years after 1945, it remained a prime, though not an obligatory qualification, to have 'had a good war' to reach senior positions in the Conservative Party. In Macmillan's case, to have been wounded 'counter-balanced many an intellectual and political eccentricity'. He did not need 'to play the political card; his body played it for him'.[32]

To the end of their lives Eden and Macmillan remained conscious of the tremendous influence which the First World War had exerted on their characters and their careers, and realized how fortunate they were to have survived. Macmillan's late recollection of his war service in *Winds of Change* was fascinating but all too brief. Eden, by contrast, when in the last year of his life, aged 79, and very ill, produced a minor classic in *Another World*. He found the writing hard going but exciting and exhilarating. Whereas his previous autobiographical volumes had been very long and lacking in sparkle, this was a concise and beautifully written little book which might easily have been the work of a young man. It is vivid, moving, even funny at times, but never sentimental. It is also remarkably modest and understated, making no mention at all of the author's winning of the Military Cross and other commendations for gallantry. As Eden's biographer justly concludes: 'In a lifetime of achievement against the odds, perhaps this was the most wonderful of all.'[33]

Afterword

It is with some sadness that I take my leave of these soldiers and airmen authors who have been my daily companions for the past two or three years. Close study of their books and careers almost persuades me that I knew them, though in reality I only met two of them – Charles Carrington and Guy Chapman – a few times towards the end of their lives. But in imagination I have travelled with them, vicariously experiencing their highs and lows in all the nondescript villages which they have helped to immortalize for generations of readers and battlefield pilgrims. Aubers Ridge, Loos and La Bassée for 1915, the year when most of them reached the trenches; Gommecourt, Serre, Mametz and Ginchy for the attritional Somme campaign; Pilckem, Hooge, Zillebeke and Ploegsteert for the even more hellish conditions east of Ypres; and Cambrai, Villers Bretonneux, the Lys and Amiens for the final roller-coaster year of the war.

Given the right circumstances, which alas so rarely occur even with parents and older friends, what a privilege it would have been to meet nearly all of them and raise questions about their wartime experiences and how they had ordered and articulated them in their memoirs. Robert Graves, with his bold irreverence and black humour, would surely have been tremendous fun, if only one could steer his reminiscences towards the Royal Welch Fusiliers and away from his poetic muse, the White Goddess. Would Frank Richards have been prepared to admit that he had invented the eerie story of the black rat who brought notice of death to his companion? Would the retiring, indolent and alcoholic Frederic Manning have been willing to discuss his marvellous book, separating fact from fiction and revealing how far he had sought to depict himself in the character of Bourne? Would Billy Bishop have been willing to revisit his remarkable number of victims or 'kills', perhaps answering later critics who accused him of inflating the total? Would Frank Crozier have been more specific about the British and Allied soldiers he alleged he had killed, and have explained when and why the martinet became a convert to the peace movement? Only a brave or foolhardy interviewer would have dared to ask the formidable Lord Reith about his relationship with Charlie Bowser or his arrogant behaviour towards senior officers, but he might have responded positively if asked why he had enjoyed the war so much – a question which could also have been put to the other fire-eater discussed – Alf Pollard, VC. Siegfried Sassoon and Max Plowman might have been persuaded to lead a superb seminar on their differing experiences of protesting against the war and their reactions to Dr Rivers' notions of therapy.

Although the war memoirs selected for discussion unavoidably have many facets in common; belonging to the same units, fighting in the same battles and experiencing comparable periods of fear, misery, despair and exaltation; nevertheless they also display a remarkable variety of attitudes and responses, both in recreating their periods of active service and in later reflections on their meaning. What they have in common is essentially, in Guy Chapman's apt phrase, that they were survivors – but survivors of a kind – all deeply and permanently affected by this searing experience of modern, industrialized warfare on a vast scale.

Perhaps the airmen, for obvious reasons, were less psychologically damaged than the soldiers, or at any rate damaged in different ways. Some of the soldiers too survived to enjoy successful careers: Oliver Lyttelton, Anthony Eden and Harold Macmillan in politics; Guy Chapman in publishing and authorship; Charles Carrington in higher education; and Blunden, Graves and Sassoon in the world of literature. Even so, the war years left most survivors with physical or psychological scars evident in their writing and their lives. By his own admission, Robert Graves was a nervous wreck in the 1920s but struggled, with considerable success, to break free and lead a new bohemian life abroad. Macmillan was in constant pain from war wounds for the rest of his life. Sassoon remained imaginatively rooted in his early life and the war years, writing obsessively about the pre-1914 idealized world and its loss. Blunden too explains with touching candour how he strove but failed to escape from the combat-induced nightmares which literally haunted his dreams and even invaded his consciousness in daytime to the end of his days. Blunden most markedly, but Chapman, Graves and others to a lesser extent experienced feelings of guilt that they had survived when so many better men had been killed. In retrospect the unique comradeship of the trenches, concentrated in an exalted myth of their battalions, acquired ever greater significance as they failed to find any equivalent or alternative in civilian life. Guy Chapman tried – and failed – to rediscover this spirit in the Second World War. As he frankly admitted, part of himself remained for ever a member of the 13th Battalion Royal Fusiliers; while even the iconoclastic rebel, Robert Graves, tried to rejoin the Royal Welch Fusiliers on the outbreak of war in 1939, and was very proud that his son David was commissioned in the Regiment, and recommended for a posthumous VC in Burma.

Perhaps few of these soldier-authors would have asserted as boldly as Guy Chapman at the end of his life that 'To the years between 1914 and 1918 I owe everything of lasting value in my make-up', but they would have understood his viewpoint and defended it against outsiders who had not served on the Western Front.

Earlier, in *A Passionate Prodigality*, he had vividly juxtaposed war's horrors and its paradoxical appeal. He concluded the negative description of the ghastly aspects of war with this summary of the dreary pattern of the infantryman's existence: 'labour, danger, boredom, insecurity, frustration, and the knowledge that this would never change.' And yet, he courageously acknowledged 'the fascination of war, the extreme pleasure, partly of the mind, more of the senses, it can give'. This might not be true for all men, but those who had once felt it could never erase it from their memory.

Guy Chapman's emotionally-charged association between war's beastliness and its seductive attractions may be less persuasive now to a generation which lacks any first-hand experience of soldiering and holds very different views of war to those prevalent in 1914 and 1939. Nevertheless this selection of stylish, eloquent, moving and extremely varied war memoirs should not only provide enjoyable reading, but also cause us to reconsider the complexity of military experience and its enduring influence on some of those who survived the trenches and published their personal recollections.

Notes

Notes to Chapter 1: Robert Graves and Goodbye to All That

1   Samuel Hynes *A War Imagined. The First World War and English Culture* (The Bodley Head, 1990) pp. 427–8.
2   Paul Fussell *The Great War and Modern Memory* (OUP, 1975) pp. 208–10. Adrian Caesar *Taking it like a Man. Suffering, Sexuality and the War Poets* (Manchester UP, 1993) pp. 175–6.
3   Robert Graves *Goodbye to All That* (Cassell, 1957) p. vii.
4   Martin Seymour-Smith *Robert Graves. His Life and Work* (Bloomsbury, 1995) pp. 188–90.
5   Robert Graves *Goodbye to All That* (Cape, 1929 edn) pp. 439–40.
6   Seymour-Smith p. 194.
7   Hynes p. 429.
8   Robert Graves *But It Still Goes On* (Cape, 1930) pp. 13–17, 41–3.
9   Fussell pp. 202–20.
10 Ibid, p. 212.
11 Ibid, p. 212–13.
12 Andrew Rutherford *The Literature of War. Five Studies in Heroic Virtue* (Macmillan, 1980) pp. 91–2.
13 Bernard Bergonzi *Heroes' Twilight. A Study of the Literature of the Great War* (Macmillan, 1980) p. 155. Caesar *op. cit.* p. 189.
14 *Goodbye to All That* (1957) p. 198.
15 Caesar p. 189.
16 Rutherford p. 93.
17 *Goodbye to All That* (1957) pp. 72, 165–6.
18 Ibid, pp. 195–6.
19 Ibid, pp. 110–13.
20 Ibid, pp. 183, 226.
21 Ibid, p. 154.
22 Keith Simpson (ed.) *The War the Infantry Knew 1914–1919* by Captain J. C. Dunn (Jane's, 1987). Editor's Introduction pp. XXXIX–XL.
23 *Goodbye to All That* (1957) pp. 125–6.
24 Ibid, pp. 201–4.
25 Ibid, pp. 231–3.
26 Seymour-Smith p. 199. Graves *But It Still Goes On* p. 56.

27   Seymour-Smith pp. 193–6, and see p. 241 for A. P. Graves's criticisms of his son's post-war behaviour and wounding memoirs.
28   Keith Simpson's introduction to *The War the Infantry Knew* pp. XXIV, XXXIX–XL, XLIV, L.
29   Seymour-Smith pp. 197–200.
30   Ibid.
31   Sassoon to Blunden 12 November 1929, Sassoon–Blunden Correspondence at the Harry Ransom Humanities Research Center, Austin, Texas.
32   Ibid: Sassoon's letters to Blunden dated 9 and 23 December 1929, 4, and 28 January 1930.
33   Seymour-Smith pp. 200–1.
34   Hynes p. 430.
35   *Goodbye to All That* (1929 edn) p. 391 Graves records that he had had to appear before an annual medical board on account of his neurasthenia and at last was awarded a pension of £42.00 per annum.
36   *Goodbye to All That* (1957 edn) pp. 304–5.
37   Frank Richards *Old Soldiers Never Die* (Faber paperback edn, 1964). Introduction by Robert Graves p. 1.

Notes to Chapter 2: Rebutting disenchantment: Charles Carrington and
A Subaltern's War

1   Charles Edmonds *A Subaltern's War* (1929) pp. 8–9, 17 (henceforth *Subaltern*).
2   Alan Clark *The Donkeys* (1961). See also Brian Bond 'Oh! What a Lovely War: History and Popular Myths in late Twentieth Century Britain' in William Roger Louis (ed.) *Yet More Adventures with Britannia* (2005) pp. 149–64.
3   Charles Carrington *Soldier from the Wars Returning* (1965) pp. 73–9 (henceforth *Soldier*).
4   *Soldier* pp. 76–9. *Subaltern* p. 19.
5   *Subaltern* pp. 192–5.
6   Ibid, 196–7.
7   Ibid, 204–5.
8   Ibid, 200–1.
9   Ibid, 205–6. It might be argued that for many keen volunteers of August 1914, like Carrington, by the time they reached the front at the end of 1915 or later, the war had long lost its romantic image and become a grim struggle of attrition.
10   *Subaltern* pp. 206–9.
11   *Soldier at Bomber Command* (1987). I am proud to have helped in the publication of this important account of the 'Bomber Barons' and of inter-service relations in the Second World War.
12   *Soldier* pp. 85–6, 114–17. *Subaltern* pp. 28–9.
13   *Subaltern* pp. 62–105. *Soldier* pp. 87–8, 121.
14   *Soldier* pp. 121–2. 143 Brigade in 48th Division was most unusual in that all four battalions were Royal Warwickshires. In January 1918 all brigades were reduced to three battalions.
15   *Subaltern* pp. 34–5. *Soldier* p. 95.

16 *Subaltern* pp. 72–83, 94, 108–10.

17 Ibid, p. 112.

18 Ibid, pp. 120–1. For a good account of the routines of trench warfare see Denis Winter *Death's Men: Soldiers of the Great War* (1978).

19 A prominent prehistoric tumulus which still looms ominously on the left of the Bapaume–Albert road. The site has been purchased by the Western Front Association in order to preserve it as a war monument. See also *Soldier* pp. 126–30.

20 Ibid, pp. 144–5.

21 *Subaltern* pp. 127, 131–9. *Soldier* pp. 188–91.

22 *Subaltern* p. 143, *Soldier* pp. 192–6. In the later account Carrington does not mention that he had shot at German soldiers trying to surrender.

23 *Subaltern* pp. 166–9.

24 Ibid, pp. 131–3. *Soldier* pp. 191–7.

25 *Subaltern* pp. 161–5, 185.

26 *Soldier* pp. 218–26, 251.

27 Ibid, pp. 252–3.

28 Ibid, pp. 259–61.

29 Ibid, pp. 262–3.

30 Ibid, pp. 264–5. Carrington admitted that he was one of the numerous authors stimulated to publish by Remarque's runaway success. On the latter's limited experience of combat see Brian Bond *The Unquiet Western Front* (2002) pp. 38–40.

31 *Soldier*, pp. 266–9. To the list the impressive German memoirs he might have added Ludwig Renn's *War* (1929), remarkable in that it reads convincingly as if written by a private soldier but was actually the work of an aristocratic officer.

Notes to Chapter 3: Survivors of a kind: Guy Chapman and Edmund Blunden

1 Guy Chapman *A Kind of Survivor* (1975) p. 280. Barry Webb *Edmund Blunden. A Biography* (1990) p. 98. Martin Taylor (ed.) *Edmund Blunden. Overtones of War. Poems of the First World War* (1996).

2 *A Kind of Survivor* pp. 25–6.

3 Guy Chapman *A Passionate Prodigality* (1933) p. 13.

4 *A Kind of Survivor* pp. 124–5 (henceforth *Survivor*)

5 Ibid, pp138, 275.

6 *A Passionate Prodigality* pp. 78, 107. See also *Survivor* p. 74.

7 *A Passionate Prodigality* pp. 44, 52, 92.

8 Ibid, pp. 119–22.

9 Ibid, pp. 179–80.

10 Ibid, pp. 205, 219

11 Ibid, p. 269.

12 Ibid, pp. 209, 217.

13 Ibid, pp. 111, 119. *Survivor* 233–4.

14 *A Passionate Prodigality* pp. 66–7. *Survivor* p. 58.

15   *A Passionate Prodigality* pp. 153, 207. *Survivor* p. 58.

16   *Survivor* pp. 63–5.

17   *A Passionate Prodigality* pp. 136–7, 188, 190.

18   *Survivor* p. 158.

19   *A Passionate Prodigality* pp. 99, 168.

20   Ibid, pp. 226, 276, 281.

21   Ibid, p. 226.

22   Margaret Storm Jameson's Preface to *Survivor* which she prepared for publication after Guy Chapman's death in 1972.

23   *Survivor* pp. 76, 264, 281–2.

24   Barry Webb *Edmund Blunden. A Biography* (1990) by Bernard Bergonzi. Entry on E.C. Blunden in *New DNB*. Paul Fussell *The Great War and Modern Memory* (1975) pp. 254–69.

25   Fussell pp. 258–9. See also the excellent introduction in Martin Taylor (ed.) *Edmund Blunden. Overtones of War* pp. 1–33.

26   Webb pp. 52–3, 64. Edmund Blunden *Undertones of War* (1928) pp. 122–30.

27   Webb pp. 65–6. Blunden *Undertones of War* pp. 141–4.

28   Webb p. 73.

29   Ibid, pp. 77–81. *Undertones of War* pp. 213, 222, 231–6.

30   Webb p. 80. *Undertones of War* pp. 263–4.

31   *Undertones of War* p. 223. See also C. Z. Rothkopf and B. Webb (eds) *More than a Brother: Correspondence between Edmund Blunden and Hector Buck, 1917–1967* (1996).

32   *Undertones of War* pp. 193, 198–9.

33   *Undertones of War* p. 41. Fussell pp. 254–5.

34   *Undertones of War* p. 119.

35   Ibid, pp. 232, 236, 265.

36   Ibid, pp. 70, 129, 165. Thomas Chatterton, 'the marvellous boy', poet and literary forger, committed suicide in 1770 aged 17.

37   Ibid, p. 208. Fussell pp. 268–9.

38   *Undertones of War* pp. 43, 177–8.

39   Ibid, p. 154. Webb pp. 95–6. Blunden had dedicated a poem ('The Veteran') to Harrison as early as 1919. See M. Taylor (ed.) *Overtones of War* p. 60.

40   Webb pp. 95–97. Fussell p. 260.

41   *Undertones of War* pp. 227–8. Blunden's 'A Battalion History' is printed as an appendix in M. Taylor *op. cit.* pp. 213–26.

42   Webb pp. 90–3, 215–27.

43   Ibid, pp. 100–1, 303. See M. Taylor (ed.) *Overtones of War* p. 74.

44   Webb pp. 98–101.

45   Quoted by Nicholas Murray reviewing *Edmund Blunden, Overtones of War*, *TLS* 27 December 1996. (See note 1 above.)

Notes to Chapter 4: Fire-eaters: Alfred Pollard, VC and John Reith

1 Captain A. O. Pollard *Fire-Eater. The Memoirs of a VC* (1932) pp. 43–4. I am very grateful to Catherine Boylan for allowing me to make extensive use of her MA thesis on Pollard published as 'Fearless Fighter, Tender Romantic: the Paradox of Alfred Oliver Pollard, VC, MC and Bar, DCM' in *Journal of the Society for Army Historical Research* 83 (2004) pp. 53–72.

2 *Fire-Eater* pp. 57–8.

3 Ibid, pp. 77–8, 82–3, 118.

4 Ibid, pp. 106–9, 113–23. See also the *New DNB* entry on Pollard by Nigel Cave.

5 Ibid, pp. 11, 24, 27. In his foreword Pollard stated frankly 'I enjoyed the war, both in and out of the line'.

6 Ibid, pp. 29, 69–70, 98–100. Boylan p. 63.

7 *Fire-Eater* pp. 106, 110–13.

8 Ibid, pp. 148–9, 164–5, 187–8. Boylan p. 55.

9 Ibid, pp. 199–200. Boylan p. 56.

10 Ibid, pp. 218–24. Boylan pp. 56, 60–1. She quotes Pollard's obituary in the regimental journal (in 1961) to the effect that his bravery was not the kind that came from a sudden impulse but the result of a careful study of all relevant factors followed by a quick decision to act regardless of personal danger.

11 *Fire-Eater* pp. 230–5. Boylan pp. 61–3.

12 *Fire-Eater* pp. 239–53.

13 Ibid, p. 150. Pollard obstinately refused to lead a raid without first undertaking a personal reconnaissance.

14 For an excellent comparison between Pollard and other warrior-authors, including Jünger and Crozier, see Boylan pp. 66–72.

15 Robert Wohl *The Generation of 1914* (Weidenfeld and Nicolson, 1980) pp. 55–9, and see also pp. 223–37 for a brilliant analysis of the nature of post-1918 disillusionment.

16 Boylan pp. 57–9. *Who Was Who 1961–1970.* Addenda December 1960 (Pollard died on the 4th).

17 Boylan p. 59.

18 Ibid, p. 66.

19 Ian McIntyre *The Expense of Glory. A Life of John Reith* (1993) p. 233.

20 Ibid, pp. 18, 21.

21 John Reith (Lord Reith) *Into the Wind* pp. 15–16.

22 McIntyre pp. 5–27 passim. *Into the Wind* p. 28.

23 Lord Reith *Wearing Spurs* (1966) p. 65. *Into the Wind* p. 28.

24 *Wearing Spurs* p. 76. McIntyre p. 34.

25 *Wearing Spurs* pp. 136, 143, 154. When Reith told five of his soldiers to read a chapter of the Bible every day he commented: 'Funny business; they added it to routine duties like cleaning their spurs' (p. 143).

26 Ibid, pp. 185–6. One feels that Reith would have gone on to collect medals for gallantry, or have been killed, had his active service not ended in October 1915.

27 Ibid, pp. 109, 125–6. See also the *New DNB* entry on Lord Reith by Ian McIntyre.

28   Ibid, pp. 191–2.

29   Ibid, p. 202. McIntyre pp. 50, 409 note 2. *Into the Wind* pp. 49–50.

30   McIntyre pp. 36–7. *Wearing Spurs* pp. 96–7.

31   *Wearing Spurs* pp. 220–3.

32   McIntyre pp. 57, 408 note 92. Reith also omitted his wife's name. After the prolonged and
      tragi-comic break-up with Charlie, Reith was close to madness. The breach between him
      and Bowser was never healed but when they met by accident in Southampton in 1940 the
      latter called out 'Good Luck, John' and they shook hands (see McIntyre pp. 102–13, 251).

33   McIntyre Preface p. xiii.

34   Malcolm Muggeridge 'Reith in the Trenches' *The Observer* 4 September 1966. Reviews
      quoted on the dust jacket of *Wearing Spurs*. The book was reprinted three days after
      publication.

Notes to Chapter 5: Grandeur and misery: the Guards

1   Oliver Lyttelton *The Memoirs of Lord Chandos* (1962) pp. 35–6 (henceforth *Chandos*).

2   Stuart Cloete *A Victorian. Son. An Autobiography 1897–1922* (1972) p. 238.

3   Allan Adair *A Guards' General, The Memoirs of Major-General Sir Allan Adair* (1986)
      pp. 44–5.

4   Simon Ball *The Guardsmen* (2004) pp. 27–9.

5   *Chandos* pp. 37–41. Ball pp. 30–3. Adair p. 18. The lion had been won by another general
      in a raffle in 1917. It was fed on horses killed in battle.

6   Ball pp. 30–2. *Chandos* pp. 40–1.

7   *Chandos* p. 37, 46–8.

8   Adair pp. 23, 35. Carroll Carstairs *A Generation Missing* (1930, new edition 1989)
      pp. 187–91.

9   G. D. Sheffield *Leadership in the Trenches* (2000).

10   Stephen Graham *A Private in the Guards* (1919). *Who's Who* entries.

11   Graham pp. 19, 90–3, 212–16.

12   Norman D. Cliff *To Hell and Back with the Guards* (1988) pp. 107–8.

13   Ball p. 395.

14   Graham pp. 22–81, 180.

15   Cliff pp. 25–6.

16   Ibid, pp. 36, 53, 86.

17   Ibid, pp. 71–2. Cliff cites a brave sergeant who successfully refused to carry out a suicidal
      attack ordered by Lascelles.

18   Ibid, pp. 45, 63, 90–1.

19   Ibid, pp. 40–1, 48.

20   Ibid, p. 59. Carstairs pp. 65–6.

21   Cloete pp. 230–1.

22   Carstairs p. 182. Wilfrid Ewart *Scots Guard on the Western Front, 1915–1918* (1934,
      Paperback edition 2001) p. 173.

23   Graham pp. 216–22. Cliff p. 77.

24 *Chandos* pp. 46–9.
25 Ibid, pp. 41–5. Ball pp. 34–8. Sir Frederick Ponsonby *The Grenadier Guards in the Great War 1914–1919* (1920, three volumes) Vol. I pp. 247–63 (henceforth Ponsonby).
26 Ponsonby Vol I pp. 290–321. Ball pp. 43–5.
27 Ball pp. 49–53. *Chandos* pp. 48–51.
28 Robin Prior and Trevor Wilson *The Somme* (2005) pp. 229–33. Ponsonby Vol II pp. 31–8. Cuthbert Headlam *The Guards Division in the Great War, 1915–1918* (1924, two volumes) Vol. I pp. 139–77 (henceforth Headlam).
29 *Chandos* pp. 58–65. Ball pp. 57–64.
30 *Chandos* pp. 82–91. Ball pp. 70–1. Headlam Vol II pp. 41–75. Colonel Harold Alexander held temporary command of 4th Guards Brigade at the age of 28.
31 *Chandos* pp. 92–6. Headlam Vol II pp. 78–85. Ponsonby Vol III pp. 32–9.
32 *Chandos* p. 96.
33 Ibid, pp. 96–9. Headlam Vol II pp. 85–91. Ponsonby Vol III pp. 40–8. Graham pp. 200–2.
34 Ball pp. 386–9. The rejected plays were Rolf Hochhuth's *Soldiers* and Conor Cruise O'Brien's *Murderous Angels*.
35 Ibid, p. 391. Brian Bond 'Oh! What a Lovely War: history and popular myths in late twentieth century Britain' in Wm. Roger Louis (ed.) *Yet More Adventures with Britannia* (2005) pp. 149–64.
36 Ball pp. 393–5.
37 Alex Danchev '"Bunking" and debunking: the controversies of the 1960s' in Brian Bond (ed) *The First World War and British Military History* (1991) pp. 263–88.

Notes to Chapter 6: Voices from the ranks: Frederic Manning and Frank Richards

1 Andrew Rutherford *The Literature of War* (1978) pp. 64–5.
2 Ibid, pp. 88, 99–112. David E. Langley 'Private Frank Richards DCM, MM, 2/Royal Welch Fusiliers' *Stand To!* No. 73 April 2005 pp. 30–1.
3 Jonathan Marwil *Frederic Manning. An Unfinished Life* (1988) and Jonathan Marwil 'Frederic Manning. A retrospective in the form of an introduction', *St Louis Literary Supplement*, 1978. It was this author who first revealed that Manning had been commissioned.
4 J. Marwil *Frederic Manning. An Unfinished Life* pp. 185–8.
5 Ibid, pp. 246–9, 254–5.
6 Ibid, pp. 273–4.
7 The Penguin Classics Edition (2000) has an introduction by Niall Ferguson. For the second biography see Verna Coleman *The Last Exquisite: A Portrait of Frederic Manning* (Melbourne University Press, 1990). See also the *New DNB* entry on 'Frederic Manning, 1882–1935' by Dominic Hibberd.
8 Rutherford *op. cit.* p. 99. Michael Howard's Introduction to *The Middle Parts of Fortune* (1977). All future references are to this edition.
9 W de B Wood (ed.) *The History of the King's Shropshire Light Infantry in the Great War 1914–1918* (Medici Society, 1925) pp. 229–33. The final stages of Manning's time with the 7th Battalion were as follows: 8 October 1916 to Mailly-Maillet near Albert; 18 October

in camp at Bus; 28 October–1 November in trenches near Serre; 4–12 November at Louvencourt; 13 November attack (in Third Division) at Serre in mud and dense fog – a failure with 214 other rank casualties; 14–15 November back at Bus in dreadful conditions; 21 November into early December on trench duties in the Serre sector. Manning moved camp at least a dozen times in his short tour with the Seventh Battalion KLSI.

10 For David Jones's close adherence to his battalion's movements before the battle at Mametz Wood in July 1916 see Colin Hughes 'David Jones. The man who was on the field. *In Parenthesis* as straight reporting' *David Jones Society* (1979) 32 pp.

11 Bourne's name was taken from the Lincolnshire town where he lived for several years. It was in the Bull Hotel there that he began to write his own memoirs. He is given no Christian name; significantly the only soldier so distinguished is 'Charlie' Martlow. See Marwil, *op. cit.* pp. 220, 260–7.

12 *The Middle Parts of Fortune* pp. 164, 227.

13 Ibid, M. Howard's Introduction pp. v–vii. Rutherford p. 99.

14 *The Middle Parts of Fortune* pp. 39, 80, 232, 246–7.

15 Cyril Falls is cited by Rutherford *op. cit.* p. 102.

16 *The Middle Parts of Fortune* p. 80.

17 Ibid, pp. 55, 92, 95, 166.

18 Ibid, pp. 49, 147, 156. Marwil p. 265.

19 *The Middle Parts of Fortune* pp. 129, 149, 193, 246–7. Marwil pp. 267–8.

20 *The Middle Parts of Fortune* pp. vii, 4, 209.

21 Ibid, p. 205.

22 Marwil pp. 179, 272–3.

23 Robert Graves's Introduction to the paperback edition of *Old Soldiers Never Die* (1964). All subsequent references are to this edition.

24 D. Langley 'Private Frank Richards' (see reference 2 above) and the same author's essay on Richards' early years in *Stand To!* No. 76 April 2006, pp. 48–9.

25 Keith Simpson's Introduction to J. C. Dunn *The War the Infantry Knew 1914–1919* (1987) p. XLVIII.

26 F. Richards *Old Soldiers Never Die* p. 108.

27 Ibid, pp. 109, 116.

28 Ibid, pp. 122, 172–5, 222–3.

29 Ibid, pp. 113, 130.

30 Ibid, pp. 118, 217, 256. It seems likely that Pinney inspired Sassoon's mordant poem 'The General'.

31 Ibid, pp. 118–19, 179.

32 Ibid, pp. 176, 254.

33 Ibid, pp. 156–7, 170, 217, 273, 308.

34 Ibid, pp. 34–7, 50, 93. For an excellent survey of the Royal Welch Fusiliers' regular officers see K. Simpson (reference 25 above) pp. XLII–XLVII.

35 *Old Soldiers Never Die* pp. 38–9, 216.

36 Ibid, pp. 294–5, 318–21. It seems particularly unjust that Richards did not receive a pension for his DCM because he was not in receipt of a Service pension; see Langley *Stand To!* No. 73 p. 30.

37   *Old Soldiers Never Die* pp. 53, 127, 135–7, 161, 201, 234–5.
38   Ibid, pp. 126–7.
39   Ibid, pp. 144–5, 197, 237, 275, 282–4.
40   Ibid, pp. 157–9, 183.
41   Ibid, pp. 221, 261–2. D. Langley as in reference 36 above.
42   *Old Soldiers Never Die* p. 223. A minor error occurs on p. 13 where General Grierson, who died in France in August 1914 as Commander of II Corps, is referred to as 'Chief of Staff to General French'.

Notes to Chapter 7: Protesters against the war: the contrasting cases of Siegfried Sassoon and Max Plowman

1   Rupert Hart-Davis (ed.) *Siegfried Sassoon. Diaries 1915–1918* (1983) p. 22.
2   Ibid, p. 26. Adrian Caesar *Taking it Like a Man* (1993) p. 67.
3   Sassoon *Diaries* pp. 50–1 Caesar pp. 68–9 Max Egremont *Siegfried Sassoon. A Biography* (2005) p. 91.
4   *Diaries* pp. 44–5, 52–3.
5   Ibid. pp. 66–7 Caesar p. 74–7.
6   Egremont pp. 103–4. Sassoon *Memoirs of an Infantry Officer* (1940 edition) pp. 343–7.
7   *Diaries* pp. 94–6. Egremont pp. 93–4. Caesar p. 71.
8   Egremont pp. 93–4. Caesar p. 71.
9   *Diaries* pp. 23, 61, 109.
10   Jean Moorcroft Wilson (henceforth 'Wilson') *Siegfried Sassoon Vol 1 The Making of a War Poet* (1998) pp. 290–1. See also Siegfried Sassoon *Siegfried's Journey* (pbk edn 1982) pp. 21–2.
11   Wilson pp. 318–19. *Siegfried's Journey* pp. 22, 39, 43. 'Old Birrell' – Augustine Birrell, author and member of the cabinet during the war as Chief Secretary for Ireland.
12   Egremont p. 118. Wilson p. 312. *Diaries* p. 121.
13   *Diaries* pp. 107, 139–40, 194.
14   Wilson pp. 318–19. Egremont pp. 128–32. *Diaries* pp.155–6.
15   *Memoirs of an Infantry Officer* p. 454. Wilson p. 356. Egremont p. 145.
16   *Memoirs of an Infantry Officer* pp. 457–8.
17   *Diaries* p. 166. *Siegfried's Journey* p. 48.
18   *Siegfried's Journey* pp. 50–1. Wilson p. 373
19   Egremont pp. 143–4, 151. John Stuart Roberts *Siegfried Sassoon* (pbk edn 2000) pp. 103–4. *Diaries* p. 174 lists the prominent people to whom a copy of the protest was sent.
20   Roberts pp. 104–5. Egremont pp. 144–5. *Memoirs of an Infantry Officer* p. 483.
21   Egremont pp. 145–6 and ibid, p. 177 for the similarly unsuccessful letter from the Marquess of Lansdowne (published on 29 November 1917) calling for a negotiated peace.
22   *Diaries* pp. 179–81. Wilson p. 380. *Memoirs of an Infantry Officer* p. 489.
23   Egremont p. 155. *Memoirs of an Infantry Officer* pp. 508–9.
24   Egremont pp. 157–8.
25   Roberts pp. 107–12. Wilson pp. 382–3. Caesar p. 87.

26 *Memoirs of an Infantry Officer* p. 512–13. Caesar pp. 87–91. *Diaries* p. 183.

27 *Diaries* pp. 196–8. Egremont pp. 162, 169–71. Roberts pp. 123–4.

28 *Diaries* p. 246. Wilson pp. 394–5.

29 *Diaries* pp. 233, 238, 242, 270–1.

30 Egremont pp. 201–4. Roberts p. 128. *Diaries* pp. 274–5. See also Vivian de Sola Pinto *The City that Shone* (1969) pp. 220–9

31 Jean Moorcroft Wilson *Siegfried Sassoon Vol 2 The Journey from the Trenches* (2003) pp. 233–41. Caesar pp. 104–6.

32 Wilson vol 2 pp. 235–6. Caesar p. 106.

33 *Siegfried's Journey* pp. 55–7.

34 Egremont pp. 157–8. 'Mark Plowman' entry by Richard A. Storey in *New DNB*.

35 Dorothy L. Plowman *Bridge into the Future: Letters of Max Plowman* (1944) pp. 29, 35–6, 90 (henceforth *Bridge*).

36 *Bridge* pp. 175–6, 247.

37 Ibid, pp. 48, 52 Letter to Hugh de Selincourt 18 October 1916, *New DNB* Entry.

38 Mark Seven *A Subaltern at the Somme* (1927) pp. 95, 136, 158, 172–3, 202–3, 210, 232.

39 Ibid, pp. 171, 184, 188, 197–8.

40 *Bridge* pp. 247, 260–2, 312–3.

41 Ibid, pp. 312–13.

42 Ibid, pp. 63–5. Samuel Hynes *A War Imagined* (1990) pp. 183–4.

43 *Bridge* pp. 68–9, 88–9.

44 Ibid, pp. 92–3, 97. Plowman's 'Reasons for Resigning' are printed in full in an appendix pp. 772–3. See also Hynes, *op. cit.* p. 184.

45 *Bridge* pp. 130–1.

46 Ibid, pp. 94, 127, 130. Hynes p. 185.

47 Plowman's later publications included *War and the Creative Impulse* (1919), *An Introduction to the Study of Blake* (1927), *The Faith Called Pacifism* (1936) and *The Right to Live* (1942).

48 Canon H. R. L. 'Dick' Sheppard (1880–1937). A saintly man and a very popular preacher. On 6 January 1924 he presented the first BBC radio broadcast of a church service. In 1934 he issued a public appeal for peace and in 1936 founded the Peace Pledge Union. He was a close friend of Siegfried Sassoon and christened his son George in 1936. When he died of overwork on 31 October 1937 he was deeply mourned; for several days tens of thousands of people filed past his coffin (*New DNB* entry by Alan Wilkinson).

49 *New DNB* entry.

50 *Bridge* pp. 260–2.

Notes to Chapter 8: Martinet, militarist and opponent of war: the strange career of Brigadier-General F.P. Crozier

1 F. P. Crozier *Impressions and Recollections* (1930) pp. 9–139. Timothy Bowman *Irish Regiments in the Great War. Discipline and Morale* (2003) p. 70. I am indebted to Dr Bowman for information drawn from Crozier's personal files at the Public Record Office.

2 *Impressions and Recollections* pp. 138–9. The first of the six lessons which Crozier sought

to inculcate was 'The subtle danger which always lurks behind alcohol when consumed as a beverage' ibid, p. 312.

3   Ibid, pp. 142–63. Bowman *op. cit.* Chapter 3 passim. Philip Orr *The Road to the Somme* (1987) pp. 46–82.

4   Bowman pp. 109–24. F. P. Crozier *A Brass Hat in No Man's Land* (1930) (henceforth *Brass Hat*). Nick Perry 'Politics and Command: General Nugent, the Ulster Division and Relations with Ulster Unionism 1915–1917' p. 110 in Brian Bond *et al., Look to Your Front* (1999).

5   Bowman p. 116.

6   *Brass Hat* pp. 46–50.

7   Ibid, pp. 48–51.

8   *Impressions and Recollections* p. 170. Bowman pp. 116–18.

9   Bowman p. 118. *Brass Hat* pp. 68–9. Orr pp. 120–2.

10   Orr pp. 142–88. Martin Middlebrook *The First Day on the Somme* (1975) pp. 174–5. Cyril Falls *The History of the 36th (Ulster) Division* (1922) pp. 41–63.

11   *Brass Hat* pp. 105–14.

12   Middlebrook pp. 178–9, 208–9.

13   *Brass Hat* pp. 112–16.

14   Ibid, p. 134. Bowman pp. 124–5. *Impressions and Recollections* pp. 176–7.

15   *Impressions* pp. 182–5. *Brass Hat* pp. 135–7.

16   *Brass Hat* pp. 145–9. *Impressions* pp. 187–90. For fuller operational details see F. E. Whitton *History of the 40th Division* (1926, reprinted 2004) pp. 58–85.

17   Whitton pp. 86–152. *Brass Hat* pp. 180–8.

18   *Brass Hat* pp. 52–60, 94–7.

19   Ibid, pp. 123, 164, 238–9.

20   Ibid, pp. 73–6, 132–3, 169–70.

21   Ibid, pp. 158–60, 244–6.

22   *Impressions* pp. 212–14.

23   *Brass Hat* pp. 195–201. Whitton pp. 165–200.

24   *Impressions* pp. 217–21. Whitton pp. 204–39, 257.

25   Crozier *The Men I Killed* pp. 49, 54, 96–7. In a newspaper article shortly after Crozier's death his devoted batman, David Starrett, says he was with his brigadier when he ordered machine-guns to fire on the retreating Portuguese and when he shot a fleeing British subaltern (*Sunday Chronicle* 5 September 1937). Even so Crozier's boastful references to the men he killed should be treated with caution.

26   WO 374/16997 Brig-Gen Crozier. I am grateful to Dr Tim Bowman for this reference.

27   *Impressions* pp. 242–9. He is vague about whether he could have remained in the Army when he returned from Lithuania.

28   *The Men I Killed* pp. 121. See also C. L. Mowat *Britain between the Wars 1918–1940* (Methuen, 1966) pp. 64–72, 76–8.

29   *The Men I Killed* pp. 157, 168.

30   Ibid, pp. 177–9, 214.

31   Ibid, pp. 216–17, 246.

32   Ibid, 253–4.

33   Bowman p. 30. Orr p. 226.

34   Orr p. 226. *Impressions* p. 207.
35   David Starrett *Batman* IWM 79/35/1. Starrett believes that Crozier was a much nicer man than he portrayed himself in his books. He had been 'like a father' to his batman and 'the pride of his life' pp. 10, 21.

Notes to Chapter 9: The war in the air: Cecil Lewis and Billy Bishop

1   Hugh Cecil and Peter H. Liddle (eds) *Facing Armageddon* (1996) p. 196.
2   Cecil Lewis *Sagittarius Rising* (1936) p. 137 (henceforth C. Lewis *Memoirs*).
3   Denis Winter *The First of the Few* (Penguin Paperback, 1983) pp. 167–9 (henceforth D. Winter).
4   Cecil Lewis *Never Look Back* (1974) and *New DNB* entry on C. A. Lewis by James Owen. W. Arthur Bishop *The Courage of the Early Morning. The Story of Billy Bishop* (1966).
5   Cecil Lewis *Never Look Back* pp. 99–109. As with Frederic Manning, it was Peter Davies who persuaded Lewis to write his First World War memoirs.
6   C. Lewis *Memoirs* pp. 48–50. C. Lewis *Never Look Back* p. 28.
7   *Memoirs* pp. 82–5. *Never Look Back* pp. 29–31.
8   *Memoirs* pp. 96–8.
9   Ibid, pp. 104–6.
10   Ibid, pp. 106–7. On Lewis' hatred of shooting as a sport see *Never Look Back* p. 25.
11   W. A. Bishop *Winged Warfare* (Penguin paperback, 1938) pp. 6–9. Henceforth 'Billy' Bishop.
12   Billy Bishop *Winged Warfare* pp. 60–2. D. Winter p. 134 quotes Sholto Douglas on Bishop's tendency to live in a 'hard brittle world of his own', but there is ample evidence to the contrary, notably in his son's biography, that he loved to socialize and 'live it up' when out of action.
13   Billy Bishop *Winged Warfare* pp. 66–9.
14   C. Lewis *Memoirs* pp. 139–47.
15   Ibid, pp. 168–70.
16   Ibid, pp. 174–84.
17   Billy Bishop *Winged Warfare* p. 114. According to his *DNB* entry there was some controversy later about Bishop's number of 'kills' since he was often the only witness. But Bishop is generally credited with 72 victims, surpassed only by Edward ('Mick') Mannock's 73, René Fonck's 75 and Manfred von Richtofen's 80. See Bruce Robertson (ed.) *Air Aces of the 1914–1918 War* (Harleyford Publications, 1959).
18   Billy Bishop *Winged Warfare* pp. 116–17, 135–6, 142, 146.
19   Ibid, pp. 155, 161–70.
20   Ibid, pp. 237–41. Compare his son's account (in *The Courage of the Early Morning* pp. 124–5, 162–3) of Bishop's nerve-wracking visit to Buckingham Palace, and his frenetic forays to boost his kills on his final morning in France.
21   D. Winter pp. 169–71. Whether Edward Ritter von Schleich (35 victories) actually took his downed opponent to finish a tennis match may be doubted, but he was noted as a chivalrous and eccentric fighter ace.
22   Ibid, pp. 172–3. C. Lewis *Memoirs* p. 26 footnote.

23   Billy Bishop *Winged Warfare* pp. 11, 83–90, 166, 214.

24   C. Lewis *Memoirs* pp. 45–6, 93, 169–72.

25   Ibid, p. 59. D. Winter p. 143. W. Arthur Bishop *The Courage of the Early Morning* p. 182.

26   C. Lewis *Memoirs* p. 61. Flying low and straight over enemy trenches to take photos required nerve and the routine demanded twice-daily flights until you were hit or went home.

27   D. Winter pp. 146, 151–4.

28   C. Lewis *Memoirs* pp. 66–7. Billy Bishop *Winged Warfare* p. 147. W. Arthur Bishop *The Courage of the Early Morning* pp. 171–3.

29   W. Arthur Bishop pp. 105–6. Billy Bishop *Winged Warfare* pp. 176–85. C. Lewis *Memoirs* p. 174.

30   C. Lewis *Memoirs* pp. 94, 120–3, 184–6.

31   W. Arthur Bishop *The Courage of the Early Morning* pp. 165–75, 192–6 and Marc Milner 'William Avery Bishop' in *New DNB* entry.

32   C. Lewis *Memoirs* p. 196 admitted he was a 'a natural seducer and not a good husband'. In his *New DNB* entry James Owen remarks that he had 'a prodigious appetite for seduction'. His obituary notice in the *Daily Telegraph* (29 January 1997) notes that 'He retained his attractiveness to women, and even at 95 might have passed for a spry 70'.

33   C. Lewis *Never Look Back. Daily Telegraph* obituary. Entry in *New DNB*.

34   C. Lewis *Never Look Back* p. 200. *Daily Telegraph* obituary.

Notes to Chapter 10: Having a 'good war': Anthony Eden and Harold Macmillan

1   Anthony Eden *Another World, 1897–1917* (1976) pp. 34–5 (Henceforth 'Eden'). Robert Rhodes James *Anthony Eden* (1986) pp. 33, 545.

2   Eden pp. 20, 67, 81.

3   Ibid, pp. 77–9.

4   Ibid, p. 81. See also entry on Eden in *New DNB* by D. R. Thorpe.

5   Eden pp. 95–8. Foljambe (1878–1962) became the 6th Earl of Liverpool in 1941.

6   Ibid, pp. 101–8.

7   Ibid, pp. 116–17.

8   Ibid, pp. 118–19.

9   Ibid, pp. 120–5. See also Louis Ackroyd 'General Sir Thomas Morland – the Forgotten Commander' *Stand To!* September 2002 pp. 46–9.

10   Eden p. 135.

11   Ibid, p. 142.

12   Ibid, pp. 147–8.

13   Ibid, pp. 148–50.

14   R. Rhodes James *op. cit.* p. 55.

15   Simon Ball *The Guardsmen* (2004) pp. 144–5, 152, 162.

16   Alistair Horne *Macmillan 1894–1956 Volume I of the Official Biography* (1998).

17   Ibid, pp. 10–12. Harold Macmillan *Winds of Change 1914–1939* (1966) pp. 56–7 (Henceforth 'Macmillan').

18   Horne *op. cit.* pp. 15–19.

19   Ibid, p.30. Ball pp. 29–31. Macmillan p. 67. The trenches near Bovingdon Green where Macmillan trained may still be clearly seen though their original purpose is less obvious today than when the author first played in them in the early part of the Second World War.
20   Macmillan pp. 70–7. Ball pp. 43–5. Horne pp. 37–40, 43.
21   Macmillan pp. 79–85. Ball p. 55.
22   Macmillan pp. 82–3. Horne pp. 40, 43.
23   Sir Frederick Ponsonby *The Grenadier Guards in the Great War, 1914–1919* (1920) Volume 2 pp. 31–8. Oliver Lyttelton *The Memoirs of Lord Chandos* (1962) pp. 58–66. Raymond Asquith, the Prime Minister's son, was killed in this bungled attack.
24   Macmillan pp. 87–9. Ball pp. 57–60.
25   Macmillan pp. 90–1. In the three days of this battle (13, 14 and 15 September) the 2nd Battalion Grenadier Guards lost three officers killed and nine wounded, 108 other ranks killed and 235 wounded.
26   Macmillan pp. 56–7, 95. Ball pp. 64–5.
27   Macmillan pp. 92–4. Macmillan reflected that, in contrast to the Second World War, the First was a singing war; he attributed this to the popularity of the music hall in 1914–18 and the fact that it was overwhelmingly a marching war.
28   Macmillan pp. 99–100.
29   Ibid, p. 98. Ball (p. 395) considers that Macmillan's feeling of guilt at surviving was retrospective. 'Guilt and anger seem to have been much more the products of his early personal and political failure than the war.'
30   Ball p. 117. Horne pp. 86–9. See also the *New DNB* entry on Macmillan by the late H.C.G. Matthew.
31   Ball pp. 176–7, 215.
32   Matthew in *New DNB* cited in note 30.
33   R. Rhodes James pp. 618–19.

Appendix. Chronology of publications

This list is not comprehensive but aims to include the best-known and most interesting war memoirs. A few titles which are not strictly memoirs have been included as significant landmarks.

1917   Bernard Adams *Nothing of Importance: A Record of Eight Months at the Front with a Welsh Battalion.*
Arthur Guy Empey *Over the Top. An American Subaltern who Went.*

1918   W. A. ('Billy') Bishop *Winged Warfare.*
R. D. Holmes *A Yankee in the Trenches.*

1919   Stephen Graham *A Private in the Guards.*
A. P. Herbert *The Secret Battle.*

1922   C. E. Montague *Disenchantment.*
Aubrey Smith *Four Years on the Western Front by a Rifleman.*

1926   Henri Barbusse *Under Fire* (first published in France in 1916).

1927   'Mark Seven' *A Subaltern on the Somme* (Max Plowman).

1928   Edmund Blunden *Undertones of War.*

1929   Erich Maria Remarque *All Quiet on the Western Front* (published in Germany in January and in English translation in March).
Ernst Jünger *The Storm of Steel* (first published in Germany in 1920).
Robert Graves *Goodbye to All That.*

1929   Frederic Manning *The Middle Parts of Fortune* (and an expurgated edition ('Private 19022') *Her Privates We*).
Charles Edmonds *A Subaltern's War* (Carrington).
Rudolf Binding *A Fatalist at War.*
Ludwig Renn *War.*

1930   Siegfried Sassoon *Memoirs of an Infantry Officer.*
F. P. Crozier *A Brass Hat in No Man's Land.*
Carroll Carstairs *A Generation Missing.*
Ernst Jünger *Copse 125* (first published in Germany in 1925).
D. V. Kelly *39 Months with the 'Tigers'.*
C. D. Baker-Carr *From Chauffeur to Brigadier.*

1931   Charles Douie *The Weary Road: Recollections of a Subaltern of Infantry.*

1932   A. O. Pollard *Fire-Eater: the Memoirs of a VC.*

1933   Guy Chapman *A Passionate Prodigality.*
        Frank Richards *Old Soldiers Never Die.*
        Sidney Rogerson *Twelve Days.*
1934   Wilfrid Ewart *Scots Guard on the Western Front.*
        Ernst Toller *I was a German.*
        Paul Maze *A Frenchman in Khaki.*
1935   Stanley Casson *Steady Drummer.*
1936   Cecil Lewis *Sagittarius Rising.*
        Siegfried Sassoon *Sherston's Progress.*
1937   F. P. Crozier *The Men I Killed.*
        P. Wyndham Lewis *Blasting and Bombardiering.*
        Douglas Jerrold *Georgian Adventure.*
1938   John F. Lucy *There's a Devil in the Drum.*
1945   Siegfried Sassoon *Siegfried's Journey 1916–1920.*
1961   Arthur Behrend *Make Me a Soldier. A Platoon Commander at Gallipoli.*
1963   Alexander Aitken *Gallipoli to the Somme.*
        Arthur Behrend *As from Kemmel Hill: an Adjutant in France and Flanders, 1917–1918.*
1965   Charles Carrington *Soldier from the Wars Returning.*
1966   Lord Reith *Wearing Spurs.*
1968   Alan Thomas *A Life Apart.*
1969   Vivian de Sola Pinto *The City that Shone.*
1971   Donald Portway *Memoirs of an Academic Old Contemptible.*
1974   Norman Gladden *The Somme, 1916.*
1975   Guy Chapman *A Kind of Survivor.*
1976   Anthony Eden (Earl of Avon) *Another World, 1897–1917.*
1977   P. J. Campbell *The Ebb and Flow of Battle.*
1978   H. E. L. Mellersh *Schoolboy into War.*
1979   P. J. Campbell *In the Cannon's Mouth.*
1980   George Coppard *With a Machine Gun to Cambrai.*
1988   Norman D. Cliff *To Hell and Back with the Guards.*

Select bibliography

WAR MEMOIRS FEATURED IN TEXT

W. A. Bishop *Winged Warfare* (1918; Penguin Books, 1938).

Edmund Blunden *Undertones of War* (Cobden-Sanderson, 1928).

Charles Carrington (pseud. Charles Edmonds) *A Subaltern's War* (Peter Davies, 1929).

Charles Carrington *Soldier from the Wars Returning* (Hutchinson, 1965).

Carroll Carstairs *A Generation Missing* (Heinemann, 1930. New edition; Stevenage: The Strong Oak Press, 1989).

Guy Chapman *A Passionate Prodigality* (Nicholson & Watson, 1933. Second edition MacGibbon & Kee, 1965).

Guy Chapman *A Kind of Survivor* (Victor Gollancz, 1975).

Norman D. Cliff *To Hell and Back with the Guards* (Braunton, Devon: Merlin Books, 1988).

Stuart Cloete *A Victorian Son: An Autobiography 1897–1922* (Collins, 1972).

F. P. Crozier *A Brass Hat in No Man's Land* (Jonathan Cape, 1930. Reissued in Florin Books, 1937).

F. P. Crozier *Impressions and Recollections* (T. Werner Laurie, 1930).

F. P. Crozier *The Men I Killed* (Michael Joseph, 1937).

Anthony Eden (Earl of Avon) *Another World, 1897–1917* (Allen Lane, 1976).

Wilfrid Ewart *Scots Guard on the Western Front, 1915–1918* (1934. New edition; Stevenage: The Strong Oak Press, 2001).

Stephen Graham *A Private in the Guards* (Macmillan, 1919).

Robert Graves *Goodbye to All That* (Jonathan Cape, 1929).

Cecil Lewis *Sagittarius Rising* (Peter Davies, 1936).

Cecil Lewis *Never Look Back* (Hutchinson, 1974).

Oliver Lindsay (ed.) *A Guards General. The Memoirs of Major-General Sir Allan Adair* (Hamish Hamilton, 1986).

Oliver Lyttelton (Lord Chandos) *The Memoirs of Lord Chandos* (The Bodley Head, 1962).

Oliver Lyttelton (Lord Chandos) *From Peace to War. A Study in Contrast, 1857–1918* (The Bodley Head, 1968).

Harold Macmillan *Winds of Change, 1914–1939* (Macmillan, 1966).

Frederic Manning *The Middle Parts of Fortune* (Peter Davies, 1929. New edition 1977).

Max Plowman (Mark Seven) *A Subaltern on the Somme* (J. M. Dent & Sons, 1927).

Alfred Pollard, VC *Fire-Eater. The Memoirs of a VC* (Hutchinson, 1932).

John Reith (Lord Reith) *Wearing Spurs* (Hutchinson, 1966).

John Reith (Lord Reith) *Into the Wind* (Hodder & Stoughton, 1949).

Frank Richards *Old Soldiers Never Die* (Faber & Faber, 1933. Faber paperback, 1964).

Siegfried Sassoon *The Complete Memoirs of George Sherston* (Faber & Faber, 1937. (*Memoirs of an Infantry Officer*) Faber paperback, 1972).

Siegfried Sassoon *Siegfried's Journey, 1916–1920* (Faber & Faber, 1945. Faber paperback, 1982).

BIOGRAPHIES AND CRITICAL STUDIES

W. Arthur Bishop *The Courage of the Early Morning: The Story of Billy Bishop* (Heinemann, 1966).

Barry Webb *Edmund Blunden. A Biography* (Yale University Press, 1990).

Robert Rhodes James *Anthony Eden* (Weidenfeld & Nicolson, 1986).

Martin Seymour-Smith *Robert Graves. His Life and Work* (Bloomsbury, 1995)

Alistair Horne *Macmillan, 1894–1956. Vol I of the Official Biography* (Macmillan, 1998).

Simon Ball *The Guardsmen, Harold Macmillan, Three Friends and the World They Made* (Harper Collins, 2004).

Jonathan Marwil *Frederic Manning. An Unfinished Life* (Durham NC, Duke University Press, 1988).

Dorothy L. Plowman *Bridge into the Future. Letters of Max Plowman* (Andrew Dakers, 1944).

Ian McIntyre *The Expense of Glory. A Life of John Reith* (HarperCollins, 1993).

Max Egremont *Siegfried Sassoon. A Biography* (Picador, 2005).

John Stuart Roberts *Siegfried Sassoon.* (Richard Cohen Books, 1999).

Jean Moorcroft Wilson *Siegfried Sassoon. The Making of a War Poet, 1886–1918* (Duckworth, 1998).

Jean Moorcroft Wilson *Siegfried Sassoon. A Journey from the Trenches 1918–1967* (Duckworth, 2003).

DISCUSSION OF WAR LITERATURE

Bernard Bergonzi *Heroes' Twilight. A Study of the Literature of the Great War* (Macmillan, 1965. Second edition 1980).

Adrian Caesar *Taking it Like a Man. Suffering, Sexuality and the War Poets.* (Manchester University Press, 1993).

Hugh Cecil *British Fiction Writers of the First World War* (Secker & Warburg, 1995).

Modris Eksteins *Rites of Spring. The Great War and the Birth of the Modern Age* (Bantam Press, 1989).

Paul Fussell *The Great War and Modern Memory* (Oxford University Press, 1975).

Rupert Hart-Davis (ed.) *Siegfried Sassoon Diaries, 1915–1918* (Book Club Associates, 1983).

Samuel Hynes *A War Imagined. The First World War and English Culture* (The Bodley Head, 1990).

Holger Klein (ed.) *The First World War in Fiction* (Macmillan, 1976).

Andrew Rutherford *The Literature of War. Five Studies in Heroic Virtue* (Macmillan, 1978).

Martin Taylor (ed.) *Edmund Blunden. Overtones of War. Poems of the First Word War* (Duckworth, 1996).

COMPLEMENTARY HISTORICAL STUDIES

Ian Beckett *The Great War, 1914–1918* (Longman, 2001).

Brian Bond *The Unquiet Western Front: Britain's Role in Literature and History* (Cambridge University Press, 2002. Pbk edn, 2007).

Brian Bond (ed.) *The First World War and British Military History* (The Clarendon Press, 1991).

John Bourne *Britain and the Great War, 1914–1918* (Edward Arnold, 1989).

Timothy Bowman *Irish Regiments in the Great War* (Manchester University Press, 2003).

Hugh Cecil and Peter Liddle (eds) *Facing Armageddon: The First World War Experienced* (Leo Cooper, 1996)

Paddy Griffith *Battle Tactics of the Western Front* (Yale University Press, 1994).

Richard Holmes *Tommy. The British Soldier on the Western Front 1914–1918* (HarperCollins, 2004).

Peter H. Liddle (ed.) *Passchendaele in Perspective* (Leo Cooper, 1997).

Martin Middlebrook *The First Day on the Somme* (Allen Lane, 1971).

Martin and Mary Middlebrook *The Somme Battlefields* (Viking, 1991).

Robin Prior and Trevor Wilson *The Somme* (Yale University Press, 2005).

Gary Sheffield *Leadership in the Trenches* (Macmillan, 2000).

Gary Sheffield *Forgotten Victory. The First World War: Myths and Realities* (Hodder Headline, 2001).

Keith Simpson (ed.) Captain J.C. Dunn *The War the Infantry Knew, 1914–1919.* (Jane's, 1987).

Dan Todman *The Great War. Myth and Memory* (Hambledon and London, 2005)

Denis Winter *Death's Men. Soldiers of the Great War* (Allen Lane, 1978).

Denis Winter *The First of the Few. Fighter Pilots of the Great War* (Allen Lane, 1982).

Index

Adair, Sir Allan 61
Adelphi magazine 111
aerial combat xvi, 131–45
    Crozier's views on 126–7, 128
Aeschylus, *Prometheus* 159
Ainsley, Mary 47–8
Amon, Horace 41
Annandale, Second Lieutenant A.J. 116
Ardee, Lord, Brigadier, Guards Brigade 70, 122
Arras, Battle of 98, 104, 131
Asquith, Raymond 69

Baldwin, Stanley 127, 162
Ball, Captain Albert, Royal Flying Corps 132, 135, 137, 139, 141, 143
Ball, Simon 68, 154
Barbusse, Henri 15, 32
Barker, William 144
Barrett, Lance Corporal L. 'Jackson', West Yorkshire Regiment 109
Barrie, J.M. 77
Bennett, Arnold 101, 106
Bennett, Sir William 160
Bernard, Lt Col H.C., Royal Irish Rifles 116
Binding, Rudolf 26
Bishop, W.A. 'Billy' 135–6, 137–9, 141, 142, 143–4
    Winged Warfare xvi, 132, 139, 140
Blackadder television series 72
Blake, Colonel Terence, Royal Fusiliers 33
Blake, William 111
Blunden, Edmund xiii, xiv, xv, 26, 27
    early life 35
    family background 35

and Graves 9–10
and Manning 78
and pastoral irony 39–40
Poems 1930–1940 42
post-war life 41–3
'Reunion in War' 42
Undertones of War xiii, 34–43
Bond, Brian, *The Unquiet Western Front* xiii
Boswell, James, *Life of Johnson* 147
Bowser, Charlie 52, 54, 56
Brassey, Lord and Lady 99
Braun, Otto 26
Brooke, 'Boy', commander 3rd Battalion Grenadier Guards 60
Brooke, Rupert 15
Brown, Lt Col W.E., Royal Irish Rifles 124, 128
Browne, Sir Thomas, *Urn Burial* 28
Browning, Robert, *The Ring and the Book* 21
Buck, Hector 38
Butler, L.J., brigadier, Guards Division 71

Caesar, Adrian 94, 105
Cambridge Magazine 99
Carpenter, Edward 101
Carrington, Charles xiv, 13–26
    'An Essay on Militarism' 15–17
    death 13
    early life 14, 17
    family background 14
    post-war life 24
    Rudyard Kipling 14
    Soldier from the Wars Returning 13, 15, 17–18, 24–5
    A Subaltern's War (pseudonym 'Charles Edmonds') 13, 15, 18–19, 21–3

Carstairs, Carroll, Grenadier Guards 61, 66

Cavan, Lord, Major-General, Grenadier Guards 61, 67, 69

Cecil, Hugh, *The Flower of Battle* xiii

Chamberlain, Neville 162

Chamberlain, Sir Austen 154, 162

Chandos, Lord *see* Lyttleton, Oliver (Lord Chandos)

Chapman, Guy xiv, xv, 27–35, 42–3
  early life 27–8
  family background 27
  A Kind of Survivor 27, 34–5
  A Passionate Prodigality 28–32, 34
  Why France Collapsed 28

Churchill, Winston 64, 102, 143, 144, 154, 161, 162

Clare, John 39

Clark, Alan 13
  The Donkeys 72

Clausewitz, Karl von 127

Cliff, Norman D. xv, xvi
  To Hell and Back with the Guards 62–3, 64–6

Clive, Percy, MP 68

Cloete, Stuart, Coldstream Guards officer 59, 66

Coldstream Guards 59, 66, 69, 71

Collyer, W.J. 41

Corry, Lt. Col. Noel 68

Craiglockhart Hospital 8, 102–4

Cranborne, Robert ('Bobbety') 60

Crawshay, Colonel 4

Crespigny, Colonel Claude 'Crawley' de 60, 157

Croft, Major, Adjutant of 5th Scottish Rifles 54–5

Crozier, Brigadier-General F.P. xiv, xv, 111, 113–30
  Angels on Horseback 125
  anti-war views 126–8
  A Brass Hat in No Man's Land 113, 115–24, 130
  family background 113
  Five Years Hard 125

Impressions and Recollections 113, 128–9, 130
  life as a military adventurer 113–14, 129
  and the Lithuanian Army 124
  The Men I Killed 115, 121, 124, 125–8, 129
  on military discipline
    and drunkenness 120–1
    and sex 119–20
  and the Peace Pledge Union 125, 126
  in the Royal Irish Constabulary 124–5
  in the Royal Irish Rifles 114–24

Crozier, James, Private 'Crocker', Ulster Division 116

Davies, Peter, publisher xiv, 77, 78

Douglas, Colonel, Scottish Rifles 54, 55

Duff Cooper, Alfred xvii, 162

Dunn, J.C., medical officer, Royal Welch Fusiliers 4, 8–9, 99
  The War The Infantry Knew 83, 85

Eden, Anthony xv, xvii, 147–54
  Another World 147, 162
  character 154
  family background 147–8
  and the Military Cross 149
  political career 154, 161–2
  and the Yeoman Rifles 148–54

Eden, Jack 148

Eden, Nicholas 148

Eden, Sir William 147

Eden, Timothy 148, 154

Egremont, Max 95–6, 101

Ewart, Wilfrid 66

Feversham, Lord 148, 149, 152

Fisher, Sir Warren 52

Fitzgerald, Scott 144

Folijambe, Major the Hon. Gerald, Yeoman Rifles 150

Fonck, René, French pilot 135, 142

Frech, Fritz 139

French, General Sir John 54

Fussell, Paul 35–6
 The Great War and Modern History xiii,
  39, 40

Gaffikin, Major George, Royal Irish Rifles
  117, 120–1
Galton, Reverend Arthur, tutor to Manning
  76
George V, King 65, 139
German offensive (March/April 1918) 69–71,
  122–4
Gort, Lord, Grenadier Guards officer 59, 61,
  68
Graham, Stephen xv, xvi
 A Private in the Guards 62, 63–4, 66–7
Graves, Nancy 2
Graves, Robert xiv, 1–11, 26, 42, 67
 But It Still Goes On 3, 8
  early life 1–2, 4
  family background 1–2
 Goodbye to All That xiii, xv, 1, 2–11, 83, 91
 Lawrence and the Arabs 3
  and Manning 78, 83
  poetry 1, 2
  post-war life xv, 2–3, 8, 10
  reported 'killed' in the First World War 2,
   4–5
  and Richards xv, 75, 91–2
  and the Royal Welch Fusiliers 4, 5–7, 8–9,
   10–11
  and Sassoon 2, 4, 5, 6, 7–8, 9–10, 101,
   102–3, 104, 106, 112
Grenadier Guards xvi, xvii, 59, 60–1, 63, 64–6,
  68, 69, 71, 155, 156–9, 160
Grey, Lady Sylvia (Eden's mother) 147–62,
  154
Grigg, Ned 70
Guards regiments 59–73
  Coldstream Guards 59, 66, 69, 71
  Irish Guards 59, 69, 71
  Scots Guards 59, 62, 66
  Training Depot, Caterham, 'Little Sparta'
   63–4
 see also Grenadier Guards

Gurdjieff, George 145
Guynemer, George 132, 141

HAC (Honourable Artillery Company) 45–7,
  48–50
Haig, Sir Douglas 31, 72
Haileybury school 17
Haking, General Sir Richard, Royal Fusiliers
  32
Halifax, Edward Wood, 1st Earl of 162
Hamilton, Sir Ian, Royal Sussex Regiment
  42
Hanmer, Bobby, friend of Siegfried Sassoon
  96, 101
Harington, Tim, Yeoman Rifles 152, 153
Harrison, Colonel George H., Royal Sussex
  Regiment 38
Harrison, George Hyde, Colonel, Royal
  Sussex Regiment 41
Harrop, Sergeant, Yeoman Rifles 149
Hefford, J.S., Royal Fusiliers 31
Hemingway, Ernest 144
Higginson, General Sir George, Grenadier
  Guards 156
Hitler, Adolf 42, 127
Hoare, Sir Samuel 162
Honourable Artillery Company (HAC) 45–7,
  48–50
Horne, Alistair 155
Howard, Sir Michael 78, 79
Hynes, Samuel 10

Iremonger, Very Reverend Frederic 52
Irish Guards 59, 69, 71

Jameson, Margaret Storm 27, 34
Jeffreys, Major G.D. (later General Lord), 'Ma'
  60, 68
Johnson, Samuel 59
Jones, David 112
 In Parenthesis 78
Jones, Ira, Royal Flying Corps 132
Jünger, Ernst xv, 26, 50
Jutland, Battle of (1916) 148

King's Own Yorkshire Light Infantry 66
King's Royal Rifle Corps 156
King's Shropshire Light Infantry xvi, 76–7
Kipling, Rudyard 14, 85
Knox, Ronald 155–6

Lamb, Sergeant Roger 11
Langham Voluntary Service 112
Lascelles, Captain (Viscount), Grenadier
    Guards 65
Lawrence, T.E. 3, 76, 77
Lees-Smith, H.B. 100
Lewis, Cecil xiv, 131, 132–5
    Never Look Back 145
    post-war life 144–5
    in the Royal Flying Corps 133–5, 136–7,
        140–1, 142, 143
    Sagittarius Rising xvi, 132, 133
Liddell Hart, Captain B.H. 127–8
Lithuanian Army 124
Littlewood, Joan 13, 72
Lloyd George, David 97
London Field Ambulance Territorial Force
    107
Loos, Battle of 3–4, 65, 67, 68, 72, 86,
    156–7
Lyttleton, Oliver (Lord Chandos) xv
    From War to Peace 72
    Memoirs xvi, 59, 60–1, 61, 64, 69–72

MacDonald, Ramsay 162
McIntyre, Ian, biography of Reith 52, 56–7
Macmillan, Harold xv, xvii, 60, 63, 72, 147,
    154–62
    early life 155–6
    family background 147, 155
    in the Grenadier Guards 60, 155, 156–9,
        160
    political career 161–2
    Winds of Change 147, 154–5, 162
    wounded at the Somme 158–60
Macmillan, Helen (Nellie) 155
Macready, General Sir Nevil, Royal Irish
    Constabulary 124

Manning, Frederic xiii, xiv, xv–xvi, 91
    family background 75–6
    The Golden Coach 76
    Her Privates We xiii, xvi, 77, 80
    The Middle Parts of Fortune 75, 77–83
    Scenes and Portraits 76
Mannock, Edward 135
Marsh, Edward 5, 101, 102
Marwil, Jonathan 77, 78–9
Massingham, H.W. 99, 101
Maxse, General Sir Ivor, Royal Fusiliers 32
Metcalfe, Lt Col H.C., Royal Irish Rifles 124,
    128
Meyer, Jacques 34
Montague, C.E. Disenchantment 15, 16
Morland, General T.L.N. 151–2
Morrell, Lady Ottoline 96–7, 99–100, 101,
    103, 106
Morrell, Philip 99–100
Mosley, Sir Oswald 42
Muggeridge, Malcolm 52
Munich agreement (1938) 42
Murry, John Middleton 100
Mussolini, Benito 112, 127, 129

The Nation 99
New Army infantry 27
Norman, Ronald 52
Nugent, Major-General Sir Oliver, Royal Irish
    Rifles 114–15, 116, 120, 128

O'Brien, Corporal Mick 95
Oh! What a Lovely War 13, 72
Olivier, Sir Laurence 72
Orr, Philip 129
Ouspensky, P.D. 145
Ovillers, Battle of 14, 18–19
Owen, Wilfred 2, 72, 103, 106

Paschendale campaign 14–15, 21–3, 160
Peace Pledge Union 111–12, 125, 126, 128
Peyton, Major-General W.B., Royal Irish
    Rifles 124
Phibbs, Geoffrey 2

Philpott, Glyn, portrait of Sassoon 99
Pinney, Major-General Sir Reginald, Royal
  Welch Fusiliers 85, 98–9
Plowman, John 107
Plowman, Max xvi, 103, 107–12
  anti-war protest 108, 110–11
  death 112
  early life 107
  literary output 111, 112
  and the Peace Pledge Union 111–12
  The Right to Live 110
  and Sassoon 111–12
  A Subaltern on the Somme (pseudonym
    'Mark Seven') 108–10
  in the West Yorkshire Regiment 108–9, 110
Plumer, General Sir Herbert 21, 23, 114, 152,
  153, 160
Pollard, Alfred xiv, xv, 45–51, 54
  early life 45–6
  family background 45
  Fire-Eater 45, 46–51
  post-war life 51
  wins VC 49
Pollard, James 45–6, 48
Pound, Ezra 76
Pryce, Captain T.T., Grenadier Guards 71

Reith, John (later Lord) xv, 133
  early life 52–3
  family background 52
  Into the Wind 52, 55
  post-war life 56–7
  Wearing Spurs xv, 51–6, 57
Remarque, E.M., *All Quiet on the Western
  Front* xiv, 8, 15, 25–6, 80, 105
Richards, Frank xiv, xv, 96
  early life 84
  family background 83–4
  Old Soldiers Never Die xv, 11, 75, 83–92
Richardson, Samuel, *Pamela* 157
Richthofen, Manfred von 132, 137, 138
Riding, Laura 2, 8
Rivers, Professor W.H.R. 8, 103–4, 110
Rotherstein, Sir William 77

Royal Auxiliary Hospital, Selkirk 110
Royal Engineers 54–6
Royal Flying Corps (later Royal Air Force)
  131, 133–43
Royal Fusiliers 28–34
Royal Irish Constabulary 124–5
Royal Irish Rifles 114–24
Royal Sussex Regiment 36–8, 40–2
Royal Warwickshire Regiment 14, 18–24
Royal Welch Fusiliers
  and Graves 4, 5–7, 8–9, 10–11
  and Richards 75, 83–92
  and Sassoon 26, 93–6, 97–9, 104–5, 112
Ruggles-Brise, Major-General Harold, Royal
  Irish Rifles 118
Russell, Bertrand 99–100, 101, 103
Rutherford, Andrew
  The Literature of War xiii
    'The Common Man as Hero' 75

Sackville, Lady Margaret 103
Sassoon, Hamo 94
Sassoon, Siegfried xiii, xiv, xv, 21, 72, 81,
  93–107, 128
  and Blunden 38
  at Craiglockhart Hospital 102–4
  diaries 93–4, 95–6, 106
  early life 93
  family background 93
  and the Garsington pacifists 96–7, 99–100,
    102, 106
  and Graves 2, 4, 5, 6, 7–8, 9–10, 101,
    102–3, 106
  and Manning 78
  Memoirs of an Infantry Officer xiii, 103,
    105
  Memoirs of a Fox-Hunting Man 93, 105
  Memoirs of George Sherston 7, 93, 105–6
  and Plowman's anti-war protest 111–12
  poetry 93, 97, 99, 106–7
  public anti-war protest 7–8, 93, 100–2
  in the Royal Welch Fusiliers 25, 93–6,
    97–9, 104–5, 112
    awarded Military Cross 95

Sassoon, Siegfried (*continued*)
   'Mad Jack' nickname 94–5, 105
   Somme offensive 95–6, 97
   Siegfried's Journey xvi, 93, 106
Scots Guards 59, 62, 66
Scott, Sir Walter, Waverley novels 157
Scottish Rifles 53–4
Second World War 11, 17, 25, 34–5, 127,
  145
Seymour, Major Lord, 'Copper' 60
Shaw, George Bernard 133
Sheffield, Gary 61
shell-shock 103, 104, 110
Sheppard, Canon Dick 111, 125, 126
Sherriff, R.C. 2
Simon, John, 1st Viscount 162
Sladen, Lt.Col. G.C., Royal Warwickshire
  Regiment 19
Smith, Colonel R.A., Royal Fusiliers 28, 30–1,
  34, 35
Sola Pinto, Vivian de 106, 112
Somme offensive 33, 36–7, 69, 108–9, 149–51,
  158–9
   and aerial combat 131, 133–5, 136
   Royal Warwickshire Regiment 17–20
   Royal Welch Fusiliers 6, 84–5, 90, 95–6, 97
Stalin, Josef 127
Starrett, David, batman to Crozier 129
Stockwell, Brigadier C.I., Buffalo Bill 87, 88

Tawney, R.H. 32
Taylor, A.J.P. 63
Terraine, John, historian 13, 72

Thomas, David 81, 94
Thorneycroft, Colonel 113
Tice, Ernest 41
Tudor, Major-General Hugh, Royal Irish
  Constabulary 124
Tynan, Kenneth 72

Udet, Ernest 132, 139–40

Versailles Treaty (1919) 25
Vidler, Arnold 41

Wells, H.G. 101
  Mr Britling sees it Through 16
Welsh Guards 59
West Yorkshire Regiment 108–9, 110
Williams, Colonel O. de L., Royal Welch
  Fusiliers 9
Wilmot, Ralph 99
Wilson, Sir Charles (Lord Moran) 59, 69
Winter, Denis 139
Wolff, Leon, *In Flanders Fields* xv
Worley, Sergeant Frank, Royal Sussex
  Regiment 41

Yeoman Rifles 148–54
York and Lancaster Regiment 14
Young, Edward, *Night Thoughts* 39
Ypres campaign 21, 29–33, 37, 39, 41, 46–7,
  50, 67, 70, 87, 101, 157–8
   and aerial combat 131
   Blunden visits post-war battlefield 42
   and the Yeoman Rifles 148–51